Report on The National Education Convention

By

The Convention Secretariat

Editor: John Coolahan

ISBN: 0 7076 0343 9

Published by The National Education Convention Secretariat
Origination by Monica Dowdall
Designed by Bill Bolger
Printed in Ireland by Cahill Printers Ltd.

To be purchased from
Government Publications Sale Office,
Sun Alliance House, Molesworth Street, Dublin, 2.

(Pn.0430)   Price: £5.00

Convention Secretariat

Chairperson: Professor Dervilla Donnelly

Professor John Coolahan —*Secretary General*

Professor Patrick Clancy

Dr. Sheelagh Drudy

Professor Damian Hannan

Dr. Thomas Kellaghan

Dr. Séamus McGuinness

Máire Uí Mhaicín

Consultants

Professor Peter Mortimore

Professor Malcolm Skilbeck

Professor Galo Ramírez

FOREWORD

Because of the extent of their joint and several learning and experience, both academic and professional, it was an honour, as Chairperson, to be involved in the authors' private good-humoured discussions, debates, balanced decisions and wise comments on the key issues for Irish education. The outcome of their deliberations is presented between the covers of this very readable and thought-provoking Report. To be further privileged with an invitation to scribe the foreword gives me nothing but pleasure.

The task of compiling a report on the topic of Education in Ireland is not an easy one. It becomes particularly difficult when the subject embraces so vast a volume of documentation arising from discussions and debates on the Green Paper, *Education For A Changing World* (1992), the *Programme For A Partnership Government* (1993), elaborations on policy by the Minister for Education in many of her speeches, and culminating in the presentation papers and Analysis of Issues summaries from The National Education Convention. What to select, what to omit, how to edit and summarise and paraphrase, and how to present the material in an intelligible form, requires, firstly, a detailed knowledge of the subject and its sources, and, secondly, an informed appreciation of what is relevant to its understanding. The authors of the Report, as educationalists and researchers under the enlightened leadership of John Coolahan, have brought both to this compilation. All the issues are dealt with in a learned yet simple manner. Without doubt the report will prove invaluable, not only to the educationalist, but to the public at large.

The inclusion of the excellent Background Paper as an appendix to the Report is very helpful in setting the context within which the National Education Convention worked, as well as highlighting the many changes occurring in Irish society, which require the planning of new policies, structures and procedures for our educational system.

In Ireland it is well recognised that education is of fundamental importance to the quality and well-being of our society. We have a long and distinctive educational tradition incorporating good and essential values. To quote John Coolahan: "Throughout our history education has drawn to its service many gifted individuals of great dedication and commitment." Indeed, from reading inputs into the many debates referred to in the Report, this country is still blessed with "gifted individuals."

The Report incorporates views from a unique, deliberative forum, enriched by analysis and interpretation by the panel of experts in the Secretariat. A perusal of the Report will enable intelligent and good advice to be given from which an informed policy should crystallise, with the added help of the Department of Education.

Dervilla Donnelly

CONTENTS

Page

REPORT

ON THE NATIONAL EDUCATION CONVENTION

Introduction

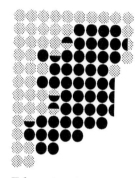

The National Education Convention, which took place in Dublin Castle from 11th to 21st October, 1993, was an unprecedented, democratic event in the history of Irish education. It brought together representatives from forty two organisations — educational bodies, the social partners and the Department of Education — to engage in structured and sustained discussion on key issues of educational policy in Ireland. The Convention was a very significant dimension of the wide-ranging consultative process on the Green Paper, *Education For A Changing World,* published in June 1992, and on the *Programme For A Partnership Government,* of January 1993. Occurring at the penultimate stage before policy is formulated for the forthcoming White Paper on Education, the National Education Convention provided a forum for mature reflection and focussed debate by representatives of many of the agencies involved. It set out to encourage participants to clarify viewpoints; to question, probe and analyse varying perspectives; to foster multi-lateral dialogue and improve mutual understanding between sectoral interests; to explore possibilities of new ways of doing things and to identify areas of actual or potential agreement between different interest groups.

To the great credit of participants, there was whole-hearted engagement with this important public forum. While addressing issues from varying perspectives and traditions, participants showed respect for different viewpoints and indicated a strong concern that the policy decisions to be taken would lead to an improved education system responsive to the rights and needs of individuals and of the community, in a rapidly changing society. Over the nine days there was a remarkable gestation of ideas, articulation of ideas, refining of ideas, analysing of ideas, challenging of ideas. **Ideas were on the move.** Existing ideas and viewpoints were being enriched and expanded through an understanding of the larger context of the overall debate. Instead of rigidity of set viewpoints there was a fluidity in the exchanges and the interrelationships which were occurring. A sense of partnership was in evidence as participants focussed in a constructive spirit on the wide spectrum of educational concerns, from pre-school to adult education. A report such as this cannot convey the character of the interactive spirit which prevailed, but it can record that a strong co-operative spirit existed.

The National Education Convention comprised the following five main elements, each of which yielded fruitful outcomes:

(i)   The preparation for the Convention involved organisations in careful scrutiny of the central issues, which promoted a more concise statement of their key concerns, priorities and viewpoints. The Secretariat analysed a comprehensive range of documentation, submitted to the Department of Education in response to the Green Paper, and prepared a Background Paper and associated material, which set the context for the National Education Convention and attempted to clarify the main issues;

(ii)   The plenary sessions featured the presentations by the organisations and the questioning by the Secretariat, which helped to promote a clearer overview of how various organisations viewed particular issues, and afforded them the opportunity to clarify their positions on those issues. They also provided an opportunity to hear the Department of Education's perspectives on various aspects of the formulation and administration of policy;

(iii)   The Analysis of Issues Sessions, in the second week, built on the work of the plenary sessions, and focussed in a structured way on fifteen key areas. Participants approached these sessions in a very committed and disciplined way and many worthwhile ideas and a good deal of consensus on important issues and priorities emerged;

(iv)   The reports of these analysis sessions which were delivered orally to the final plenary session, clearly indicated a host of important ideas and understandings which received the concentrated attention of participants;

(v)   The final element is the preparation by the Secretariat of this Report on the Convention.

As well as contributing directly to the work of the National Education Convention by making a presentation and engaging in extended discussion on it, senior officials of the Department of Education attended all plenary sessions and listened intently to the discussions and reports. The Minister for Education, Niamh Bhreathnach, T.D., formally opened the Convention and gave a policy address at its conclusion. She honoured the Convention by her continual presence at the plenary sessions. In her closing address the Minister remarked, "Together, we have produced a most powerful dynamic during these days of intense debate. The forces unleashed by this dynamic will ensure that policy making in Irish education will never be the same again." She went on to say, "As I go forward to determine the shape of the White Paper and the Education Act, I will rely immensely on the outcomes of the National Education Convention."

Even before the publication of the White Paper, the Minister undertook to publish an official position paper on intermediate educational structures, which was called for at the Convention.

The presentations and discussions of the Convention were available directly to the Minister and her Department through their participation in the Convention.　They have also received copies of the stenographers' report which includes the formal addresses, the text of the presentations made by the participating organisations, the text of the questioning sessions and the Analysis of Issues Reports. As well as this extensive written record, Radio Telefis Éireann has made available the visual and oral record of the plenary sessions. This record has also been deposited in the National Archives. Thus, from the point of view of policy making and from the historical archive perspective, it is gratifying that such a comprehensive written, oral and visual record of the proceedings of the National Education Convention is available. Of course, the Department of Education also has the texts of responses made by all individuals and organisations to the Green Paper and the *Programme For A Partnership Government, 1993/1997* to consult in its policy-formulation.

The role of the Convention Secretariat was to organise, assist and facilitate the process of the National Education Convention. It took on this task prompted by the view that the Minister for Education's initiative was one of significant public importance and in the interests of the educational system at this time. The Green Paper and the *Programme For A Partnership Government,1993/1997* provided a comprehensive set of proposals for educational change.   The responses to these documents by the invited organisations, and their submissions to the Convention, provided the basis on which the Secretariat conducted its questioning, and promoted dialogue among the participants in relation to the government's proposals. Subsequent to the Convention, it was the task of the Secretariat to draw up an independent Report on the work of the Convention, with a view to helping the policy-making process leading to the White Paper on Education. Despite the time constraints imposed by other professional responsibilities, the Secretariat has endeavoured to perform this task without undue delay so as to maintain the momentum of consultative deliberation. The Secretariat is very conscious that it is not a policy-making body; its role is purely one of assistance, and it has approached its work in that spirit, towards all involved parties.

The Secretariat's Report on the National Education Convention proceeds on the basis that the comprehensive record, alluded to above, is available for consultation purposes by policy-makers, researchers and the interested public.   The Report does not set out to be a summary of the proceedings of the Convention.   Such a summary would be unduly long and not particularly helpful to the on-going work on policy-formulation.   Many important points of detail were made in presentations and discussions, and these are contained in the more comprehensive record. While such points could not be included in the Report, in no sense does their omission mean that they are lost from considerations of policy, or from the record.

The Secretariat's Report obviously relies very heavily on the presentations, debates and discussion sessions of the Convention.   Its task is to try to report succinctly on these and to analyse, interpret and contextualise the perspectives put forward.   To be useful for the policy process the Report seeks to avoid too much detail and focuses on the essence of contributions to policy issues.   It aims to lead the debate forward, to make some recommendations and to pose options for policy.   The document is oriented towards issues and policies. As far as possible, it seeks to remain true to the content and spirit of the National Education Convention's deliberations.   Where it is conscious that a recommendation may not have emerged from deliberations at the Convention, the Secretariat signals that this is a view of the Secretariat itself.

The Report is not a comprehensive review of all aspects of Irish education, nor did the Convention debate all the proposals contained in the Green Paper.   In line with its terms of reference, the Secretariat paid particular attention to areas where divergent views seemed to exist within mainstream education and there was a need to explore possibilities of more agreement.   It also sought to examine elements of the educational system being affected by changing social conditions.   The Secretariat bore in mind the categorisation by the Minister, in her Framework Document for the Convention, of "main" organisations and "other participating" bodies, in the emphases given to presentations, questioning and the issues being analysed.   The Convention's deliberations also reflected areas of particular emphasis in the Green Paper and the *Programme for A Partnership Government, 1993/1997,* as, for example, equality issues.

The Secretariat is conscious that some important areas of education do not receive significant attention in its Report.   Among such areas are vocational training and youth affairs.   In this regard, however, the Secretariat draws attention to the significant report by the NESC, *Education and Training Policies For Economic and Social Development,* published in October, 1993, which provides comprehensive treatment of the training area.   Concerning youth affairs, it is the view of the Secretariat that this is an important but complex area of policy at present, and that it would benefit from a more specific and specialised study than could be accommodated within the ambit of the Convention Report.

The Report on the Convention has seventeen sections, containing various subdivisions. As could be expected, some topics, such as, the role of the inspectorate, the school plan, equality issues, while featuring in a specific way in some sections, also permeate the comment in other areas. The Report covers a wide spectrum of educational issues. There are complex elements involved in each of the themes. To do full justice to all the issues would require a very extensive report, and, to some extent, it would be repetitious of material already submitted to the Department of Education by various organisations. While individual interest groups might wish for more detailed treatment of their areas of particular concern, the Secretariat considered that the Report would be most useful as an analytical overview of the debate on the main issues, if it reflected a pattern of coherence and provided a framework for development of the overall system.

The proposals for change set out in the Green Paper, and the educational commitments of *The Programme For A Partnership Government, 1993-1997* will involve very significant additional expenditure on education, if they are to be realised. As issues were explored at the Convention, it became clear that many reforms were being recommended by participants which would have significant cost implications. High expectations of improvements were also in evidence. The Secretariat was aware that, on accumulation, the overall cost of reforms being discussed would be formidable. In its presentation to the Convention the Department of Education submitted some projections of the costs involved. To be true to the debate at the Convention, the Secretariat records the type of reforms being proposed. The Secretariat realises that it would be extremely difficult to undertake all proposed improvements contemporaneously and that a planned, prioritisation policy will be necessary. Nevertheless, it has to emphasise its view that the process now underway cannot hope to be successful without significant extra resources being available for educational expenditure. A hopeful sign in this regard is the availability of increased structural and cohesion funds from the European Union, over the next six years, but these will need to be supplemented by increased national investment in education. The issue of resources is returned to in the final section of this Report.

The Secretariat sought to write the Report in a style which is free from professional jargon and in a way which may commend it to a wide readership. The comprehensive debate on education, which has taken place since June 1992, has confirmed the very wide level of interest of the Irish public in educational developments. It is hoped that this Report will be of significant assistance to the debate leading up to final decisions on educational policy.

In recognition of the nature of the participation at the Convention, the Secretariat considered that it would be helpful, and useful for reference purposes, if some selective documentation of the Convention were published as appendices to the Report. This is particularly so in the case of the Background Paper, which was circulated to invited organisations in advance of the Convention. In the interest of consistency and coherence of approach, the treatment of issues in this Report follows, to a large degree, the sequence of issues set out in that Background Paper. The appendices also include reports from Analysis of Issues Sessions, the Programme of Events and some of the official addresses, which will help to convey information on the organisation, character and some of the contents of the Convention.

1. Philosophy of Education and Policy-Formulation

 It is acknowledged that education makes a fundamentally important contribution to the quality and well-being of Irish society. It will play an even more crucial role in the social, intellectual, cultural, economic and political life of the country as it faces into the new century. Ireland has a long and distinctive educational tradition incorporating important values. Throughout our history, education has drawn to its service many gifted individuals of great dedication and commitment. Parents and other social groups made great sacrifices to obtain the benefits of education for Irish citizens, but particularly for the younger generations. The quality and depth of this educational tradition, the achievements in expansion and development of the education system in recent decades, and the informed awareness of, and interest in, educational issues among the general public, should be a source of significant confidence to Irish society as it charts the way forward towards a new era in Irish education.

Within an improved overall policy approach and framework, attention to a philosophy and aims for the education system should be a matter of priority. The Background Paper to the National Education Convention pointed out that, while there had been broad endorsement of the statement of educational aims in the Green Paper, there had been criticism that the aims had not always permeated subsequent sections of the Green Paper. There was also extensive criticism of the lack of an adequate philosophy of education. It was considered that this omission occasioned a distortion in the rationale of the Green Paper, giving an over-emphasis to utilitarian and commercial concerns. Statements by Ministers Brennan and Bhreathnach, subsequent to the issuing of the Green Paper, aimed at redressing this imbalance, would appear to have influenced attitudes at the Convention, resulting in less dissatisfaction being expressed on the issue. Given that every educational action unavoidably presupposes a philosophy of some kind or another, the provision of an adequate philosophical rationale, from which both structures and practice draw their coherence and strength, remains a priority. The need to work anew for such a rationale was the keynote of the John Marcus O'Sullivan Memorial lecture delivered by Minister Bhreathnach in Tralee in March 1993. The state has a responsibility to set out educational principles and rights within which educational institutions may set out their philosophical approach, while respecting such rights.

At the National Education Convention it was clear that participants were willing to share in the task of contributing to formulating a philosophy of education. In successive contributions to the Convention there was a new awareness of the legitimate plurality of educational purposes and evidence of a mature commitment to the achievement of balance in educational aims: to the pursuit of a harmony between academic achievements and spiritual qualities, between liberal learning and vocational aptitude, between artistic capabilities and technical endeavours, between personal accomplishments and social responsibilities. Within such a balance, the key concern would be to enable each pupil to discover the nature and scope of his or her particular potentials and limitations; to enable each and **every** pupil to make the most of these potentials; to overcome limitations wherever this is possible; to mitigate their effects wherever it is not. In short, educational policy and endeavour would be concerned to enable each pupil to appropriate from moral and spiritual tradition, and from the plenitude of human learning, something of an abiding and sustaining sense of identity, amid the ubiquity of change in contemporary society.

The commitment to a balanced education is also endorsed by the social partners in the NESC report *Education and Training Policies for Economic and Social Development* (1993), (pp.294-296). The view set out in the NESC report emphasised that concern for links between the education system and social and economic development need not, and did not, undermine the valuation of a balanced approach. This was also reflected in the Convention's deliberations. The participants accepted the value of qualities such as enterprise, innovation, self-reliance and problem-solving as legitimate and desirable characteristics to be promoted among our people. The dissatisfaction had been that, in the Green Paper, these qualities were too narrowly associated with a technological and commercial idiom. The cultivation of the imagination, creativity and divergent thinking ought to be objectives and outcomes of many features of educational experience. While promotion of vocational and practical subjects and of work experience were regarded by the Convention as important features of the educational system, a too narrow approach to them could distort the educational process. All subjects should be approached in a truly educational way and thus transcend old dichotomies of liberal versus vocational.

Successful educational planning and policy-formulation are very complex tasks in modern society. They require great expertise, an intimate knowledge of the dynamics of the system, research guidelines, time, resources, and the backing of government. The implementation of policy is even more difficult and its success is dependent on many variables. While recognising the difficulties, they must not be avoided. A number of analyses have indicated the need for a significant reform of Irish education to bring it into line with the changing needs of individuals, changing societal developments and improved insights from educational research and practice at home and abroad. It is also necessary to remove anomalies, achieve greater equity and set new goals for the quality of Irish democratic life.

In recent years, education has come to form a central dimension of governmental strategic policy. This is reflected, for instance, in the *Programme for National Recovery* (1987) and the *Programme For Economic and Social Progress* (1991). In its *Programme For A Partnership Government* (1993) the present government stated, "We regard education as the key to our future prosperity and to equality and equal opportunities for all our citizens."(p.29). The strength of the "knowledge base" will play a very significant part in the future development of Irish society. Ireland's *National Development Plan, 1994-1999* acknowledges this when it states, "Ireland's future prosperity will rest on a highly educated and skilled workforce and a continued growth in productivity." (p.77).

The backing of government for education is based on a number of factors, including the realisation of the multi-faceted influence of education on societal improvement, but particularly on economic development. This, coupled with the heavy national investment in education, tends to stress economic concerns with regard to educational outcomes in periodic statements made by government and by the social partners. Such concerns need to be balanced by the other dimensions which should be integral to educational policy-making. An over-emphasis on economic and instrumentalist considerations in educational policy-making could have distorting effects, with deleterious consequences. The shaping of the educational future is a prerogative of the Irish people. There is a responsibility on all those holding positions of authority to try to ensure that, in restructuring the educational system to bring it into line with changing individual and societal needs, the common good and a future-oriented perspective are kept to the fore in people's consciousness. The decisions taken now will be potentially of historical importance. Great care is needed to ensure that the best possible foundations are put in place which will be durable and supportive of educational success in a new era. While building on Irish experience and on the insights and research of personnel close to the realities of the Irish educational system, note should also be taken of what guidance can be gleaned from research and best practice of other countries which have been engaged in similar restructuring of their education systems. However, the approach taken to educational change in Ireland is very different from that prevailing in some other countries. Here the keynote is consultation and partnership, as distinct from rule by dictat or prescriptive imposition. Ireland can also learn from the mistakes of other countries and give examples of good practice itself.

The quality of educational policy and the character of its formulation will be of central significance in shaping the future well-being of the system. Some commentators have been critical of Ireland's policy-making record and structures. For instance, in its *Review of Irish Education,* in 1991, the OECD expressed misgivings about the situation governing policy-formulation, and the impediments which existed, stating, "The Department is over-stretched simply to administer the system.   Furthermore, it is neither conditioned nor appropriately equipped to advise systematically on policy." (p.39).   The National Economic and Social Council (NESC) (incorporating the social partners), in its recent report, *A Strategy For Competitiveness, Growth and Employment* (1993), stated in this regard:

> The record suggests that, in the past, educational policy has not been
> based on a complete or coherent view of the educational process.
> Ad hoc initiatives and schemes exist at all levels, but there has been
> little linkage or continuity between the various initiatives.......... It
> is the Council's view that a more rigorous approach to the
> formulation of educational policy would result in more successful
> attainment of stated objectives. (p.494).

The Green Paper, in its brief outline of the future role of the Department of Education, (p.156) stressed the importance of its policy role.   The Paper expressed the hope that by "divesting itself of its excessive involvement in day-to-day administration," the Department "will be in a position to address itself to its key tasks in a more dynamic and effective manner."   In its submission to the National Education Convention, the Department of Education referred to the significance of education policy as follows:

> It touches on every aspect of public policy. It reflects the aspirations
> of society, is strongly grounded in philosophical bases, reflects many
> social objectives and also reflects many economic policy
> objectives......... (Stenographers' Report, p.4)

In reply to questioning at the Convention, the Secretary of the Department stated "If there is a significant devolution achieved, well then, the Department has more time for policy analysis, policy-formulation and that, in turn, will require a change in our behaviour." (p.14)

The Secretariat of the Convention endorses the priority which now seems to be given to the strategic policy role of the Department of Education and considers that it is necessary to take a range of measures to ensure that this can become a reality.   These would include a significant departure from long-established, inherited procedures within the Department of Education, the genuine devolution of some responsibilities from the Department, fostering an orientation towards policy-making within the Department, improving communication networks, continuing the improvement of statistical procedures, and the harnessing of research towards policy-formulation.   In these ways, the Department can develop its capacity for leadership and establish a more assured basis for policy initiatives.   Work in these areas is already under way and, in the Secretariat's view, deserves support and resourcing from central government to allow it to develop satisfactorily. The consultative processes on the Green Paper, and the nature of the Department's engagement with them, also indicate a progressive policy of dialogue with involved parties and an openness to the ideas of agencies external to the Department, which is praiseworthy, and should be developed further. Close links ought to be fostered and sustained between the Department of Education and research agencies in Ireland. An openness and receptivity to comparative research studies should also be promoted.

The size of the Irish education community and the character of the partnership which exists between agencies should be utilised in helping to build a system distinguished by its commitment to excellence in the service of all students, to policy formation, to the quality, communication and co-ordination of research, to comprehensive statistical data, to informed awareness of educational problems at home and to trends and developments abroad.

2.   Administrative Change and the Role of the Department of Education

2.1   The General Context

 The administrative and organisational development of the education system was an issue of central concern and debate at the Convention. While it was emphasised that the most crucial aspect of the educational process was the quality of the educational experiences of participants at all levels of the education system, it was also understood that this depended on the character and efficiency of the policy and administrative framework of the system. At a period of profound change and remarkable expansion of the education system, there was general acceptance that reforms in the long-established, inherited framework were desirable. However, Convention participants also made it clear that great care and thoughtful planning were required so as to ensure that the outcomes of the reforms would be satisfactory, in alignment with demonstrated needs and, as far as possible, capable of winning the allegiance of key agencies within the system. In this context, the opportunity for debate and multi-lateral dialogue provided by the Convention was appreciated by participants.

Sections 3.2 and 3.3. of the Background Paper for the Convention had outlined, in summary form, the key proposals for change as set out in the Green Paper and the *Programme for A Partnership Government*, together with some reactions to them. The key proposals involved a new role for the Department of Education, new roles for Boards of Management of Schools and the establishment of local educational authorities. Many of the presentations by organisations at the Convention made reference to such proposals. The issues were also raised by the Secretariat in the questioning sessions, and several of the Analysis of Issues sessions focussed on administrative matters. It was generally concluded that, if the projected division of powers and responsibilities was to become a reality, then this would involve a historically significant restructuring of the education system. It was also recognised that the achievement of major educational change was usually a complex and slow process. Traditional rights, allegiances and working procedures would need to be altered. A striking feature of the Convention was an openness to discuss possible change, but also a concern that people should be convinced of the value of change, and of the need for consultation and good communication if an ownership of such development was to be fostered among involved parties.

As well as the Department of Education, there are a number of other national agencies which play a significant role in the education system and which have close links with the Department. Two of these, the Higher Education Authority (HEA) and the National Council for Educational Awards (NCEA), are statutory bodies with significant functions relating to higher education. It is planned to develop and expand their remits, and these will be discussed later. The National Council for Curriculum and Assessment (NCCA) is not a statutory body but has important advisory functions relating to curricular and assessment issues. The Green Paper proposed that a new agency would take over responsibility for curricula and examinations and this would have important consequences for both the NCCA and the Department, which require careful analysis and planning. The National Council for Vocational Awards (NCVA) is of more recent origin and may develop new links with the NCEA and the NCCA. It is desirable when setting out the new organisational profile of the Department of Education to treat of the relationships which will exist between the Department and such national bodies.

3.   Intermediate Educational Tiers

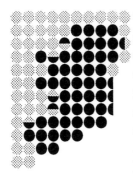 The issue of regionalisation of authority for education has been a recurrent one in the history of Irish education. However, with the exception of the vocational education sector, local education structures have not been established. As has been noted, the Department initiated moves towards establishing regional education structures in the mid-seventies and the mid-eighties, but without success. Now, in the nineties, the *Programme For A Partnership Government* of January 1993 has declared that "democratic intermediate structures for the management of first and second level education" will be established. The absence of a clear and more comprehensive statement of what is intended by such "intermediate structures" has been a disadvantage with regard to promoting an informed debate on such structures. Nevertheless, the issue of an intermediate tier has been a central one in much of the general debate on proposed developments for the future of Irish education. Between the polarities of a "disengaged" Department concentrating for the future on strategic policy, budgetary and quality assurance roles, and the individual schools being required to be more autonomous and self-reliant, the issue of a middle tier being established between the Department and the individual schools has come more to the fore.

Among key questions raised with regard to local educational authorities are: the authority and powers which would be devolved to them and the nature of their relationships with school trustees and Boards of Management; the structure and composition of such authorities; the form of their accountability to the Department and to schools; the geographical area to be designated to them; the resources which would be available to them and the timing of their establishment.

It would seem that a considerable change of attitude has occurred with regard to local educational authorities since the proposals were mooted in the Green Paper of 1985, *Partners in Education.* This may be influenced by the declared intention of the Department to disengage from day-to-day involvement with schooling issues, but it may also be affected by changing social attitudes, demographic trends, and economic circumstances. Traditionally, the owners of "private" schools have been anxious to preserve their independence and relate directly with the Department of Education on many matters. If this were to be no longer possible, then they might consider it desirable to look to another agency for assistance.

As well as a concern about intrusive powers of local authorities on individual schools, those less favourably disposed to local education structures have expressed concern about the danger of more bureaucratisation within the education system. Linked to this is a fear that such bureaucracies might swallow up resources to the detriment of the educational services to schools. This is associated, in turn, with a fear that resources made available for the regional authorities would be inadequate to service the envisaged needs. A concern was also expressed about the dangers of politicisation, in the party sense, of the administration of local education. Such concerns and apprehensions were raised during the debates at the Convention. Nevertheless, there was general agreement that an intermediate educational tier could have a valuable role in supporting the quality of educational provision within the system. The apprehensions need to be addressed in the White Paper, and, if dealt with satisfactorily, it would seem that there could be widescale support for such structures within emerging new circumstances.

The realisation of the need for greater professional support services to schools and the need for co-ordination and effective utilisation of such services have fostered a more favourable attitude towards local educational authorities which might provide such services. Many schools are small and face declining pupil populations, with consequent anxieties about future survival. A local educational agency potentially could be of great assistance in helping to rationalise school provision. It could also have a useful role to play in preventing unfair competition between schools in a multi-school, "free for all" educational environment. Such authorities might also play a significant role in preventing, or limiting, inequalities and disadvantage in districts where the "between-school" rivalries may lead to inequalities and inadequate curricular provision for some pupils.

A strong emphasis was placed by many at the Convention on the co-ordinating, support and service role which such structures could play. Among the services proposed were: the organisation of inservice education for teachers, and other staff; psychological, medical, para-medical and social services (in association with the local health board); education for special needs; a counselling service for pupils and teachers; curriculum development initiatives; library services; remedial services; facilities for pre-schooling; a teacher supply service; organisation of adult and community education; specialist visiting teacher services; transport services; legal advisory services; school/industry links and co-ordination of European Union intervention programmes and funding mechanisms.

The strategic planning role of an intermediate tier for its region was considered by some participants such as the Conference of Major Religious Superiors and the Irish Vocational Education Association to be an important function. This would include taking an overview of needs and existing provision in its area, engaging in forward planning, and co-operating with other local authority agencies on matters of mutual concern.

The question of the authority and powers of the intermediate tier was a matter of particular concern at the Convention. The ideal situation from the point of view of the IVEA, which has had the experience of over sixty years of local education authority activity, was that, on a gradual basis, the proposed intermediate tiers should own or lease all the schools and be the formal employers of all teachers. Other organisations disagreed strongly with such a perspective and saw the new structures as being primarily support agencies to schools, without interfering in the institutional independence which the schools currently had.

Following further discussion, it was agreed in the analysis session that, to function effectively, the tiers, as well as being support agencies, needed to have "some regulatory powers." Sustained attention needed to be given to this dimension in the context of the powers which would be devolved to the new structures. It was felt that a model could be developed which would accommodate both differences in school types and variations in ownership, and it was suggested that a number of models should be devised and examined by the various interest groups. Flexibility in the type of relationships which schools might have with an intermediate tier was seen to be important. Different schools might wish to have different relationships with the local tier.

At this stage, the majority view was that teachers should be employed by their Boards of Management and support staff such as psychologists and counsellors might be employed by the intermediate tier. This structure could also play an important role in the redeployment of teachers and the organisation of supply staff to schools.

The intermediate tier was seen as playing an important role in developing a variety of links at all levels within the system, downward to local schools and communities, laterally with other local tiers and upwards with the Department of Education. In this respect, the strategic role of an intermediate structure in identifying local needs and priorities and communicating these to the Department, was regarded as very important. Local educational authorities should liaise with other local development structures as set out in chapter seven of *The National Development Plan, 1994-99.* Links could also be developed with other agencies serving the systems, particularly with a Teachers' Council, if established.

The issue of resources was discussed at length. It was stressed that power and decision-making in this area must be devolved from the centre. Significant additional resources would be required in order to nurture a cultural climate which would enable the new structures to develop and gain the confidence of those they served.   Authority would be dependent on the budget allocation.   It was suggested that a degree of realism was required with regard to resources, and that an important task for the new tier would be to draw up a five-year costed plan of requirements for the institutions in its area, with an identification of priorities.

The geographical boundaries of the new structures received only brief discussion at the Convention because of time constraints.   It was stated that the area should be small enough so as to facilitate real local involvement and that account should be taken of existing boundaries which people understood and could identify with.   To allow the sense of local engagement with the authorities, the county structure would seem to recommend itself in terms of geographical spread.   However, if the intermediate tiers were to have the authority, resource allocation and planning functions, outlined above, the Secretariat considers it difficult to see how they could work effectively and economically, if they were to operate totally on a county basis. It would seem necessary to establish remits where several counties with small populations could co-ordinate efforts for the provision of some services.   It would seem particularly important that counties would cluster with regard to the provision of specialist services such as inspectorate, psychological services, curriculum development units, and draw from a more regional base rather than the individual county.   An alternative approach might be to set up a small number of regional authorities, with county sub-committees, focussing on issues which can best be dealt with at a more local level.   Without more clarity as to what powers and budgetary discretion are to be given to the proposed intermediate tiers, it is not possible to be precise on the optimum framework for such tiers.   The forthcoming Departmental paper on intermediate tiers should help to clarify relevant issues.

Representation on intermediate tiers should reflect appropriately the balance of interests involved, including public representatives, but in a minority role. The intermediate tiers should have an executive with significant authority and accountability. The accountability relationship to the Department of Education would need to be set out clearly and an appeal procedure to the Minister or the Department of Education would need to be put in place.   Obviously, the powers of the new tiers would be linked to their budgetary strength and the criteria devised for the provision of services.   Thought must also be given as to how they could interact with existing school authorities concerning aspects of local and regional educational planning.   Their regulatory powers would need to be clearly defined.   It would be desirable if the new authorities could operate with flexibility in their arrangements with different types of schools. The authorities ought to incorporate responsibilities for primary and post-primary schools in their areas, but also have responsibilities ranging from pre-school to adult education.

If established, confidence and trust in the new structures would need to be fostered. In this context, time is crucial and it may be that a gradual, transitional approach might be adopted beneficially to facilitate the growth of such trust and new forms of partnership. It would seem desirable that such new structures would subsume the existing vocational education committees, but be influenced by their commitments, such as to the disadvantaged, promoting technical education, adult education provision, curriculum development initiatives. On the other hand, in terms of their powers, composition and functions, they would need to be understood as a new beginning with a much broader remit than the vocational educational sector. If all sectors were to be expected to participate wholeheartedly in the new structures and evolve new partnership arrangements, then it would seem necessary that a new start, albeit influenced by older traditions, be undertaken.

As an earnest of their interest in the intermediate tiers it was agreed at the Analysis of Issues session that organisations would engage in further discussions and seek to devise and explore models for structures which might accommodate varying interests. It was also proposed that, to promote informed debate, the Department of Education should draw up a position paper in advance of the White Paper, setting forth its concept of the new structures. This the Minister undertook to do in her closing speech to the Convention. Such a position paper would provide a sense of direction, and prompt the necessary detailed discussion on possible powers, composition, accountability, resourcing and mode of functioning by interested organisations.

4. The Governance of Schools

The Green Paper referred to "the drive to promote greater autonomy for schools" and stated the Department's intention "to devolve the maximum degree of responsibility for the management of its affairs to the school." (p.141)   Within this policy, there may be an underestimation of the extent to which individual schools already exercise discretionary powers and the scope they have for decision-making when compared to schools in some other countries. While the OECD *Review Of Irish Education* (1991) emphasised the centralised administrative structure of the Irish education system, a recent OECD (1993) survey showed that Ireland is rather exceptional among OECD countries in the extent to which certain decisions are made at the level of the school. A high percentage of decisions are made at the school level relating to the organisation of instruction (e.g. methods, choice of textbooks), planning and structure (e.g. establishment or closure of a school, defining the syllabus), personnel management (e.g. appointment of staff), and allocation and use of resources in schools. This is partly explained by the absence of any other authority between the great majority of schools and the Department of Education. This tradition of decision-making may be helpful in promoting greater self-reliance and autonomy in schools.

As was noted earlier, Management Boards are relatively new features of Irish schools, and some schools do not have them at all. Historically, patrons and trustees have been the key authority agencies as regards school management in the majority of schools. The fundamental question is whether appropriate adjustments and adaptations can be made to bring the governance of schools into line with very changed economic, social and political circumstances, while respecting the rights of various involved parties and winning the allegiance of the relevant partners within school communities. The great majority of the schools are privately owned but are predominantly state funded. The Irish people have a high regard for the great contribution of religious in the provision and management of schooling in the past. While maintaining that regard, there is also a strong public desire for new forms of partnership which will reflect changed circumstances and attitudes.

Nowadays, the state pays over 80 per cent of capital costs of buildings and facilities, and over 90 per cent of current expenditure, if one includes teachers' salaries. Bearing this in mind, and in view of the pace and direction of economic, technological, social and cultural change occurring in Ireland, and increasing demands for more democratic participation of parents and teachers in the governance of our schools, the Green Paper had proposed that the Patrons/Trustees should cede many of their powers and functions to schools' Boards of Management. The Green Paper envisaged all schools having Boards of Management with significant responsibilities such as the quality of student learning, appointment of staff, quality of teaching, and school plan and review. It also proposed a common form of management board for all aided secondary schools and for different categories of primary school, and suggested that the chairperson would operate on an elective, rotating basis.

The Green Paper intended that the Boards would receive the necessary authority to fulfil their duties from the owners/trustees, "on the basis of clearly defined roles and responsibilities and embodied in appropriate instruments and articles of management." (p.143). The establishment of Intermediate Tiers as recommended in the *Programme For Government,* (1993) would also have implications for the operation of school Management Boards.

Quite clearly, the Green Paper proposals would involve very significant changes in the roles of Patrons, Owners and Trustees in their relationships with their schools. Dissatisfaction was expressed by all the religious authorities at the National Education Convention on the extent of such proposed changes. This was exacerbated by the neglect or inadequate understanding, which was implied by the Green Paper, of the rights and roles of Patron and Trustee. Neither had the Green Paper spelled out what "appropriate instruments and articles of management" might involve and how they might safeguard the concerns of patrons/trustees. Patrons and Trustees drew attention to constitutional and legal rights in support of their position, their key concern being the safeguarding of the religious ethos and character of their schools.

Substantial clarification of the roles of Patrons, Trustees and owners in Irish educational provision emerged in the course of the National Education Convention discussions. The different religious authorities, and indeed other ethically or culturally motivated groups such as the multi-denominational schools or Gaelscoileanna, who set up and operate schools do so because they wish to ensure that certain fundamental beliefs, values and culturally valuable practices are effectively taught and learned/internalised within the schools they set up. These fundamental beliefs, values and cultural practices are to be expressed not only in explicit curricular programmes — such as religious instruction classes but, also, clearly incorporated into the overall organisational character and enlivening ethos of the school. The Patron/Trustee in this sense stands for, or acts on behalf of, a body (usually organised) of people who wish their children to be educated within a particular religious, ethical or cultural tradition. Discussion at the Convention also clarified various functions of the Patron/Trustee with regard to the establishment, operation and closure of schools, and these are referred to in the report of the analysis of issues session. The vocational school sector offers a different model of trusteeship from the majority of schools, and is embedded in a more democratic concept of schooling provision.

With more educated parents, most of whom exhibit keen interest in their children's education and are more conscious of the constitutional prerogatives of parents than formerly, the older model of patron "acting on behalf of" such people is coming under challenge. This was clearly in evidence at the Convention. It is also the case that a more pluralist society, with many emerging interest groups, may give rise to pressures for new forms of schooling in alignment with their interests. The state may have to strike a balance in responding to pressure groups so as to prevent an undue fractionalising of the school system.

In the course of a comprehensive and constructive debate at the Convention it was made clear by all parties that they were not opposed to change. The key concern was that forward-planning would respect rights which had their corresponding responsibilities, would be based on clear and realistic rationales for the exercise of authority of the various responsible agencies, and would be flexible and amenable to accord with what was educationally distinctive and defensible in tradition, as well as meeting the challenges of evolving social contexts.

Discussion of existing managerial models indicated a clear diversity of forms of relationships between Patrons, Trustees and Boards of Management in the different types of school: between the Catholic bishops and primary school management; the VECs and their schools; the Catholic Religious orders and their schools; the Protestant Patrons and their school management; lay owners and their schools. Given that variation, it will require considerable negotiation to secure a common Board of Management structure which will incorporate equality of participation by the Trustees' nominees, parents and teachers.

In all cases where Boards of Management existed, the Patrons/Trustees considered that their establishment had been valuable, but all conceded that improvements were desirable. The view was that the Boards generally created a greater sense of collegiality and engagement on the part of the partners and could have great potential if developed further. While most Trustees were prepared to promote Boards of Management, they considered that more consideration should be given to the functions they could perform beneficially. Some backed the functions as set out in the Green Paper. It was also emphasised that, while Boards should have significant and clearly delineated powers, they must also accept responsibility and implement in an unambiguous manner the, sometimes, hard decisions which have to be taken.

Autonomy of Boards could not be absolute, but Patrons/Trustees were in favour of a greater degree of independence.

It was suggested at the Convention that devolution of powers from the Department of Education to the Boards could be more significant than devolution from the Patron or Trustee. It was also considered that, if new responsibilities were to be taken on by Boards of Management, it would be essential that the budgetary allocation to them would be adequate to allow them fulfil such responsibilities. It would also be necessary to improve greatly the training opportunities for those participating on Boards of Management. Extra support would be needed, particularly in areas of disadvantage, where parents could sometimes be alienated from schools or reluctant to get involved. In view of the competence and experience required for efficient and effective engagement in Boards of Management, it was questioned if a three-year term of office was sufficiently long.

It was accepted that Boards of Management should be responsible for the educational work of the school. However, the Green Paper was rather unclear as to the degree of responsibility for the quality of teaching of individual teachers, as between Boards of · Management, Principals and the Inspectorate. The Green Paper's proposal — "it will be a matter for the principal, in the first instance, to ensure the quality of teachers' work in the school" (p.169), was accepted generally at the Convention. Since the Board of Management would not have the expertise to evaluate directly in this area, it may have to rely more on external expertise if it is to fulfil its general responsibility. In this context, the withdrawal of the Inspectorate from the evaluation of individual teachers' work, should be planned with great care. There is a need for discussion between the Department, management bodies and teacher representatives to ensure that satisfactory procedures would be put in place.

The composition of Boards of Management remains a contentious issue. At the National Education Convention, the National Parents' Council (Primary), made a very strong case in favour of equal representation with other partners on the Boards, and post-primary parents favoured the same, without insisting on it in all cases. All of the teacher organisations made a case for equal representation with trustee nominees on Boards of Management. New models for the composition of Boards were tabled by the primary school parents' representatives, the Educate Together movement and Gaelscoileanna, in keeping with their aims. The general view was that the Green Paper's suggestion of eleven members for schools of five teachers, or more, was too unwieldy. There were also serious reservations by some about involving the school principal as a voting member of a board. The patrons and trustees of Catholic schools considered that they needed to appoint majorities on the board and nominate the Chairperson so as to protect the religious ethos and social mission of their schools. However, both the Catholic Bishops and the CMRS declared they were open to discussions with the Department and other relevant bodies on possible alternative, effective mechanisms by which the continuing religious ethos and social mission of their schools could be protected.

Protestant school managements faced particular difficulties. They have to deal with a very scattered and low-density population, with less clear bonds to local parish communities at primary level, and almost no such connection at post-primary level. In addition, a substantial proportion of children attending their schools are not Protestant. In such a situation they feel strongly that the Patron's right to nominate the majority on Boards of Management is essential to maintain the Protestant ethos of the school. Even if Deeds of Trust enshrined the religious ethos of the school, they feel strongly that a significant non-Protestant presence on the Boards of Management could erode the continuing religious ethos of the school. In addition, it was felt that the "reserve power" of Patrons/Trustees could not be effectively utilised to ensure the continuing Protestant ethos of their schools when Boards of Management were not effectively carrying out their duties. At post-primary level, also, it was felt strongly that the current structure of Boards of Governors/Guardians had such substantial advantages for the welfare and ethos of their schools that they would not wish to lose the expertise involved. However, the representatives indicated that they would be willing to discuss possible new structures.

The Vocational schools, on the other hand, are the only schools which operate under a clear legal or statutory framework in which Boards of Management operate as subcommittees of the VEC (VEC Act, Section 21, 1930). Although there is substantial variation across VECs in the presence, composition, powers and operation of Boards of Management, it is, nevertheless, the stated policy of the IVEA to increase the democratic representativeness of Boards of Management and to devolve more power to them. The IVEA is also anxious to ensure that its values and priorities would be shared by the Boards of Management.

The issue of school ethos is a pervasive one in the debate on school governance. The debate could benefit from a detailed analysis and exposition of the concept of ethos, and what it entails. In discussion at the Convention the Secretariat indicated its unease at a view of ethos as being "determined by Trustees," and seen as something which could be handed on, as it were, to a school community and be "guaranteed" to operate. In the view of the Secretariat, the statement set forth in the submission on the Green Paper by the Irish Commission for Justice and Peace has much to recommend it. It stated:

> An ethos foreign to the lived experience and struggle of the school
> and its component groups, and for which they felt no responsibility,
> would exist at best on paper rather than in reality.   While trustees
> insist, and rightly so, on certain minimum requirements as
> facilitating the creation of a particular ethos, there are intangibles at
> the heart of a living ethos which cannot really be compelled.   Ethos
> is best expressed, helped to develop, and enriched within the school
> community as the result of the continuing interaction between a
> **shared dialogue on the core values of the school,** embracing the
> patron, trustees, board, principal, staff, parents and students, and the
> **daily practice which endeavours to embody those values.**
> (original emphases)

Quoting from the Vatican Council and other church documents, it concluded, "In
regard to ethos this must signify the structured and continuous involvement of all the
groups which constitute the school community" (Irish Commission for Justice and
Peace, 1993, pp.21,22).   If the school ethos is to be an enlivening one, this dynamic,
participative approach, which would draw on qualities of school leadership,
partnership and the moral energies of the school community, would seem to have
much to contribute.

Looking to the future, there is a significant, but not insuperable challenge ahead to
devise management structures which would accommodate the diverging views.   In
the context of contemporary and evolving educational, economic and social
circumstances, the state seeks Boards of Management with genuine responsibility,
more democratic participation and effective accountability procedures.   The teachers
and most parents seek equal representation with trustees' or patrons' nominees on the
Boards.   The majority of Trustees/Patrons are reluctant to depart from a guarantee of
a majority of nominees on the Boards and the appointment of a Chairperson, in the
interests of protecting their denominational concerns.

The Secretariat submits the following reflections which may be of assistance in the
on-going planning for management change.   The roles, rights and authority of
Trustees/Patrons in Irish education provision for all types of school need to be much
more clearly articulated in state documents.   The main current mechanism which is
perceived by religious managements to guarantee the character and enlivening ethos
of religiously run schools is by the Trustee/Patron nominating the majority on Boards
of Management. The actual growth in demand for greater participation by parents
and teachers, and more openness and transparency at the level of each individual
school will, in many cases, require a much more democratic form of school
management than we have had in the past.   These expectations and trends do not
necessarily run counter to the legitimate interests of the Trustee/Patron in seeking to

protect the continuing ethos of the school; but they do directly challenge the current main mechanism used by Trustees/Patrons for this purpose.

In this context, note should be taken of the responses of the CMRS, and of the Episcopal Commission at the National Education Convention which stated that they would be willing to enter discussions with the Department of Education and others to find alternative effective mechanisms to protect the continuing religious ethos and character of their schools. In such discussions, the following considerations are relevant to the construction of a model of relationships between Trustee/Patron and management:

- A clearer specification of the functions of patronage and management, such that the interests of Trustee/Patron are protected and the concern for the greater democratisation of school management boards may be accommodated;

- Agreed Deeds of Trust and Articles of Management to be drawn up, within the ambit of which the Board of Management would operate, and departures from which could lead to its being called to account;

- Boards of Management to be primarily concerned with functions such as: the educational objectives of the school; approving school plans and school reviews; appointments, promotion and dismissal of teachers and other staff; arrangements on inservice education and replacement teaching; budgets and expenditure programmes; maintenance of buildings; relations with parents; discipline codes agreed with teachers and parents;

- The method of selection of the chairperson is an important matter deserving of discussion and negotiation between the involved parties;

- School Plan to include aspirations or aims for the kind of ethos to which the school community might become committed and work towards achieving. The means adopted might, thus, be part of, and emerge from, a collaborative planning activity. The school plan and the annual review of progress to be referred by the Board of Management to the Trustee/Patron.

In such a governance framework, with clear Deeds of Trust and Articles of Management, the Board would have clearly defined functions and responsibilities. The Board would be equally representative of Patrons, teachers and parents, and could co-opt individuals from the local community. This would address the interface of responsibilities between Trustees/Patrons and Boards of Management, could alleviate current concerns and lead forward to a more democratic and constructive partnership in the years ahead.

The Secretariat reiterates earlier statements which emphasise support for management training, adequate budgets for Boards of Management and, possibly, a longer term of office than three years for Board members. Planning for the functions of Boards of Management should be done in conjunction with planning for proposed Intermediate Educational Tiers. In this context, attention should be paid concurrently to relative responsibilities of the Department of Education, of the Intermediate Tiers and of the Boards of Management, with an articulation of the nature of the linkages between them.

5. Provision of Multi-Denominational and Secular Education

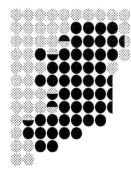 Denominational schooling has been the dominant form of schooling in this state since independence. In recent decades Irish society has been experiencing changing patterns in religious belief and practice. While the great majority of parents would seem to retain a preference for denominational education for their children, there are minorities which seek alternative schooling provision. A striking example of this is the emergence of a parental movement which favours multi-denominational education for their children. They have grouped together in the Educate Together movement. This group was represented at the National Education Convention, and some attention has been paid to its concerns in the previous section "Governance of Schools." The pressure for the provision of other than denominational schooling is likely to grow and it is important for the state to have an informed policy on this developing situation. The Green Paper declared Departmental support for the establishment of such schools on the same terms as are available for denominational schools. This was challenged at the Convention when it was demonstrated that, as a matter of policy, the Department only grants "provisional recognition" to such schools for up to five years before it will pay any capital grant, a constraint which is not present for Church organised schools (The problem of "provisional recognition" is also encountered by Gaelscoileanna and is linked to Departmental concerns about the longterm viability of such schools initiated by groups of interested parents). It was also pointed out that all other member states of the European Union provide publicly owned buildings for basic, compulsory education. Ireland was seen as unique in requiring citizens to provide privately-owned accommodation for this purpose. In its presentation to the Convention the Department of Education acknowledged the emergence of a more pluralist society and the demands of different groups of parents for other than denominational schools.

There would seem to have been unanimous agreement among participants at the Convention that the rights of parents to multi-denominational education should be respected and facilitated. There was also appreciation of the problems groups face such as "provisional recognition," the great difficulty of providing a site for a school and of raising the necessary 15 per cent of the total cost of school buildings.

In this regard, the issue of unused or underused church-owned school property became an issue of discussion. With limited exceptions, it appears to be the experience of the multi-denominational school bodies that it is proving extremely difficult to get the agreement of church authorities to rent, lease or even sell such property to multi-denominational school organisations.   Although predominantly state-funded, these properties are in private hands, though limited in their possible usage and with significant liens by the state on the realisation of their market value, once no longer needed for educational purposes.   This is an area in which it would seem desirable for the state to initiate discussions with the religious authorities so that vacant school buildings could be made available on reasonable conditions to multi or non-denominational groups of parents where there is significant evidence of sufficient continuing demand for such new types of schools.   In this respect, it would appear unacceptable for the state to have to buy back school buildings at current values, where the historical costs were, predominantly, originally paid for by the state.   The establishment of intermediate education tiers could be a useful mechanism in assisting the provision of multi-denominational education.

In general, the Department needs to recognise the growth of alternative forms of "patronage/trusteeship" to that of traditional religious organisations, and recognise in its administrative arrangements the greater difficulties these new forms of ethically/culturally inspired groupings have in meeting conventional Departmental rules for capital grants and current expenditure.   These appear to be balanced against the newer forms of school organisation: i.e. their greater difficulty in raising the necessary starting finance for school sites and the 15% for school capital as well as the greater difficulties they face with "provisional recognition" rules.   The idea put forward by Educate Together, that school buildings and sites could be publicly owned or provided and leased out to school authorities, would seem to be worth exploring.

It was suggested to the Convention that the next national census will show that there are at least 30,000 children aged between 4 and 12 years who do not adhere to the Catholic, Church of Ireland, Presbyterian or Methodist faiths.   The state needs to take more responsibility in assisting the rights of minority religions for educational facilities which would respect their outlook.

A representative of those seeking secular education at the Convention fully accepted the rights of the majority to denominational education but pointed out the conscientious dilemmas which existed for non-believing parents who had no choice but to attend religiously-run schools.   Some painful experiences of unacceptable discrimination towards such parents and children were reported to the Convention.   It was the general view of the Convention that respect for the views of such citizens was essential, and church representatives stressed that greater sensitivity should be promoted among school authorities in this context.   The Convention seemed to adopt the view of the Background Paper which stated, "While protecting the rights of majorities, the rights of minorities must not be just tolerated, but treated with respect, and an out-going policy be adopted to facilitate the accommodation of their needs." (p.10).

The main issue here is that, in many cases, parents not only do not wish their children to attend religious instruction classes but they also object to their children being educated within schools whose dominant ethos is not of their faith/beliefs.   These parents have the right, of course, to withdraw their children from religious instruction.   But, besides the possible peer-stigmatising effects such withdrawal may bring, the point has been made strongly that an issue of civil liberties may be involved for such pupils/parents attending schools where religion is fully integrated with the rest of the curriculum and where the ethos and "hidden curriculum" fully reflect the religious ideals of the school.   This dilemma was put most sensitively by the CMRS to the National Education Convention: "We recognise, however, that issues of civil liberties remain because of genuine conscientious objections on the part of some families to the principle of the integration of religion with other aspects of the curriculum."   The dilemmas and challenges posed for policy makers and school authorities require not only dialogue at the school level but the development of "good practice" guidelines by a suitably qualified and representative working party convened by the Department.   Such a working party might also explore legal and, perhaps, constitutional issues which may be involved.

Without affecting the rights of religious authorities to establish schools with a clearly defined ethos, and to be aided by the state, there needs to be much wider agreement on the rights of nonbelievers, or other minorities within schools whose dominant ethos is not that of the majority.   In this situation, the Secretariat suggests that the Department should enter discussion with the main religious authorities to try to promote understanding of, and sensitivity to, the issues involved.

6.   School Rationalisation

6.1   Overview

While the Green Paper envisaged dramatic reductions in the number of schools at primary and post-primary levels in the coming years, it gave very little attention to the complexities involved in this process or to the sophisticated planning required to minimise its potentially harmful side-effects.   The issue of school rationalisation was a major one at the National Education Convention, with many representatives extolling the virtues of the small school and others deploring the inadequate policies which existed with regard to school amalgamations. There is no doubt but that good planning for school provision, in the context of significant demographic decline and new curricular policies, is one of the major issues of this decade and needs sustained and skilled attention by all authorities involved .

6.2   General Factors Affecting School Size

The Green Paper identified a number of reasons why smaller primary and post-primary schools are becoming less viable and, therefore, amalgamations become more necessary.   These underlying trends or pressures are very likely to intensify over the coming decade.   They include the following elements:

(a)   Declining pupil numbers at both primary and post-primary levels; with the number of primary pupils expected to decline by over 100,000 between 1991 and 2001, although it is only after 1996/7 that the numbers in post-primary pupils are expected to decline significantly.   These are national figures, however, and hide large regional and local variations in the rate and timing of decline;

(b)   The rapid decline in the number of religious who are teachers and principals in schools will also increase pressure for school rationalisation, because of the loss of the voluntary contributions of religious to their schools but, also, because their very departure from smaller schools makes it more likely that amalgamations will be considered;

(c)   As the rate of participation to Leaving Certificate level increases rapidly, with a much wider ability and aptitude range among the students, there is a necessity to broaden and enrich both the junior and senior cycle curricula at post-primary level.   This is very difficult to achieve in small schools.   Also, since most of these small schools are in multi-school catchment areas it would be highly inefficient to multiply costly additional curricular provision in essentially competing schools catering for the same community;

(d)   The envisaged rapid expansion of vocational/technical education at senior cycle level, and also in post Leaving Certificate courses and in continuing education and training, emphasises the importance of extensive and more differentiated curricula, and therefore larger schools.

However, it should be borne in mind, for all schools, that school size *per se* is not perfectly correlated with curricular range and effectiveness of provision and teaching across the whole ability/curricular range. So, there is some degree of freedom available to small schools, at both primary and post-primary levels, to provide effective education despite their small sizes, and this needs to be strongly taken into consideration in any decisions on amalgamations. There is not, in other words, an argument for amalgamating smaller schools into larger units unless the education provided is going to be more effective for the majority of pupils affected.

Yet, given current trends and the rapidly increasing significance of the role that education and vocational training, at both school and continuing education levels, play in the viability and productivity of modern technologically advanced economies, school size and curricular diversity are likely to become more critical factors in educational delivery in the future. This is likely to become even more critical for rural and small town communities. In order for those communities to adapt or transform themselves fast enough, given the central role that education and vocational training and retraining now play in rapid economic adjustment, it will become even more critical in future that they have effective, more curricular rich and, therefore, larger schools.

6.3   Criteria and Considerations for Primary Schools
There will always be some small schools in the country, given the distribution of the population and the need to serve minority religious groups. Indeed, groups such as Gaelscoileanna or Educate Together, who require a certain form of schooling, may contribute to the number of small primary schools. Other considerations also apply. The young age and early development stage of primary school children make it less appropriate to have a long transport time to and from school. Very young children going to local schools integrate their parents into local parish/community life to a far greater extent than at second level. Amalgamations of local schools and bussing to distant larger schools tend to exclude parents from everyday interaction with their children's teachers and schools. The growing independence of children from their parents as they mature makes this a far less emotionally sensitive issue for older children. Parents may also prefer the more intimate character of small schools,

sometimes accompanied by better discipline for their children.   Among the disadvantages of small schools, however, are possibly more limited curriculum, limitations in physical resources available, difficulty in providing services such as remedial teaching, the professional isolation of teachers and the disproportionate effect which a persistently under-performing teacher would have on the educational careers of the children in such a school.

While the Minister for Education is no longer aiming to establish schools in rural areas with a minimum of four teachers, the number of very small schools cannot be ignored as a policy issue.   In 1991. 43 per cent of all primary schools had three teachers or less and it appears that, over time, such small schools have been declining faster than larger schools.   However, a blanket bureaucratic decision that all schools of a particular size should be closed would not be satisfactory.   In the view of the Secretariat catchment area studies are needed which would provide detailed information on the present situation in terms of age and condition of schools, distances between schools, demographic projections, unit costs and associated data. Studies on the effectiveness of small schools are also needed.   The main criterion should obviously be educational quality and not school size *per se.*

The Secretariat considers that it would be helpful to devise minimum standards and criteria for small schools against which arguments for closure or amalgamation could be assessed.   One would need to be assured that gains in effectiveness actually occur from school closure in remote rural communities or small villages.   Such small schools may serve important local identification, social and cultural functions.   The alternative to keeping effective small schools open, even where the numbers do not justify it, but where their effective operation would need outside help from a local or regional educational tier, should be considered sympathetically.   The decision here should encompass both educational effectiveness and local community needs.   When decisions are made to close small schools it should be in the light of sophisticated investigation, with the educational well-being of the pupils as the main concern. The importance of consultation with management, parents and teachers should not be under-estimated, even when the relevant educational authority may have to overrule their preference.

6.4   Criteria and Considerations
Regarding Post-Primary School Rationalisation

Almost 25 per cent of Irish post-primary schools have less than 250 pupils.   Despite the six year cycle and higher retention rates, demographic projections indicate a significant decline in pupil enrolments from 1996-1997.   Besides demographic decline, constraints on curricular provision on small schools are likely to become far more serious in the future.   With increasing participation in the senior cycle, the consequent necessity to cater for a wider range of abilities and aptitudes and prepare the below average or "weaker" academic ability students for occupations which hold promise for their particular abilities and aptitudes, will require a much wider curriculum and teacher specialisation, as well as extra rooms, laboratories and facilities. The marginal costs of adequate additional curricular and teaching resources are likely to be just too great for many small schools.

School size is highly correlated with curricular range, though the latter is not completely determined by the former. Effective management and good planning by small schools, and poor management and planning by larger ones often mean little difference in curricular provision or effective schooling between schools that may vary by a few hundred students (Hannan, Breen et al., 1983). Nevertheless, small schools of less than 250 pupils with, say, 10 to 12 teachers, are necessarily limited in their curricular possibilities, so, if the curriculum options are to be extended, it appears to be a very difficult and very expensive task.

In the case of post-primary schools, therefore, amalgamation pressures appear much less resistible than in primary schools. In any case, most small post-primary schools are in multi-school catchment areas. Significant difficulties exist for school managements in such areas to plan for a better future.

It is unlikely that many local catchment area school managements can suddenly overcome their competitive interests, accurately perceive the wider interests of the communities or local economies, and organise spontaneously to keep a local competitor school in operation, particularly if they are gaining from its closure. Some outside authority, whether the Department or a local/regional educational authority, needs to act as a planning agency. Otherwise, the local community loses heavily, and the taxpayer will have to replace the curricular shortfall in the longterm. So, where there are a number of small schools in an area and the population is falling, rationalisation should ideally take place before damage is done to any of the schools, and their co-operation in the process of creating a new comprehensive school for their community is gained before competition destroys goodwill, and perhaps good schools!

In areas where separate viable schools are possible, each with a separate mission/goal (i.e. boys', girls', vocational/technical), inter school co-operation in maximising access to the widest curriculum by all pupils should be encouraged. However, the difficulty of achieving such co-operation and agreed division of labour, in the equal provision of specialised subjects and levels to all pupils in all schools needs to be appreciated. Some outside neutral and authoritative facilitator or monitor would appear to be essential to gaining such effective co-operation and ensuring equality of both provision of, and access to, educational services by the individual schools, which in most cases have been competitors.   This is where an Intermediate Tier with both legitimacy and authority and some control over discretionary resources could play a very important role in monitoring and moderating competition and in promoting co-operation.

There are a number of small, "stand-alone," post-primary schools serving a large hinterland with a scattered population, and their role in the life of their community is crucial.   Such schools should be given special consideration and support to help them fulfill their educational and social roles.

Besides, any role it might play in securing effective amalgamations, an Intermediate Tier could also play a very important role in providing specialist services and facilities on a shared community basis to groups of schools, and coordinating access and use of these. Specialist technology centres, specialist laboratories, modern office facilities, computer and Information Technology facilities, should be made available in the larger schools; but for even most medium size schools (300-500 pupils) such facilities would be very expensive, and hardly justifiable if they had to be provided to a number of such schools in the same catchment area.

6.5   Managing the Process of Amalgamation

The main problem identified by Convention participants regarding school amalgamation is the absence of any clear Departmental policy, even the absence of publicly available basic statistics on current and projected demographic trends for school catchment areas and regions.   Even where agreements have been reached by individual school managements on amalgamations, they have been left waiting for long periods by the Department, primarily, it would appear, because of the absence of any capital funding for such projects.   Given the size of the problem, clearly identified in the Green Paper, the Department should play a much more proactive role in bringing about successful amalgamations.

The Secretariat suggests that the Department should publish detailed statistical projections for each catchment area and region, its expectations for school amalgamations, and its order of priorities in such amalgamations.   In cases where school areas are low on the priority list, the Department, or local educational authority needs to develop a clearly defined policy on both promoting co-operation amongst local schools and moderating destructive competition.   In addition, it would need to be clear to all participants that the seriousness of the government's commitment to school rationalisation is matched by the earmarking of the substantial capital funding required for school amalgamations.

Once a group of schools in a catchment area is scheduled for amalgamation then a clear strategy and organisational arrangements need to be put in place in order to achieve the most beneficial results. These might include:

(a)   Prohibiting competition amongst schools;

(b)   Setting up an organising committee which would include not only the local owners/managers of the individual schools but, also, some Departmental or local educational authority representative. The use of an external, national, or regional, independent planning and arbitration body for amalgamations would be extremely helpful. It was clear at the Convention that, if a local educational authority were to attempt to do this it would need to be much differently structured and much more widely acceptable than the current VEC structure;

(c)   Owners and managers of schools in areas scheduled for amalgamation should organise themselves long before a crisis emerges (easily foreseeable if good demographic projections are available). Such anticipatory planning, with outside expert help, should help to maximise agreements and overcome opposition to effective amalgamations.   In this respect, it was considered that the use of formal representative bodies of proprietors, managers, principals, teachers and parents, could be a suitable organisational approach;

(d)   Guidelines on good practice in securing successful amalgamations could be derived and published, and some expert group should be financed by the Department for this purpose.

6.6   Planning for the Success of the Amalgamated School

The newly amalgamated school has not only the problem of creating a new organisation to achieve new objectives with a much larger and more diversified staff, but the major problem of uniting two or more separate, or originally competing teams of teachers, principals and other post holders into one team around a new leader and new objectives. It also faces the major difficulty of creating a new school culture, ethos and team spirit.

Again, this is an issue to which, it would seem, that the Department has paid insufficient attention, and, like the difficulties of arranging the process of amalgamation itself, it needs a good deal of outside assistance. The Secretariat recommends the following procedures:

(a)   The appointment of the Principal, and a planning team to work with the Principal to plan for the new school, at least for one year before the amalgamation takes place. The Principal should be involved in all decisions relating to the appointment of main post holders;

(b)   Intensive inservice courses for Principals, Vice-Principals and the middle management team;

(c)   Extreme sensitivity in planning the integration of the "losing" Principals and Vice-Principals into the new school. The provision of counselling and support for such personnel in their adjustment to the new school should be considered;

(d)   Inservice training is required for all teachers, but, particularly, for those moving from single sex to coeducational classroom situations. Ensuring gender equality in school curricular provision and access, as well as in classroom practice, does not arise spontaneously and teachers need inservice training to ensure effective coeducational teaching.

7.   The Internal Management of Schools

7.1   Overview

Education is a labour intensive enterprise with almost 40,000 teachers employed in approximately 4,100 first and second level schools, and about 80% of the annual recurrent budget allocated to teachers' salaries and pensions. This represents a huge investment in human resources and, in terms of quality, effectiveness and accountability, presents a major challenge to those responsible for the management of the system. Much of this responsibility, in the first instance, rests with the internal management personnel in the schools. The research literature consistently identifies good leadership as one of the key features of successful schools. Providing this quality of leadership is likely to present an even greater challenge in future years as schools respond not only to the curricular and organisational changes planned for the education system, but also to the wider changes in society which impinge on the work of the schools. The proposal in the Green Paper to give greater autonomy to schools will also add significantly to the responsibilities of the management in these institutions.

Considerable time was devoted at the Convention to discussing the internal management of schools.   At the post-primary level, presentations on these issues were made by the three principals' associations, the relevant patron and management organisations, the National Parents' Council (Post-Primary), and two teacher unions. A separate Analysis of Issues session was also devoted to discussing internal school management.   At the primary level, management issues were raised in the presentations by the primary management associations, The National Parents' Council (Primary) and the Irish National Teachers' Organisation.

While the responses to the proposals on the internal management of schools presented here reflect the outcomes of these discussions, the presentation is weighted towards schools in the post-primary sector.   This merely reflects the broader level of representation from this sector at the Convention, which, in turn, reflects the variety of school types and management structures at this level.   In the case of the primary sector, comments, for the most part, are based on the written responses to the Green Paper and the formal presentations at the Convention.

7.2   The Role of Principal

(i)   Proposals in the Green Paper
Consistent with the aim outlined in the Green Paper to devolve greater decision-making and responsibility to the individual school unit, particular emphasis is given in the document to the responsibility of the Board of Management in ensuring that the school provides a high quality education for all the pupils.   In practice, direct day-to-day responsibility for the smooth and efficient running of the school is vested by the Board of Management in the principal. The principal is supported in this task by the vice-principal and the post of responsibility holders.

The role of the principal is given particular emphasis in the Green Paper. The principal is seen as occupying a pivotal position in the school with responsibility for determining the educational aims of the school, devising strategies to achieve them, gaining the commitment of the staff to support them, and developing the school's curriculum and assessment policies. Managing the teaching staff, affirming and evaluating their work, identifying their development needs and fostering good relationships between teachers and parents and the rest of the community are also cited as important dimensions of this role (Green Paper, p.148). The development of a school plan, and the conduct of an annual review based on the plan, form an important mechanism through which this role can be exercised. (Green Paper, pp. 146-147).

The proposals on the role of the principal are consistent with the research findings on school effectiveness. This research has identified a strong relationship between positive school leadership and institutional effectiveness, and describes the successful principal as providing skilled instructional leadership for the staff, creating a supportive school climate, with particular emphasis on the curriculum and teaching and directed towards maximising academic learning, having clear goals and high expectations for staff and students, establishing good systems for monitoring student performance and achievement, promoting on-going staff development and inservice, and encouraging strong parental involvement and identification with, and support for the goals of the school.

(ii)   Response to the Proposals
The responses to the Green Paper and the subsequent presentations and discussions at the Convention, in general, were supportive of the above proposals. There was general agreement that the principal had an important leadership role in the school, although there was somewhat less evidence, as judged from the discussions, that this role was at present being exercised as portrayed in the Green Paper. The principal

was described as occupying the position of first teacher — *primus inter pares* — in the school, with responsibility for managing and supporting the staff in their work. There was little support for the title of chief executive as proposed in the Green Paper. It was stated that the role of the principal as instructional leader clearly distinguished this position from that of the manager or chief executive in a business environment, and this was also given as the reason why school principals should be recruited from the ranks of teachers, rather from those of professional administrators.

It also emerged from the Convention discussions that there was a fundamental mismatch between the role of the principal as outlined in the Green Paper and as agreed by the participants, on the one hand, and, on the other hand, the manner in which that role is being exercised at present in many of the schools. Instructional leadership, according to the participants, was the most neglected aspect of the principal's work in the school. Pressure of time, with the urgent taking precedence over the important, and insufficient back-up support services, were cited as the main reasons for this neglect. No great difficulties were reported when dealing with cases of serious misconduct by a teacher. While this, at any rate, is a rare occurrence, both the responsibility of the principal and the procedures to be followed are clearly defined. Neither was there reported to be any difficulty when taking responsibility for the first stage involved in dealing with the under-performing teacher. In this context, principals saw their role as providing advice and support to the teacher, but, if the problem was not being resolved, responsibility was then passed on to the Department of Education. While acknowledging that these seriously under-performing teachers form a tiny minority of the 40,000 teachers in the system, it was agreed that the procedures for dealing with this issue were inadequate and that relevant support services for these teachers were not readily available. It should be noted that, while there was general support at the Convention for tackling this issue, there is considerable frustration among the public at large, as reflected in the contributions of the parent organisations, at the lack of progress in this area. This problem requires immediate attention.

Although promoting and supporting the professional development of all the teachers in the school was regarded as an important task for the principal, this role is rarely exercised. The restoration of the support services which existed up to the cutbacks introduced in the 1980s, the provision of school secretarial and maintenance services, and a more effective middle management structure would, it was stated, free the principal to concentrate on this aspect of the role. Teaching principals in the primary sector, who form the majority of primary principals, have a particular problem in finding the time to promote and support staff development. Many of these schools also have neither office accommodation, secretarial services nor basic office equipment.

It emerged from the discussions, however, that more time and the provision of the support services identified may not in themselves be sufficient to enable the principal exercise the instructional leadership role envisaged in the Green Paper and supported by research literature. This may be due to a misunderstanding of the full implications of what is involved in providing instructional leadership in schools. The frequent requests, both in the submissions and the discussions, not to withdraw the inspectorate from their advisory role in schools, indicate a reluctance on the part of management to accept the main responsibility for the quality of education being offered to the students. The Green Paper proposal may be too drastic and, perhaps, should be preceded by a period of phased withdrawal. Some doubts were expressed about the competence and confidence of the principals to undertake this task. Neither may they have the authority to do so. At present, procedures for observing teachers in their classrooms, whether by the principal or by the inspectorate, are unclear and practice varies. It is also questionable whether the supportive climate necessary for this role to be exercised exists at the present time in the system. Appraisal of teachers, who traditionally work apart from their colleagues in the isolation of their classrooms, and who value highly and defend their independence, is a very sensitive issue, and, because it is more frequently viewed as threatening rather than supportive, is strongly resisted.

Nevertheless, observing teachers in the classroom, whether by colleagues or by superiors, and providing them with specific, positive and constructive feedback, as well as promoting teacher discussion about good teaching practices are strongly supported by research literature on effective teaching, and can make a significant contribution towards improving the quality of education being provided in schools. To accomplish this, the instructional leadership of the principal is critical and this can be demonstrated most effectively by a sound knowledge of learning theory, instructional methodology and relevant research. In this way, the findings of research on effective teaching can be translated into practical staff development activities directed towards improving classroom instruction and student outcomes. These findings have profound implications for the preparation and subsequent inservice training of principals, which, in fairness to them, cannot be avoided if they are expected to be accountable for implementing the proposals contained in the Green Paper.

The transition from the classroom to the principal's office can be difficult for a newly-appointed principal, and the concept of management which views the principal as first among equals may not be helpful in making this transition. Moreover, this view of the principal's role would also seem to be at variance with the concept of management envisaged for the principal as instructional leader in the school.

Nevertheless, the notion of the principal as first among equals would appear to be firmly grounded in the culture of the schools and underpins the expectation which the principals may have of themselves, as well as that which their staff have of the role. Some principals experience a feeling of guilt about abandoning their classroom role; there is a strongly held belief among them that it is necessary to continue to teach some classes in order to "keep in touch" and to maintain their credibility among the staff. This adds to their already heavy workload. Some teachers, on the other hand, believe that principals who are removed from the classroom lack credibility as instructional leaders. They also argue that promotion to principalship removes the most able practitioners from the classroom and thus devalues their role as teachers. This can create a "them and us" culture in schools in which the exercise of management is not seen as important, at least when compared with teaching. Yet, ironically, it is argued that principals should be recruited from the ranks of teachers. When, moreover, principals, both at the stage of transition to this position and thereafter throughout their careers, do not have the support of good inservice programmes in management theory and practice, they also can feel abandoned and their work undervalued. A more precise specification of the role of the principal and a better understanding of the distinction between this role and that of the teacher would be of benefit in this situation.

(iii)   Selection of Principals

More precise specification of the role and functions of the principal, it was suggested, would also assist in the selection of candidates for this position. The role and functions should, it was added, be derived from an analysis of the concept of leadership. This was defined as including the ability to formulate a vision for the school, to build a corporate structure embodying that vision, to engage in strategic planning at all levels, and to put in place effective communication systems, both within and without the school. Leading the staff by supporting and developing new curricular initiatives, identifying areas of greatest need and diverting resources towards them, providing opportunities for extending the skills and competencies of the staff and deploying these to best effect throughout the school, encouraging good practice and promoting teacher development, and identifying and managing inservice provision, were identified at the Convention as important dimensions of instructional leadership.

It was stated that particular difficulties arise in matching these qualities with the track record of candidates. Because of the middle management structure operating in many of the schools, teachers are afforded limited opportunities for gaining relevant experience in management as their careers advance. This, it was added, makes the selection process a bit of a gamble, more serious because new appointees do not usually serve a probationary period, and suitable exit arrangements are not available for those wishing to withdraw and return to the classroom.

The proposal in the Green Paper that principals should hold office for a period of seven years received little discussion, mainly because there was insufficient information on how such a policy would be implemented. However, the proposal was seen as having many potential attractions, especially if, in the first instance, it could be introduced on a voluntary basis for principals seeking early retirement or wishing to return to full-time teaching. The nature of the allowances which principals could retain on resumption of teaching duties or have included in their pension entitlements, as well as the pattern of redeployment, were among the issues requiring further clarification. In an era of limited teacher mobility, redeployment back into the same school could in time lead to over-staffing, especially in smaller schools. The hope was expressed that this proposal would be developed in greater detail in the White Paper.

(iv)   Composition of Selection Boards
Given that the selection of the principal is the most important appointment in the school, the composition of selection boards received considerable attention. There was some disagreement with regard to teacher and parental representation on selection boards. One view stated that parents had a sense of the ethos of the school as well as an intuitive sense of the personal qualities needed for this role and should be included on all selection boards. Another view held that neither should be included in a representative manner, but rather on the basis of their expertise and experience. It was agreed, however, that members should be appointed by virtue of their expertise and experience in selecting staff at this level, and that a balance of local and external perspectives and of gender should be ensured.

7.3   The Role of Vice-Principal

While the role of the principal is relatively well defined, that of the vice-principal is rather vague. Indeed, some division of opinion is apparent on how this position fits into the overall management system in schools. One view is that the principal and vice-principal form the senior management team in the school, while another is that the vice-principal is a member of the middle management team. To a large degree, views are formed on the basis of the functions assigned to this postholder in the individual school and the concept of management in operation.

The role and functions of the vice-principal were not addressed in the Green Paper and received little comment at the Convention. Procedures for the selection of candidates for this position, which potentially offers the best practical training and preparation for promotion to principalship, vary across the different sectors within the post-primary sector. The position is filled by open competition in the case of Community and Comprehensive schools and in schools in the VEC sector. In the vast majority of cases this position is advertised internally in the voluntary school sector, and, generally, allocated on the basis of seniority. In the primary sector, all posts below the level of principal are advertised internally.

In the post-primary sector, the position of vice-principal in schools of 500 pupils and upwards is ex-quota. All vice-principals are allocated some teaching hours. The number of hours, which vary between 8 and 15, is determined by the size of the school.

It was suggested at the Convention that this position should be ex-quota in all post-primary schools, and that all the posts be filled by public competition. A second proposal, that large schools (say 700+ pupils) should be allocated more than one vice-principal, was designed to take into account the additional administrative and managerial responsibilities which arise in such cases. It was also suggested that schools which had a substantial evening/night adult education programme should have a vice-principal specially designated to direct this programme. The Secretariat endorses these proposals.

It was stated that, ideally, the principal and vice-principal should operate closely as the senior management team in the school, sharing duties on an agreed basis so as to ensure the smooth running of the school in the absence of either. For this reason it was felt that the duties and responsibilities of the vice-principal should not be specified in detail, but rather should be agreed in accordance with the particular needs of the individual school. In general, it was reported that the vice-principal operated more or less as the front house manager in the school, assuming the main responsibility for drawing up and implementing the timetable, organising classes, managing substitute teachers, as well as for a broad range of student related issues such as time-keeping, absences, pastoral care and discipline. In order to meet these requirements, it was stated, vice-principals should have much reduced teaching commitments.

7.4 Posts of Responsibility

The present structure governing posts of responsibility in the post-primary sector evolved historically in an unstructured manner, and, to a large degree, unrelated to the management needs of the schools. It should be added that, in the past, schools were rather less complex institutions, and the management needs were less demanding than is the case at the present time. Posts are allocated to schools on the basis of a points system which is computed according to the ages of the students enrolled. Procedures for defining the functions attached to posts, the advertising of posts and the appointment of staff vary across sectors, and sometimes between schools in the same sector. A serious lack of published research data on many aspects of this system makes it difficult to offer generalisations in this area and runs the risk of doing an injustice to the system and, in particular, to post holders in some of the institutions. Local agreements compound this difficulty. Nevertheless, the following are offered as valid generalisations on the operation of the system.

All A and B posts are advertised internally in community, comprehensive and voluntary secondary schools. In the VEC system, the first A post is advertised externally, and all other posts internally. However, even in this instance, the post is usually allocated to an internal candidate.

Differences also arise in relation to the specification of functions to be attached to posts at the stage of advertising. In ommunity schools and those in the VEC sector, a specific function, or more usually a number of alternative functions, are listed in the advertisement, and, in the latter case, the functions are agreed with the successful candidate. In the voluntary school sector and generally in the comprehensive sector, the specific functions are agreed after the appointment has been made. Specific functions are listed in the advertisement in the case of primary schools, but since these functions are capable of being performed by any member of staff, the actual specification does not influence selection.

Criteria for the selection of candidates are based on a combination of capability and suitability to administer the responsibilities in question, and seniority. The application of these criteria, and, in particular, the balance to be struck between suitability and seniority has proved to be problematic. As a general rule, seniority is the criterion applied when appointments are being made in the voluntary sector schools and in primary schools, whereas elsewhere this is not the case. However, variations occur in many of the schools where local agreements are frequently devised. In some schools where two teacher unions are represented, agreements have resulted in a sharing out of posts proportionate to the membership of the different unions. In such circumstances one agreed candidate applies for the vacancy. In the VEC sector, where suitability is the main criterion, it was stated at the Convention that a proportion of appointments are made on the basis of seniority, as a means of keeping the peace. In the voluntary sector, appointments made on a basis other than seniority, when a more senior teacher in the school is an applicant and is not selected, are usually appealed.

In short, the procedures in this area are unsatisfactory, and their application can be divisive and contentious. Boards of Management have limited discretion both in the selection of candidates and in assigning duties to post holders.

Examples of duties which can be assigned to post holders at post-primary level include year-head, examination secretary, curriculum/subject coordinator and adult education in the case of A posts; and librarian, organising audio visual resources and equipment, health education, and organising school tours in the case of B posts.

It would be unfair, however, to conclude that the present middle management system, despite all of its drawbacks, does not operate successfully in many schools. While it is difficult to generalise for the reasons already stated, the present system would appear to work reasonably well in the community and VEC school sector, and less well in some comprehensive schools and in voluntary schools. Once duties have been agreed, post holders are conscientious in carrying out their responsibilities.

The main criticism of the system is that it evolved at a time when the management of schools was relatively uncomplicated and now is less well suited to the modern-day needs of the institutions. The lack of clearly defined procedures for the selection of post holders, the need to define responsibilities commensurate with the posts in question, and the facility to allow some flexibility so as to match these with the particular needs of the school, are among the defects associated with the system. A general finding is that post holders are unwilling to accept any responsibility for the management of staff in the schools. This does little to relieve the burden of the principal.

There is general agreement that this system is unsatisfactory and should now be redesigned in such a manner as to reflect the present management needs of the schools. However, there is less consensus on how this might be accomplished. The view that promotion to management which results in the withdrawal of good practitioners from the classroom somehow devalues the status of the classroom teacher and teaching as a profession, was evident in many of the responses to the Green Paper, and, later, in the discussions at the Convention. The structure of middle management was considered to be divisive in schools by creating a "them and us" culture. A promotional structure for teachers which would recognise and reward good practitioners, and thereby encourage them to remain in the classroom, it was suggested, would be the ideal solution to the problems of middle management. One view was that the hierarchical nature of the present management structure in school was built on an out-dated industrial model and was unsuited to the needs of the institution. In its place an organic model, based on a collaborative concept of management, was proposed. This would seek to involve all of the staff in the management of the school and would promote group planning and management through a consensus approach.

This, however, would add significantly to the management costs of schools, involving, according to some suggestions, the granting of B, and later, A posts to all of the teaching staff after a certain number of years' service, and in return for which teachers would accept responsibility for the management functions in the school. To facilitate this engagement in management, teachers would have reduced class contact time, which, in turn, would lead to the creation of additional teaching posts. How these management functions could be distributed to members of staff in a manner which would ensure that a fair and equitable distribution of responsibilities resulted, and that agreement could be reached between individuals and management so that a realistic match could be achieved between the range of experience and expertise available and the management needs of the school, was not demonstrated. It also assumes that every member of staff would wish to be involved in management and that there were sufficient management functions to be distributed to all staff. Neither is it clear where the ultimate responsibility lies in this collaborative management system. In short, it differs little from the manner by which the present structure was designed and would appear to be based on the assumption that the system should be conceived as a means of rewarding teachers on the basis of seniority, rather than as a means of providing a supportive management structure for schools.

However, the proposal recognises a major defect of the present middle management system, namely, that many of the functions associated with the management of schools cannot be deferred to that part of the day when teaching ends. Rather, they have to be attended to during the normal working period when the staff are otherwise engaged. In this sense, the proposal that teaching hours could be exchanged for involvement in management duties merits serious consideration. Whether this should involve all the staff in the school is open to question.

7.5   Proposals for
the Re-Organisation of the Middle Management System

Bearing in mind the extent of the dissatisfaction with the present arrangements, and the significant costs attached to the present structures, the Secretariat offers the following considerations for reorganising the system. In doing so, it recognises that considerable discussion and negotiation will be required before any changes can be put in place. Such discussions may be arranged more appropriately under the auspices of a reconstituted Conciliation and Arbitration scheme.

Firstly, in conducting any review of the middle management system in the schools it will be important not to create the impression that the allocation of posts of responsibility to teachers is to be regarded as payment for seniority in the profession. This is unfair to post holders. Other means can be found to reward teachers for length of service, if this is deemed desirable.

Secondly, a more rational basis for determining the number and grade of posts which can be allocated to schools should be devised. The present method of calculating posts does not appear to have a clearly defined rationale.

The suggestions made hereunder for the re-organisation of the middle management system are aimed at matching the responsibilities linked to posts to the central tasks of the school, creating a career structure for teachers which does not result in having to withdraw from the classroom, and providing opportunities for teachers to assume major responsibility in the school for instructional leadership and the management of staff.

This would result in teachers not having to assume responsibility for duties of a routine administrative nature, better support services for all the teachers in the school, thereby freeing them to concentrate their energies on academic and pastoral work, and reducing significantly the workload of the principal so as to concentrate on the more central aspects of instructional leadership.

The present middle management system has been criticised because of the mismatch between the responsibilities which can be attached to posts and the academic needs of the schools. It has also been stated that the system does not help to create a career structure for the classroom teacher. The creation of senior teacher positions, such as a head of department, with responsibility for the management and administration of a subject, would help to forge a closer link between the responsibilities which could be attached to a post and the academic work of the school. This post would involve responsibility for the design of programmes within a department, the implementation of the programmes, the allocation of students and teachers to classes, the development of assessment policy, the management of resources, financial management, the identification of staff development needs and the organisation of inservice programmes, the development of a school plan for the subject/curriculum area, and evaluating and reporting on the work in the department. Posts with responsibility for a curriculum area, rather than for a subject could be created in the case of a small school, or as a curriculum specialist or co-ordinator in the case of a primary school,

Similar posts could also be created in other sections of the school, such as in curriculum development, pastoral care and staff development. The creation of these posts would signify to the school community the commitment of management to the academic goals of the school, provide opportunities for the staff to take responsibility in areas which closely match their training and experience, and give official recognition to their professional role in the school.

The specific responsibilities could be clearly and unambiguously defined and the suitability of candidates could be matched to those duties and be subject to occasional review. The qualifications, experience and track record of applicants, rather than their seniority, would form the main criteria for appointment to posts of this nature. Post holders should be given some reduction in class contact hours. However, since much of the work involved would have to be undertaken outside of the normal working day, holders of these posts should be adequately remunerated.

Other functions which are mainly administrative in nature and not directly related to the academic work of the school need not, and some would argue, should not be undertaken by the teaching staff. Many of the duties attached at present to B posts come under this category, and are, as described at the Convention, task rather than management oriented. The performance of these duties requires a level of training well below, and different to, that which teachers have, and does little to advance their professional careers. Those posts could be converted into new positions of a secretarial, administrative, technical nature and thus meet the needs of the school administration in these areas, as was so frequently articulated at the Convention.

This would result in a reduction in the number of posts available to teachers. However, the creation of back-up secretarial, administrative and technical assistance of this nature would also provide much needed support to all the teaching staff in the school and enable them to concentrate on their professional work. In this way, schools could make a significant contribution towards improving the quality of education they provide.

The position of vice-principal may also need to be re-defined. This post holder, in addition to sharing some of the general management functions with the principal, could also assume responsibility for co-ordinating the work of the senior post holders. The detailed functions to be attached to this position would depend to some extent on the degree of complementarity between the management expertise of both the principal and the vice-principal, and the size and particular circumstances of the school.

An important concern at the Convention was the disproportionate burden on management in very large schools. In common with all other schools in the system, they have only one vice-principal. The suggestion that these schools (700+ pupils) should have more than one vice-principal is endorsed by the Secretariat.

Devising senior teacher posts which assign responsibility and accountability to teachers for the academic and pastoral programmes in the school would reduce considerably the workload of the principal. Were this to happen, the principal would have more time to concentrate on the central aspects of management generally associated with this role.

7.6 Managing the Transition

This re-organisation of the middle management system, if adopted, would require detailed negotiation and may need to be introduced on a gradual basis. The expanded structures proposed for Conciliation and Arbitration could facilitate this process.

As a first step in this process, the funding mechanism for the management of schools should be examined. A separate budget could be devised for schools according to an agreed formula and be so designed as to take into account the total administrative costs of the institution, including the provision of secretarial, administrative, technical and maintenance support services. This could be incorporated into the budget proposals for schools as proposed in the Green Paper (p.153).

Secondly, the transition from the present system to the new one could be organised in a number of ways, of which the following are examples:

(a)   The present system could be terminated following agreement between the relevant organisations and the new one put in place. Existing post holders could be given the choice of opting into the new system or negotiating the termination of their post;

(b)   The present system could be gradually phased out by converting the old posts as they became available, due to retirements or resignations, into the new structure.

7.7 Management Training

Irrespective of the way in which the management system should be re-organised in the schools, there is an urgent need to put in place a properly structured system of training for those who wish to become involved. The haphazard preparation of teachers for management positions in schools, up to recent times, received much comment at the Convention. This, it was stated, gave the impression that administration and management skills can easily be mastered by teachers, and for the most part be acquired on the job. In recent years, the number of courses in educational management available through university education departments, colleges of education, teachers' centres and other agencies, has increased considerably, and this criticism no longer holds.

Ideally, preparation for management should begin early on in teachers' careers and proceed on a gradual basis as they assume greater responsibility and gain more practical experience in management. Principals have an important contribution to make in this respect by identifying good potential candidates for management positions and giving them the opportunity to gain experience across a range of administrative areas in the school. Providing advice and support, and encouraging them to enroll on relevant courses will assist them in developing their potential, and also ensure that the knowledge and skills acquired on courses can be applied in the workplace. Once such a system has been put in place, the difficulties mentioned at the Convention of matching a candidate's track record to the specifications of the position should not be so difficult.

Courses being provided should be closely related to the management needs of the school, and matched to the types of leadership required at the different management levels within the system. For example, the specific responsibilities outlined earlier for the senior teacher position of head of department could form the main components of a course for such personnel.

Induction courses for new principals should be provided and should be taken well in advance of taking up appointment. Thereafter, back-up and advisory services during the early years of transition to management, should form essential elements of a development service for principals. If, as stated in the Green Paper, the principal is expected to assume additional responsibilities for preparing school plans and annual reports, for supervising probationary teachers and for the general quality of education in the school, the need for these services becomes all the more urgent.

8.   The Quality of Education within Schools

8.1   Overview

 Improving the quality of education within schools should be a central goal of any education reform movement. The quality of education depends on many variables, including the competence of staff, school leadership, the quality of planning, pupil-teacher ratios, support services, the social context and level of parental and community support. This section of the Report deals with four aspects — the school plan, the inspectorate, psychological and guidance services, and support services to schools.

8.2   The School Plan

(i)   The Green Paper Proposal

The proposal in the Green Paper that the maximum amount of decision-making and responsibility be devolved to the individual school implies that each institution will be required to furnish evidence with regard to the quality of education it provides. The proposed withdrawal of the inspectorate from their traditional role to schools adds to this responsibility.

A number of proposals aimed at assisting schools in providing a quality education are contained in the Green Paper. One of the most central of these is that which states that all primary and secondary schools should develop plans. The plan would set out the school's goals and policy objectives as well as its key strategies in relation to curriculum provision, approaches to teaching and learning, assessment practices, school/home/community liaison and enrolment policy. The plan would be prepared annually by the principal in consultation with the staff and other partners, and approved by the Board of Management. The plan would also form the basis of the report to be presented to the annual general meeting of the parents' council. Each school, it is stated, would report to the parents and the local community on its performance and achievements by reference to its school plan; the presentation of reports would be modest and functional. The publication of the school plan would enable parents to understand the aims of the school, while the annual report would provide a means for assessing performance against the plan. Inspection of the schools would include the review of achievements against the plan. The Department of Education will offer guidelines to the schools on drawing up plans.

The school plan proposal, which is aimed at assisting schools in setting down, in a formal manner, their aims, policies and practices, is commendable, and, in the relation to school improvement and quality enhancement, is potentially the most important proposal in the Green Paper. A school planning document provides a framework against which practices can be compared with intentions, and interventions planned where a gap is found to exist. Around it a practical model for conducting in-school evaluation can be constructed. Important outcomes of school effectiveness research can be incorporated into policies at individual school level by means of the plan, and implemented in such a manner that they penetrate right down into the deep culture of the individual classroom. This has been the central aim of schools plans developed elsewhere.

Understandably, the discussion on the school plan in the Green Paper was limited. The description of the plan outlined is very general and vague, and does not appear to encapsulate the important link between planning, development and improvement. The elements of the plan, as outlined above, give the impression of a document being prepared which contains general statements of a school's policy in relation to its main activities. Such a document could be prepared with little difficulty, and in a short space of time. Indeed, many schools already have such a document. However, the influence of school plans on school practice and on quality enhancement could well be minimal.

An important difference between the school plan as outlined in the Green Paper and those developed elsewhere is, that in these latter cases a development section is incorporated into the plan. Indeed, the title given to such a document, School Development Planning, highlights this emphasis on development. These documents set out not only school policy and practices, but also contain a small number of development or action plans designed to address areas of concern. These action plans, which have statements of objectives to be achieved and intended outcomes, form the basis of small scale projects which can be implemented in a short time span. In this way, small incremental improvements can be made to practice.

(ii)   Reaction to the Proposals
General approval was expressed for the school plan proposal both in the responses to the Green Paper and in the discussions at the Convention. Primary schools have been engaged in this process since about 1980 and some post-primary schools have become involved more recently in this exercise.

Involving the various partners in drawing up school plans was regarded as a valuable mechanism for promoting a collaborative culture in schools through engaging patrons, management, staff, parents, and, where appropriate, the wider community, in defining a mission and more specific objectives for the school, devising policies for implementing programmes and monitoring progress. There was some disagreement about the degree to which the different partners within the school community should become involved in this exercise. Involvement would depend on the particular task or element of the plan being developed. Parents would play a more significant role in the formulation of the general aims of the school and in the development of programmes in areas such as health and social education, and religious education, in drawing up discipline and homework policies and in promoting home/school/community links. The professional staff in the school would have responsibility for that part of the plan concerned with the delivery of the curriculum and the implementation of policy; parents would have a consultative role in these matters.

The degree of importance which should be given to the two main dimensions of school plans — the product and the process — gave rise to much discussion at the Convention. The benefits to be derived from engaging in the planning process appear obvious and were not a cause for concern. However, it emerged that there is sometimes a reluctance to produce planning documents, especially if it appears likely that these will be widely available outside the school. This arises for a number of reasons. Firstly, there is a concern that the publishing of a planning document might give an impression of finality to the whole planning process and convey the message that this is a once-off exercise culminating in a document carved in stone. This, of course, would be contrary to the ongoing development dimension of the planning process and would contribute little to the improvement of the quality of education in schools.

Secondly, there is a concern that the production of a final document might be used as a rigid accountability mechanism for evaluating schools. Should this occur, school planning documents, it was stated, may not convey the realities of school but rather become marketing devices for the purpose of impressing a wider public and creating a more positive but unreal image of the school. The link proposed between the school plan and the annual report also gave rise to such concerns. An over critical public could undermine the good development work which a school was undertaking and thus inhibit innovation.

It was evident from the discussions that there was little shared understanding of what was involved in the process of formulating and implementing school plans. There is general confusion in relation to the purposes of developing plans, their content, about who should prepare them and approve them, and to whom they should be made available for inspection. Indeed, decisions on this last issue could have a significant bearing on what a plan might contain.

Obviously, much more development work needs to be done in this area, and the publication of guidelines by the Department of Education to schools, as indicated in the Green Paper, would be an important first step in this process. The Secretariat offers the following comments on the benefits of school planning, and a proposal for the further development of this initiative.

(iii)   Advantages of Planning for the School

The concept of development planning includes the identification of priorities within an institution, the selection of a limited number of priorities for immediate action, the devising of action plans to address them, the specification of targets to be achieved and the monitoring of the entire process. The specification of targets and the evaluative dimension, frequently tend to be neglected with the result that development plans are more likely to be vague and ambiguous, objectives general rather than specific, and progress difficult to monitor. In such a situation, staff are likely to become disillusioned, if only because they will not receive precise feedback on their efforts. Success will be difficult to identify, and stagnation, rather than development, could follow.

Should school plans be envisaged as final documents which rarely change and are only occasionally reviewed, their influence on school improvement may be marginal. Systematic evaluation of school practices needs to be conducted on a regular basis. In this way, incremental improvements can be made and quality can be enhanced. School development plans can provide a formal focus for this activity. At the same time, schools must be given the freedom and the time to plan and implement innovations without having to report in detail to a wider public while a particular innovation is in process. The Board of Management should, of course, be kept informed by means of regular progress reports.

The potential benefits to be derived from schools engaging in the planning process include the following:

(a)   Putting in place a formal procedure, adapted to the needs and resources available in each individual institution, can assist schools in the process of implementing and managing change;

(b)   The development of plans and priorities, identified on the basis of an internal evaluation of the school, can make a significant contribution to the improvement of the quality of education being offered to the pupils;

(c)   The process of planning provides an opportunity for engaging staff in collaborative planning and teamwork by focusing on whole-school issues and, thereby, counteract the isolation which teachers traditionally experience within the narrow confines of their own classrooms;

(d)   The planning process provides an effective vehicle for incorporating national, local and school priorities into the work of each individual school;

(e)   The development of action projects, arising out of an evaluation of school needs, provides an efficient and effective method for identifying the resources needed to introduce innovation and improvement into the school, and so promote quality enhancement;

(f)   Engaging in the drawing up of school plans and establishing priorities requiring action, provides an effective means of identifying teacher development needs, and enables more precise specification of the inservice provision that would meet both the needs of the teachers and schools; and

(g)   The process of planning can afford a means of empowering teachers within a school by extending their professional skills and gaining a greater degree of ownership over the central issues which influence their work.

(iv)   Policy Proposal

As a way forward, it is recommended by the Secretariat that school plans should be conceived as having two components, or parts. The first component should comprise, what may be termed, the relatively permanent features of school policy. These would include such elements as the ethos, aims and objectives of the school, curriculum provision and allocation, approaches to teaching, learning and assessment, and policies on home/school/community liaison, homework, discipline and enrolment.   This section of a school plan could be published in a separate document and any modifications or revisions could be reported each year.   Such a document would inform parents and others about the school and its general policies. This document could be circulated widely.

The second component of the plan, which might be titled the development section, would be devoted to outlining and reporting on the specific planning priorities which the school was undertaking. The concept underpinning development plans is that each school would undertake, on an ongoing basis, a limited number of small-scale development projects which the staff have identified as important priorities. These priorities for development would arise out of an internal evaluation of the school's policies and practices, covering both curricular and non-curricular areas.

Such projects should be capable of being implemented over a short time-span of one, or, at most, two years. The selection of a particular project would be dependent on the willingness of staff to undertake the work and the availability of resources, including time. All of the staff in a school would not be required to become involved in implementing any one action plan, although over a period of years they would all have become involved and have gained experience in this development work. This would help to ensure that work overload and innovation fatigue could be avoided. Introducing small-scale, short-term projects of this nature, matched to the needs and capabilities of the school and having the commitment of the staff, would help to ensure that innovations could be implemented and that gradual, incremental improvements in the quality of education could be incorporated into all schools. In this way, rolling innovation and improvement can be promoted in schools. Teachers can feel a greater sense of ownership of and commitment to those action plans which they themselves have selected, designed and implemented.

The content of these development plans would be of a professional and technical nature, mostly of relevance to the staff and management of the school. It would not be necessary to publish them on a wider basis. However, progress reports on developments underway could be incorporated into the annual report. Once an action/development plan has been successfully implemented, it can be incorporated into the general school plan as part of the policy statement of the school.

(v) Resource Implications

While some schools have made considerable progress in this area, many would benefit from assistance in various forms.

In the first instance, the publication of guidelines on school plans and annual reports would go a long way towards clearing up some of the confusion and suspicion which is evident. These guidelines should give a clear indication of what the school plan should include. They should not be too specific or too restrictive as, otherwise, schools will not be able to adapt them to their own particular needs. In particular, sample or model school plans should not be published, as experience elsewhere would suggest that schools may merely adopt them rather than design their own. The guidelines might evolve beneficially through a dynamic process, with inputs from principal teachers during inservice courses.

Secondly, school staff will need to acquire a range of skills, notably observation, communication and evaluation skills in order to engage in this process. Much of this development work should be conducted at school level, with the provision of external assistance where appropriate.

Thirdly, management, and, in particular, the principal will be expected to take a leading role in promoting the development of school plans. The ability to encourage a collegial climate and teamwork approach among the staff, to identify teacher development needs and match these with appropriate inservice provision, and to provide the leadership which will motivate them to engage in whole school evaluation and planning will be important.

Fourthly, the provision of specific resources such as secretarial assistance, reproduction equipment and curriculum materials will be necessary. Above all, staff will require adequate planning time if they are to be expected to engage in this exercise. It should be noted that the failure to provide this in other countries at the time school plans were being introduced set back the innovation for a considerable period. Progress was not made until this deficiency was remedied. The six days mentioned in the Green Paper (p.150) for school planning, may be helpful in this context.

Fifthly, the provision of advisory services can be most helpful to schools when they are beginning this process.

Sixthly, this proposal should be introduced into schools on a gradual basis. The temptation to devise sophisticated plans, often borrowed from elsewhere, should be avoided. Schools should be encouraged to start with small-scale projects, experience success, even if it is modest, and then build on this. In this way skills can be gradually developed and applied.

8.3   The Inspectorate

(i)   Green Paper Proposals
Proposals in the Green Paper that schools be given greater autonomy, and that Boards of Management have responsibility, in the first instance, for the quality of education in their schools have important implications for the role of the inspectorate. It is proposed that the inspectorate withdraw from direct involvement in the detailed activities of schools and concentrate on evaluating the more general functioning of the system. Observing, monitoring, evaluating and reporting on the implementation of policy, contributing in a more formal manner to the development of new policy and linking more closely to the administrative section of the Department of Education, are among the key aspects of the new role envisaged for the inspectorate in the Green Paper.

An important dimension of the inspectors' work will involve monitoring the quality of education in schools. This will be achieved by a system of whole-school inspection in the context of the School Plan, and conducted by a team of inspectors drawn from a unified professional grouping. The outcomes of these inspections will form the basis of the annual report on the performance of the system. This report will be prepared by the inspectorate and published independently of the Department of Education.

The success of these proposals will be dependent on the achievement of a related set of proposals which are directly linked to quality effectiveness and assurance in the system. These include the ability of Boards of Management to assume the main responsibility for the quality of education being provided in their schools, the agreement of the inspectorate to relinquish some of the many functions it now undertakes, the establishment of other agencies to take over some of these functions, the provision of suitable training for members of the inspectorate so as to prepare them for their new role, the provision of adequate support services so as to enable them to carry out their new responsibilities efficiently and effectively, a better management structure to co-ordinate the activities of this group, and a better appreciation at official level of the contribution which a well trained and organised inspectorate can make to the successful implementation of many of the proposals contained in the Green Paper.

The Secretariat is concerned about the consequences for schools if proposals related to the inspectorate are implemented without first examining the implications these may have for schools, and, in particular, for the enhancement of quality in the system. The sudden withdrawal of the inspectorate from their present role in the system will add significantly to the responsibilities of Boards of Management and school principals, especially with regard to quality assurance. They report that they have neither the expertise nor the experience to undertake this responsibility. The fact that there are no indications in the Green Paper that school boards will be given adequate training in this area would seem to suggest that the authors have seriously underestimated the complexities involved in monitoring the quality of education being offered in schools. The hasty implementation of this proposal, without first ensuring that school management is adequately prepared for its new responsibilities, could seriously put at risk many of the other proposals relating to quality assurance and school improvement.

The new role envisaged for the inspectorate, particularly in relation to monitoring the quality of education being offered in individual schools, is also ambiguous. The conduct of whole-school inspections, the frequency with which these will be conducted in individual schools, the responsibilities and the authority which will be invested in the inspection team, especially in relation to the provision of advice and support to schools experiencing difficulty and, more importantly, ensuring that appropriate action is taken by the schools to address weaknesses, and the provision of extra funding for schools needing special assistance, are not discussed in the document. A period of, for example, five years between inspections may be too long in the case of a school experiencing difficulties. Whether the team of inspectors who conduct whole-school inspections and make proposals for action should also become involved in the implementation of these proposals is also questionable, and could give rise to role conflict.

This raises the issue of the need to provide a two-tier inspectorate in the system — a national inspectorate for the purpose of conducting whole-school inspections, co-ordinating the collection of data for the preparation of reports, both general and specialist, on the performance of the system, and a local inspectorate, as part of the intermediate tier or regionally organised, with responsibility for providing an advisory and support service to schools, implementing proposals arising out of whole-school inspections, and organising and managing teachers seconded to work with the inspectorate and the Visiting Teacher Service.

(ii) Response to the Proposals

The response at the Convention to the proposals for the inspectorate was varied. Neither management, teacher organisations nor parent associations was supportive of the proposal to withdraw the inspectorate from its present role in the schools. The inspectorate is held in high regard by these groups; they appreciate the inspectors' role in the system, have high expectations of their contribution in supporting schools and the teachers in their work, and are apprehensive of the implications of their withdrawal from their traditional contact with schools.

Paradoxically, it is also recognised that visits to schools by the inspectorate have been so drastically curtailed in recent years, especially at the post-primary level, that the support and advisory service which it provides is no longer expected. In this respect, the proposal that teachers with subject and pedagogical expertise, be seconded to the inspectorate to provide this advice and support to the teachers, was warmly welcomed.

While inspectors are regarded as having an important supportive function in assisting schools and teachers, less emphasis is given to their evaluative role in schools. The exercise of these two roles — advisory and evaluative — gives rise to confusion on the part of teachers who find it difficult to determine which of the two roles the inspector is exercising at any given time. Teachers, it was reported, are reluctant to engage in meaningful dialogue with an inspector about aspects of their practice, if it is perceived that their performance will be judged in a summative manner.

Guidelines for distinguishing between these two functions, and clear definitions of the purposes of each are necessary, especially if they are to be performed by the same individual in the course of the same visit. It is also evident that formalised procedures relating to the inspections of schools and, in particular, of teachers, need to be drawn up and agreed. Present practice with regard to the inspection of teachers varies between primary and post-primary schools, as well as between the different school types in the latter case. In many instances, the quality of teaching has to be inferred from questioning of the class by the inspector. Such practices can hardly be regarded as the most valid or defensible method of evaluating teacher performance. Addressing the problem of the underperforming teacher was regarded by some participants at the Convention as one of the most urgent needs to be resolved in the schools.

(iii)   Interpretation

It is acknowledged, both in the responses to the Green Paper and the discussions at the Convention, that the inspectorate has an important and unique role to play in contributing to the effective implementation of many of the proposals contained in the Green Paper, especially those directly related to enhancing the quality of education in the system.

However, there has been a failure at official level to recognise and develop the potential of this group of professionals. Analysis of the work of the inspectorate, especially in the post-primary sector, indicates that they perform a wide range of duties, some of which are only indirectly related to what is generally regarded as their main function. Thus, the practice of inspectors serving on the management boards of community schools and on selection boards for the appointment of teachers, of having the main responsibility for the examinations, and a heavy involvement in the organisation and delivery of inservice, deflects them from what is regarded as their main functions of visiting schools, reporting on the performance of the system and contributing in a more formal manner to the development of educational policy. Many of the above functions could be easily discarded and performed by other groups or organisations in the system.

The reluctance of both management and teachers to have the inspectors withdrawn from close contact with the schools raises fundamental questions about the advisability of this proposal, and supports the view of the Secretariat that this withdrawal should be introduced on a gradual basis. This is not to imply that the Green Paper proposal should be rejected. Advances made in the quality of teachers entering the system and in the professionalism of teachers, indicate that schools should take more responsibility for the quality of the education they provide. However, adequate preparation will be necessary in order to prepare schools for this responsibility.

The secondment of teachers as advisors to schools should be regarded as providing specialist expertise to the system, rather than as an excuse for not bringing the membership of the present inspectorate up to a more realistic level. Seconded teachers will also require training for this role.

(iv)   Training Implications

The proposals in the Green Paper signify a new, more professional and a more demanding role for the inspectorate.   However, no indication is given as to how this role might best be exercised, or as to what kind of inspectorate it might require.   In such circumstances it is difficult to judge whether the inspectorate is equipped to take on this role, more especially since the views of this group are not known. Traditionally, inspectors have been recruited from the ranks of teachers on the basis of their qualifications and teaching expertise, and, until recently, have been given very limited preparation for their role in the system.

A much improved induction programme is now being provided for new members of the inspectorate, and a development programme aimed at preparing those already in the system for their new role, is also operational. The Secretariat is encouraged that the Department of Education has already taken these steps to prepare the inspectorate for their new role and wholeheartedly supports these initiatives. Such development programmes will, it is hoped, become a regular feature of support for the inspectorate.

Inspectors will be required to be knowledgeable in a broad range of areas including methodology, curriculum innovation, assessment, evaluation, management, counselling, research, the writing of specialist reports and policy development. The ability to work as a member of a team, to network with educational and research institutes and to collaborate with inspectors in other countries, will also be essential requirements. Few of these can be acquired by experience or casually on the job. Most importantly, inspectors will need to be given time to engage in private study and research.

Moreover, there will be an increasing need for individual inspectors to acquire specialist skills in key areas related to their work, and to be able to lead specialist teams set up to address particular needs as they arise in the system. Setting up teams to evaluate schools requiring special assistance, particularly in relation to the remediation of inequalities and disadvantage, by collecting data, identifying needs, proposing interventions, implementing action plans and evaluating outcomes, are examples of tasks which will require such skills.

It will also be important to ensure that inspectors with specialist skills be distributed throughout the system, rather than be deployed centrally from headquarters. In this context, the deployment of an inspectorate as part of the intermediate tier, or the further development of regional centres for this service, may be required.

8.4   Psychological and Guidance Services

The provision of a comprehensive psychological and guidance service for schools was considered a priority at the Convention. However, issues relating to the nature of the needs for such services, or of the precise services that would meet those needs, were not explored in detail. That needs exist is clear. Some pupils are failing in the system. Teachers, especially in large classes, have difficulty in dealing with these pupils as well as with ones with behavioural problems.   At post-primary level, educational guidance has achieved greater significance with the increase in differentiation in curricula, though vocational guidance may have decreased in importance as the majority of students do not proceed directly to the labour market from secondary school.

The provision of services to meet these needs is recognised to be inadequate, resulting in a long waiting list for assessment of children, and a total lack of service in some areas.   There is not a sufficient number of psychologists or counsellors to deal with the variety of demands that is made on them, including the diagnosis of pupils' learning difficulties, providing a support service for teachers in dealing with pupils' learning and behavioural problems, and providing educational and vocational guidance and counselling for students.   Given this wide range of services, it would seem that there is a need for an in-depth appraisal of the role of the psychologist and counsellor in relation to the needs of the educational system.   While the nature of the psychologist's role will vary at primary and post-primary levels, there would seem to be a need for a greater emphasis on educational guidance at both levels, and a greater integration of the work of the psychologist with that of the teacher.   In recognition of the fact that many problems which exhibit themselves in school do not have their origins in the school, greater attention should be given to the development of linkages between school, home, community, and health and social welfare services.

In the context of a re-organised Department of Education and of the inspectorate, the role of the educational psychologist should also be incorporated as an integral part of new planning. Their perspectives could be beneficial in strategic policy-formulation and they could also provide worthwhile inputs into whole-school inspections.   If intermediate educational tiers are established, they ought to have a pool of psychological expertise to draw upon.   If set up at county level, it might be more feasible to have the local psychological and inspectoral services available through a structure involving a pooling of such specialist services between a number of county educational authorities.   The psychological service ought to be developed as an integrated one for both primary and post-primary schools. The experiences of the two pilot projects at primary level in West Tallaght/Clondalkin and South Tipperary, which will be reported on in the Spring of 1994, should provide valuable guidance to the Government's declared policy of expanding the psychological service to cover the whole primary sector. It was the view at the Convention that this service should be introduced on a phased basis, with priority given to disadvantaged areas.

It was also a view at the Convention that greater benefit could be derived from psychologists working as teams rather than as isolated individuals. While individual case work with pupils would still be necessary, the emphasis of the psychological service should be on interactionist, preventative approaches, operating in close collaboration with teachers, other significant adults in relation to pupils, and associated local services, such as home-school-community liaison programmes and local health and welfare services. Psychologists could help school staff in promoting the Green Paper's concept of the health-promoting school and the pastoral care dimension of school life. The assistance of psychologists was regarded as of great importance in the education of children with special needs. In particular, their assistance in the policy of integration of such pupils into mainstream schooling would be very significant.

8.5   Support Services to Schools

In comparison with other developed countries, educational support services to many Irish schools are spartan. Many participants at the Convention considered that the quality of education within schools suffered from the lack of necessary and desirable services. The inadequate provision of secretarial and caretaker and technical services to many schools was a serious disadvantage. It was also regarded as essential that all schools should have a telephone and photocopier, regardless of school size.

At a pedagogical level, Convention participants considered that the development of new technology in broadcasting and communications provided tremendous possibilities for promoting the quality of education in Irish schools. As the Minister for Education mentioned in her closing address, the Convention provided "a valuable highlighting of the issues of educational broadcasting." There was also support for the statement in the Green Paper that, "It is intended to explore the possibilities of drawing on the resources and potential of Ireland's educational broadcasting and to initiate discussions with the relevant agencies in this regard." The concern was that this expression of intent should be converted into action without further delay. Other forms of new technology should also be provided for and encouraged in schools. The potential of technologies such as computers, interactive video and electronic mail, mentioned in the Green Paper, was highly significant and schools of the future would need to incorporate such technologies in their activity, if they were to keep abreast of the world outside the school. It was also considered that the use of modern technology could be of great assistance to small, remote schools in allowing them to enrich the educational experience of their pupils.

The availability of library services to all schools was also regarded as highly desirable. With new approaches to self-directed learning and more active pedagogy with a project-oriented focus, library resources and familiarity with their usage are an important aspect of modern learning.   The role of local library services for adult education was also emphasised. It was suggested that intermediate education tiers, if established, should help to promote and co-ordinate appropriate library services. Local educational structures could also help to improve the resources of teacher centres and to provide assistance of various kinds in curricular materials and curricular innovations. Similarly, enrichment experiences for pupils in the arts could be facilitated.   Schemes such as theatre-in-education and dance-in-education companies visiting schools, writers and artists-in-residence schemes, and visits from creative artists to schools, can be of great value.   The Arts Council has been very supportive and innovative in such areas, and close liaison between the Department of Education, local educational authorities, the Arts Council, and regional arts officers could prove to be highly productive and beneficial for schools in the years ahead.

The concern at the Convention for improved, qualitative services to Irish schools was accompanied by a strong sense of realism that all desirable supports could not be provided in the short-term.   What was sought was a seriousness of purpose and intent giving rise to a strategic plan in this area.   Priorities should be established and their provision planned for in a reasoned and co-ordinated manner. Local knowledge and expertise, including that of parent councils, should be drawn upon, with prior claims accepted for the people and areas in greatest need. It was also proposed that schools be allowed some budgetary discretion in the type of support services they would procure.

9. Curricular Issues

9.1 Overview

Curriculum, though a crucial element of the educational system, was not a major discussion issue at the Convention. This should not be taken as an indication of a lack of appreciation of its centrality. The reasons for not emphasising it were twofold. Firstly, primary school and junior cycle curricula had recently been comprehensively reviewed and, secondly, curriculum issues are considered by the National Council for Curriculum and Assessment (NCCA) on a continuing basis. By 1995, the NCCA will have carried out a review of all elements of the primary school curriculum thus introducing a "new look" to the curriculum which was introduced over twenty years ago. While efforts to duplicate any of this work at the Convention would not have been appropriate, some matters relating to curricula inevitably arose. Discussion for the most part focussed on the primary school and on two areas of change at the secondary level — the Junior Certificate programme which was introduced in 1989 and senior cycle programmes, in which changes that have been occurring in recent years can be expected to become more widespread and institutionalised in the coming years.

9.2 Primary School Curriculum

Topics relating to the primary school curriculum which received special attention in the Green Paper were literacy and numeracy, science, a modern European language, physical education, religious education, size of school, and assessment. All were also discussed in responses to the Green Paper and at the Convention. Each, with the exception of size of school, which is discussed elsewhere in this report, is briefly considered in this section.

(i) Literacy and Numeracy

A central task of the primary school is to provide pupils with levels of literacy and numeracy that will be adequate for further education and for the development as individuals who are able to function effectively in society. Data from international studies of reading literacy and of mathematics achievement during the period of primary schooling (when pupils are 9 years of age), and around the end of primary schooling and beginning of secondary schooling (when pupils are 13 or 14 years of age), indicate that the performance of Irish pupils is average when compared with the performance of pupils in other countries. However, these studies also indicate — and the Green Paper recognises — that a minority of pupils, (estimated at about 10 per cent), do not acquire satisfactory levels of literacy or numeracy while at primary school. Furthermore, in this country and elsewhere, expectations of society and employers are rising and are likely to continue to rise.   Increasingly, work situations are requiring higher levels and a broader range of knowledge and skills, with the result that young people with low levels of achievement, particularly in the areas of reading and oral communication, are at a serious disadvantage in the labour market and in their social life.

To address this problem, the Green Paper proposed a greater emphasis on early identification through the use of appropriate assessment methods, the expansion of the school psychological service, an expanded home-school links programme, in-career training programmes for teachers, and analysis by schools of their reading programmes and staff deployment policies.   Only one of these proposals gave rise to controversy in responses to the Green Paper and at the Convention.   While there was not disagreement that the early identification of learning problems was important, there was considerable opposition to the Green Paper's proposal that all pupils at ages 7 and 11 should take standardised tests to measure their progress and to help identify pupils who might require particular help.   There was also opposition to the Green Paper proposal that the results of tests would be made available in aggregated form to the Department of Education.   The issue of assessment is discussed below.

(ii)   Science

The performance of Irish pupils (at ages 9 and 13) in science has been found to be poor in international studies.   The Green Paper has endorsed the proposal of the Review Body on the Primary Curriculum that a new science programme be developed for primary schools and that relevant preservice and inservice courses be provided for teachers.   While parents welcomed these proposals, teachers were of the view that science should not be introduced as a core subject because of an already over-loaded curriculum, but should instead be taught as part of social and environmental studies.   However, as it is already possible to teach science as part of social and environmental studies, some effort will be required to ensure that science receives more attention in primary schools than it did in the past.   To achieve this, attention will have to be given to the needs of teachers in preservice and inservice courses.   Consideration will also have to be given to the possibility of greater specialisation in science in teacher preparation courses.

(iii)   Modern European Language

The Green Paper proposed an "awareness programme" (which could include an introduction to a selected modern European language) in primary school.   While there was some support for this proposal, a number of problems relating to time constraints and teachers' qualifications were foreseen.   It would seem reasonable to focus on the awareness aspect of the proposal rather than on introduction to a language.   This could be done, to some extent at any rate, in the context of history and geography.

(iv)   Physical Education

The Green Paper foresaw the need to provide a new momentum for physical education in schools to enhance the health and physical well-being of children. It is generally accepted that physical education receives inadequate attention in schools because of lack of facilities, teachers' perceived lack of competence, and fear of litigation. All these areas will need attention if the objectives of the Green Paper (from which there is no real dissent) are to be achieved. Consideration should be given to the development of specialisms among staff inservice education, the use of peripatetic teachers, and the use of facilities in post-primary schools and community resources.

(v)   Religious Education

The right to denominational education, while acknowledging the right of parents to withdraw their children from religious education, received broad support in the Convention. A more difficult issue, however, relates to the notion of an integrated curriculum and, in particular, the religious ethos of a school. There was an acceptance that a problem arose for parents who did not wish to have their children influenced by religious doctrine when a religious ethos infused all the work of the school. There may be a need in some schools for a greater sensitivity to this problem (See also the section on multi-denominational and secular education).

(vi)   Assessment

There is a general concern among practitioners and the Department of Education that achievement standards in schools should be raised and, in particular, that serious problems of under-performance should be tackled. It is clear that under present conditions, some children slip through the net and are not being identified until it is too late. The fact that there is no external examination that might bring such failures to light through the primary school and right up to the age of 15 years, serves to underline the need to establish procedures for obtaining information in the functioning of primary schools. The need for a system of quality assurance will be all the greater in the future, if greater authority is devolved to individual schools.

The proposal of the Green Paper that all pupils should take standardised tests at ages 7 and 11 years, was not supported at the Convention. Opposition to the idea focussed primarily on the proposal that test results for schools should be made available to the Department of Education. A number of difficulties with the Green Paper proposal can be identified. Firstly, if the results of testing are made known to outside bodies (e.g. the Department of Education, a Board of Management, parents), this would be likely to create a high stakes accountability situation which would have a negative and narrowing effect on the primary school curriculum. Secondly, it is difficult to devise tests that serve differing purposes (diagnosis, monitoring) such as the Green

Paper proposed, in an equally satisfactory manner. And thirdly, practical problems could be anticipated in controlling the conditions of testing from school to school and in handling data aggregated at the national level.

There is substantial agreement on some issues regarding quality assurance and the early identification of under-achievers in primary schools, and disagreement on others. Agreement exists on the assessment of individual pupils and on monitoring of the performance of the educational system as a whole, while there is disagreement on the provision of information on the performance of schools to outside bodies. There is general agreement that all schools should have, as part of their school plan, a system for the evaluation of the progress of individual pupils. The system should specify procedures for assessment and for reporting assessment results for individual pupils to parents. The assessment results should also be considered on a whole school basis. There is an obvious place for standardised tests in such a system to provide normative and diagnostic information as a basis for devising teaching programmes. The use of such tests is not opposed by teachers. Many already make use of them.

While there is opposition from teachers to the provision of test information to the Department of Education and Boards of Management, it may be that if schools could be assured that test results would not be used for accountability purposes, they might allow access to results in aggregated form. But it would be difficult to devise a system in which schools would be convinced that test results would not be used to make judgements about schools that might have a negative impact on them.

At a national level, a system of monitoring standards based on the regular assessment of the performance of representative samples of schools should be established to provide information to the Department of Education and the general public. Only some schools, which would not be publicly identified, would participate in such an exercise. This is not a controversial matter.

Problems are greatest in developing an acceptable method of quality assurance that would inform interested parties about the performance of individual schools, and would provide information for the Department of Education regarding the allocation of additional resources where these were deemed necessary. The Convention was not successful in identifying a system that would be acceptable to all parties. However, if a national testing programme in all schools is deemed not to be suitable for this purpose, other methods of quality assurance, which will give due recognition to the variety of achievements of the primary school, will have to be devised. One way of achieving this would be to have schools provide test information with normative data to the Department of Education on a voluntary basis, when seeking additional resources, as they do at present when applying for a remedial teacher.

9.3   Secondary School Curriculum

At the Convention there was general commitment to a balanced holistic curriculum at second level. General support was expressed for the main thrust of the Junior Certificate programme.   However, problems were raised about its implementation. These related to the adequacy of resourcing, particularly for practical subject areas and in small schools, more inservice for teachers, the need for time for curriculum planning, the scarcity of textbooks in the Irish language, and the requirements of students with special needs. The need for styles of pedagogy which engage and involve all pupils more actively in the teaching-learning interaction than was traditional, was also realised.

Issues were also raised about curriculum levels and student differentiation.   One related to the fact that the introduction of Foundation courses may have led to some students following courses at a lower level than they are capable of, thus contributing to an overall lowering of standards of achievement in schools.   Another issue related to the longer-term effects for access to courses in senior cycle when students get locked in at an early stage to particular course levels. Both these issues merit attention and careful monitoring.

A lack of consistency was evident in views about the Junior Certificate Examination. On the one hand, support was expressed for the examination in its present form.   A number of reasons were given for this support.   The examination is the first occasion on which external objective information is available on students; it may provide useful information to students and parents in choosing further educational and career options, and it provides certification for students who are leaving the system at the end of compulsory education.

On the other hand, it was recognised that the examination can create distortions in the curricular experiences of students. By focussing on the knowledge and skills assessed in the examination, schools were neglecting areas and approaches to development regarded as important in the Junior Certificate programme, including active learning and student activity.   The examination was also encouraging an emphasis on rote learning and a teacher centered approach to teaching and learning in which a passive role was assigned to the student.   Furthermore, subjects which are not formally assessed in the examination, tend to be undervalued. The form of the examination may also serve to reinforce the subject centered nature of teaching and learning.   Despite the intentions of the curriculum designers, there seems to be little cross-curriculum work in schools and efforts to develop general thinking or problem-solving skills in students are inhibited.

The problems of students who are not served by the examination and leave school without certification, still need to be addressed almost eight years after the Curriculum and Examinations Board (1986) in its document *In Our Schools* said that "all students should have available to them some certification of their achievements on reaching the end of the period of compulsory school attendance, whether or not they have completed three years of the junior cycle certificate" (p.34).

It is the view of the Secretariat that the present system of assessment at Junior Cycle is inadequate and unless reforms are introduced the objectives of the Junior Certificate programme will not be achieved. The proposal of the Green Paper, that the Junior Certificate examination should consist of an externally conducted examination and a complementary school-based assessment, a practice not unknown in other countries, has much to recommend it. The continuation of an external component should allay any possible fears about a deterioration of standards. At the same time, the concerns of teachers in terms of the extra burden which school-based assessment would place on them and the pressures that might be brought to bear on them, must be recognised. However, it is also clear that pressure at the time of the Junior Certificate examination is not as great as at the Leaving Certificate examination or as it was at the Intermediate Certificate in the past, since important educational or vocational decisions are not made on the basis of examination performance.

The place of the arts, physical and health education, and social and political studies are areas of concern in the Green Paper, and in the responses of many commentators regarding the availability of a balanced education. Problems exist as to how satisfactory provision is to be made for such areas of experience. The view of the health-promoting school, as set out in the Green Paper, has won general endorsement and there is widespread support for its promotion. Current pilot work on social and political studies should lead to a satisfactory incorporation of this important aspect of democratic education within the system in future. A very high degree of concern has been expressed about the neglect of the role of the arts in education. Both in response to the Green Paper and at the Convention, a variety of agencies have argued cogently for the centrality of education in the arts, for a balanced educational experience. Many specific proposals have been made, in submitted documentation, which hold much promise for future action. The Minister for Education recognised this when she remarked in her closing address, "The widespread concern we have heard for the place for the arts in education provides us with an agenda for action in this area." It is not possible in this report to go into detail on recommendations, but it is the view of the Secretariat that a co-operative initiative by the Department of Education, the NCCA, the Arts Council and representatives of arts teacher associations, could lead to necessary progress in the place of the arts in Irish education.

Although religious education is part of the available programme for all pupils, with due regard to parents' constitutional rights concerning the participation of their children in religious instruction, many responses to the Green Paper considered that it did not pay sufficient attention to religion and its role within Irish education. Some participants were in favour of religion as an examination subject at Leaving Certificate.

Many reactions to the Green Paper were critical of what was perceived to be its utilitarian, instrumentalist view of education, which appeared to be led primarily by economic considerations. Such a perception, however, may not have been entirely warranted. For example, for the post-compulsory period of second-level education, when utilitarian views might be expected to be most in evidence, the Green Paper had advocated a comprehensive approach to curriculum rather than the dual system of academic and vocational education which is common in other European countries and had been proposed in the Culliton report. However, the frequent references in the Green Paper to "enterprise culture" and the proposal that a subject termed Enterprise and Technology Studies should be compulsory for all students, initially at the Junior Certificate level and later extending to the Leaving Certificate, lent support to an interpretation of education as utilitarian and work-oriented. There was considerable opposition at the Convention to making Enterprise and Technology Studies compulsory for all students.

It is clear that the variety of curricula that is emerging at the senior cycle level is going to cause problems for schools, parents, and students. The problems will be particularly acute for small schools which will not be able to offer the full range of options to students. The problem will not be resolved by school amalgamation. While there will be cases where amalgamation is appropriate, the problems of small stand-alone schools in sparsely populated areas will remain, and special provision will be required to allow them serve their pupil clientele.

There was a lot of enthusiasm at the Convention for the transition year option. It was noted that students matured during the year and sometimes revised their subject and career choices. Particular benefits, by way of improved self-esteem, seemed to accrue to lower-achieving students. However, it was felt that there was considerable variation from school to school in the quality of transition year programmes. It was considered that provision during the transition year would be likely to improve if schools had to submit a programme annually, if schools were inspected, if information on good practice was more widely disseminated, if additional resources were provided and if more time was allocated to the co-ordinator's work.

While the need for an alternative to present provision at the Leaving Certificate was universally accepted, lack of information on the precise nature of the proposed Leaving Certificate Applied Programme (L.C.A.P.) created problems. (Such information has been more widely disseminated since the time of the Convention). There was general approval for keeping the applied programme under the general umbrella of the Leaving Certificate, however, a number of problems were anticipated. Would the L.C.A.P. be perceived as having low status in schools? What prospects awaited students on completion of the programme? The NCCA has ruled out the possibility of university matriculation on the basis of this form of the Leaving Certificate. This seems to assign an inferior status to the certificate. Again, we can ask what effect the Applied Certificate will have on the ordinary level Leaving Certificate? How can it be provided as an option in anything but very large schools? These are all issues which need to be kept in mind in the design and implementation of the applied option.

The introduction of the L.C.A.P. will do much to counter criticisms made of Vocational Preparation and Training Programmes which it will replace. For one thing, students will in the future be awarded certification. However, since the course will not lead to formal vocational qualifications and the course's certificands may only progress to limited courses of post-secondary education, there is a distinct danger that it will be seen as a "soft-option" track and of limited value by students unless it is carefully planned and designed to respond to student needs. Continual review of the operation of the programme will be essential if this situation is to be avoided.

10. The Irish Language

10.1 Background Context

 The initiatives proposed in the Green Paper for an Irish Language Action Plan are underpinned by the Government's policy for the Irish language, as outlined in the *Programme For A Partnership Government* in the section entitled "Fostering our Language, Culture and Heritage" pp.54-55. The recognition of the integral and creative role which the Irish language has to play in defining Irish identity leads the policy-makers to "accept that the State must play a leading role in expanding the degree of bilingualism in Irish society and, in particular, to achieving greater usage of Irish." Planned programmes of action for these purposes are to be prepared by Bord na Gaeilge and to be implemented by Government Departments and public sector agencies.

The *Programme For A Partnership Government* recognises the major role that the education system will have to play in placing a new and creative emphasis on our own language, culture and heritage. It also commits the Government to intensifying the linguistic, social, physical and economic development of the Gaeltacht. The Green Paper proposed that particular attention would be given to the needs of schools in Gaeltacht areas, and that special initiatives would be needed to provide more structured help and support for the schools in their communities.

The Green Paper specifies its commitment to increase the allocation of marks for oral and comprehension abilities in Irish state examinations at second level. It also affirms the Government commitment to continue to support Gaelscoileanna and to provide them with all the necessary back-up support, especially textbooks and teaching aids.

10.2 Implications for a National Policy for Irish

During the Convention it was noted that the absence of a national policy for Irish in the past had put undue pressure on certain elements within the education system. Teachers in schools frequently felt isolated in their efforts to maintain the Irish language without a broader-based community support. Whenever the State decides to enunciate a clearly defined national policy for Irish, in the broadest community sense, the concomitant implications for the education system will have to be addressed. In order to achieve the policy aim of enabling people to be truly bilingual it will be necessary to provide access to effective teaching of both Irish and English for every child in the State. To aim for fluency in both languages, students would need to study them from primary school to senior-cycle level. A national policy for Irish would be expected to include achievable aims and targets, and take into account implications for educational policy such as curriculum, teaching aids, teacher education, research, assessment, the role of parents, especially at management level, and the structure and planning of the education system

10.3   Specific Issues for the Education System with regard to the Irish Language

(i)   During the Convention it became clear that there was a need to look at the various transition stages of the Irish education system in order to facilitate continuity and progress and to avoid areas of overlap from primary to post-primary and from post-primary to third-level. The teaching of Irish should be seen as a continuum and learners should be facilitated to achieve levels of competence steadily and according to their ability. During the Analysis of Issues session it was recognised that there is a need to provide resources to promote a remedial teaching programme for learners of Irish.

(ii)   The increased emphasis on the fostering of pupils' communicative skills was welcomed at the Convention, but the Green Paper's specific proposal to allocate 60% of marks in State examinations for oral and comprehension abilities was greeted with disquiet in many submissions to the Green Paper and also in presentations and discussions at the Convention. Such a large allocation would have implications for the role of literature in school syllabi, for the perceived differences between the assessment procedures of Irish and English, for the attitudes which could ensue for the teaching of Irish in the Gaeltacht, and for the standard of Irish at third level. The spirit behind the proposal of increasing the allocation of marks for true communicative skills was to be welcomed, but the Convention received a strong message to investigate further alternative weightings in the context of the different levels of courses being offered in the post-primary system. A substantial course in literature was seen as an integral part of the middle and higher levels of the Leaving Certificate course.

(iii)   *Teacher Education.*
If policy aims for the Irish language are to be achieved within the education system there needs to be a commitment to address the following issues. Every teacher who teaches Irish must be fully proficient in speaking, writing and teaching Irish. The responsibility to achieve this can be met by the provision of suitable initial and inservice programmes in teacher education. If there exist within the system teachers who are less than confident about their competence in Irish they should be given opportunities of availing of

renewal courses in Irish. Teachers must also be facilitated to acquire skills to teach other subjects through Irish at both second and third levels. The current growth of Gaelscoileanna at first and second levels makes this a matter of some urgency. The implications for teacher education involve the need for courses in bilingualism, inservice courses which would target the needs of all-Irish medium education, and courses in second-language methodologies for various age-groups and for educationally disadvantaged children. A higher standard of Irish at entry-level for intending student teachers in the colleges of education was emphasised on more than one occasion during the Convention. If more emphasis were placed on Irish in the course of their studies in the colleges, greater progress would be achieved in the provision of the kinds of language proficiency deemed necessary for effective language teaching, particularly in communicative language courses.

(iv)   *Increasing the Usage of Irish.*

Both the Green Paper and the *Programme For A Partnership Government* point to the importance of placing the teaching of Irish in the context of Ireland's heritage. This point was referred to frequently by many of the participating organisations at the Convention. If the Irish language is used positively in the development of civic, social and political education at post-primary level, the participative nature of the pupils' involvement could enhance their attitudes towards the language and encourage its use. Guidelines should be prepared to enable schools to make greater progress in the use of Irish, both as a medium of instruction for other subject areas and as a medium of communication in the school environment, in order to create a supportive background in the schools for bilingualism.

(v)   *All-Irish Medium Education.*

During the Convention frequent expression was given to the opinion that the Department of Education should be proactive rather than reactive in its approach to the development of all-Irish schools. Instead of adopting the passive role of waiting for demands from voluntary groups, a properly planned approach should be taken by the State to facilitate access to Irish-medium education for the public, especially in the newly-developing suburban areas. The increasing demand by parents for Irish-medium pre-school playgroups has given rise to a thriving network of naíonraí throughout the country. The symbiotic relationship of the naíonraí to the scoileanna lán-Ghaeilge is worthy of note.

(vi)   *Education in Gaeltacht Areas.*
         The Green Paper stated that particular attention would be given to the needs of schools in Gaeltacht areas, and that special initiatives would be needed to provide more structured help and support for the schools in their communities.

         The Convention was made aware of the urgent need for Gaeltacht schools to be supported, in the light of the many problems they now face. A significant proportion of Gaeltacht children whose home-language is not Irish, are now attending school. This is leading to an increasing linguistic mix within Gaeltacht classrooms, and poses problems for Irish language maintenance in an educational context. School rationalisation carried out since the 1960s has led to new post-primary schools being provided in locations serving catchment areas that included both Gaeltacht and non-Gaeltacht populations. Little account appears to have been taken of their impact on Irish-using communities (c.f. Bord na Gaeilge, 1986, p.12). During the Convention attention was drawn to the fact that many of the smaller schools in the Gaeltacht are in poor condition and have the added constraints of poor quality teaching aids and resources, and lack of access to remedial teaching. Such schools need to be treated with greater equity, as it was alleged they do not benefit from the recognition and the supports enjoyed by all-Irish schools outside the Gaeltacht, schools in educationally disadvantaged areas, and large schools which enjoy better levels of financing and support. The Convention heard proposals for a comprehensive plan for education in the Gaeltacht, which would take cognisance of the sociolinguistic factors and which would ensure a quality education for each Gaeltacht community. Such a plan would need to include features such as the following: pre-school education; pupils in the Gaeltacht whose home-language is not Irish; specific first and second language syllabi in Irish and English for the Gaeltacht; provision of textbooks and teaching resources; home-school links; remedial education; teacher education; school rationalisation/ amalgamation; different dialects; community and parental attitudes; the importance of Irish to the Gaeltacht's economy; third-level education. Concern was expressed about the outcomes for the Gaeltacht regions of the implementation of the local education structures, as it was alleged that the current socio-economic needs of these regions are not being met satisfactorily under other local structures.

(vii)   *Higher Education.*
         As part of a national policy a broad choice of third-level courses through Irish should be on offer and provision for planning and resourcing such courses should be organised by building on the foundation already in operation. The need for a plan for Irish in every third-level institution was

endorsed. During the Convention it became evident that some third-level colleges were diligent in such planning, but it was equally clear that large differences existed between colleges in this regard. It was suggested that a concerted effort should be made to develop an Irish *milieu* in these colleges. Criteria to examine the targets which should be set down for Irish should be established, and, in particular, at the planning stage it must be ascertained if such targets are achievable, and at the review stage it must be asked if they have been attained. The role of the HEA in encouraging and facilitating third-level colleges to develop plans for Irish was noted.

The Irish-language entry requirement to third-level colleges was discussed. Dissatisfaction was expressed that a number of institutions have a total lack of an Irish entry requirement. The view was expressed at the Convention that it seemed strange that an independent government, with a commitment to the Irish language, did not see fit to include an Irish-language entry-level requirement in the legislative framework for the establishment of new third-level colleges and universities. The anomaly now exists whereby the National University of Ireland colleges alone bear the responsibility of a compulsory Irish entry-level requirement. Their acceptance of this responsibility would be greatly enhanced if resources were provided to equip such institutions with a range of language facilities of the kind currently available in University College Galway, to enable the implementation of specific communicative courses to meet the bilingual requirements of different careers and professions in their dealings with the Irish public. This would facilitate students' exposure to and usage of the Irish language. The view was expressed that a system which necessitated exposure of all students to the use of Irish within a third-level college might be preferable to an entry-level requirement to a college which would subsequently neglect to provide opportunities for usage for its students. The new degree course through Irish announced by Dublin City University was welcomed at the Convention, as it signalled a recognition of the need to meet demands created by students whose previous educational experience has been through the medium of Irish.

10.4   Structures and Planning

Concern was expressed during the Convention about the quality of service local education structures would provide for all-Irish schools and for Gaeltacht schools. As matters stand currently, there is a perceived need for Gaelscoileanna and the VECs to arrive at some solutions for problems at post-primary level, especially in areas where difficulties exist with an all-Irish stream within an ordinary post-primary school. Serious longterm arrangements will have to be made to deal with the special difficulties of Gaeltacht schools and all-Irish schools.

(i)   With regard to the Gaeltacht a number of options emerged:

•   A strong case was made for the establishment of an Údarás Oideachais which would seek to ensure the co-ordination of a quality education for each Gaeltacht community, or

•   Special sub-committees could be established, under the intermediate structures, which would operate under a legal obligation to ensure that the needs of the Gaeltacht communities were being met. A co-ordinating committee, with membership drawn from the different Gaeltacht regions, would need to be put in place to monitor the operations of such sub-committees, or

•   The current position of Gaeltacht schools under a centralised structure could be maintained.

(ii)   In any event, it was felt that the administrative structures of the education system should be able to operate bilingually in order to have them reflect government policies as enunciated in the *Programme For A Partnership Government* in the section *Fostering Our Language,Culture and Heritage*, and in its follow-up pamphlet, *Expanding Bilingualism in Irish Society — Guidelines for Action Programmes in the State Sector,* and that as state-subvented authorities they should reflect the State's commitment to be to the forefront in the expansion of bilingualism; that emphasis on the usage of Irish in such administrative structures be increased, taking into account the citizens' rights to deal with the State in either of the two official languages, and that this work be done in a planned manner.

(iii)   The Convention heard the proposal for an independent structure for the patronage of Gaelscoileanna to promote the cultural ethos of these schools and to ensure the continuity of their status as all-Irish schools. Such a structure would be vigilant that policies deleterious to the schools' ethos should not be imposed on them. A Foundation, established for such purposes, would hold the deeds of trust of all-Irish schools, and would ensure the continued use as all-Irish schools of the school buildings whose title deeds are currently held in trust by the Minister for Education.

(iv)   *Boards of Management.*
         A support service for Boards of Management of all-Irish and Gaeltacht schools is deemed necessary. With the proposed added responsibilities on Boards of Management a training system for board members will be required

to enable them to carry out the various necessary tasks and to do these through the medium of Irish. Because of the high level of parental involvement in the establishment of all-Irish schools it is anticipated that parental participation in Boards of Management will be significant.

(v)   During the Convention it was made apparent that a need has been identified for research in teaching through the medium of the second language in Ireland, as well as an assessment procedure to estimate outcomes of learning through a second language. Effective language learning resources for Irish need to be prepared, and made available. Within a restructured Department of Education it was proposed that a planning, research, development and resources unit be established. Its remit would encompass research, planning and development at national level for Irish-medium education, in order to facilitate a network system of primary and post-primary all-Irish schools, and to co-ordinate both levels of schooling on a geographical basis. It would also facilitate the provision of necessary teaching resources and materials and foster and co-ordinate links between educational interests in the Gaeltacht and the all-Irish medium schools. It could also build on links with educational organisations in other countries with minority languages.

10.5   Irish and the European Dimension

In the preface to Chapter 3 of the Green Paper it is stated "Irish education policy must seek to ensure that our young people acquire a keen awareness of their own heritage and identity, as well as a genuine sense of European citizenship." The European Union recognises that cultural and linguistic diversity is a significant feature of its make-up. The major language attitude surveys carried out in Ireland over the past two decades reveal the public's understanding of the importance of the Irish language as a necessary element of our cultural identity. The effect of our European commitment to the Irish language was discussed at some length during the Analysis of Issues session. The importance of the European dimension as an aspect of the curriculum was recognised. Greater thought needs to be given as to how the Irish language and heritage is to be entwined into an educational experience encompassing European education and culture. The European Bureau for Lesser-Used Languages (EBLUL) which has its headquarters in Dublin, has initiated and supported schemes such as Euroskoalle, which afford opportunities to pupils in Gaelscoileanna to participate in activities with pupils of other lesser-used language backgrounds. The study-visit programme run by EBLUL has afforded opportunities to many involved in the areas of education, the public service, the media, and voluntary organisations in Ireland, to become aware of the diversity of lesser-used language experiences in the European context and to establish worthwhile linkages. EBLUL has also been instrumental in establishing the Mercator information networks. One of these four networks, Mercator Education, is developing a database on the teaching of lesser-used languages and on their use as a media of instruction. EBLUL is about to establish an Education Secretariat in Luxembourg with the support of the Ministry of Education in that country, with a view to developing programmes which would facilitate the teaching of lesser-used languages, teacher education in lesser-used languages, and the integration of lesser-used languages in the European dimension in school curricula. A relevant role for the Irish language and culture should be ensured in the EU schemes, such as Erasmus and Lingua, which are implemented in Ireland, and it was suggested that the Department of Education should endeavour to increase the scope of visits by Irish students abroad in order to heighten the awareness of the diversity of European cultures.

11. The Teaching Profession

11.1 Overview

 The quality, morale and status of the teaching profession are of central importance to the achievement of desired reforms in the decades ahead. The Convention addressed various aspects of the teaching profession including initial formation, induction into teaching, in-career development, diversification of role, remediation of persistent under-performance by teachers, seniority positions, roles of principals, relations between boards of management and senior staff, teacher-parent relationships, and the desirability of a Teaching Council. (The roles of principals and senior positions are dealt with in the section on Internal Management of Schools in this report).

Views expressed at the Convention clearly indicated a high valuation of the professional and caring tradition of the Irish teaching force. Concern was expressed that the status and profile of the teaching profession should be maintained and developed so as to attract applicants of high quality, both male and female. To ensure that the teaching profession would be in a position to respond satisfactorily to the challenges which lie ahead, it was generally agreed that a number of initiatives should be undertaken. There was wide support for the policy proposal of the Green Paper which viewed the teaching career as a continuum involving initial teacher education, induction processes and in-career development opportunities, available periodically throughout a teacher's career.

11.2 Initial Teacher Education

With regard to initial teacher education, a strong preference was expressed for the retention of the concurrent and consecutive modes of teacher preparation, as serving appropriately the needs of different categories of teachers, with varying professional roles. However, some participants put forward the view that the three year B.Ed. programme was too short a time-frame to achieve all that was needed in primary teacher education, while, the single year devoted to the Higher Diploma in Education was also regarded as pressurised in seeking to achieve the various objectives of the course. In the context of many new changes in aspects such as subject content, pedagogical style, assessment procedures, relationships with parents and community, changes in the pupil clientele and social conditions, new approaches to in-school planning, new technologies and the more extended role of the school, new approaches and responses are required from initial and inservice teacher education. While it was acknowledged that preservice teacher education courses, such as the B.Ed. and Higher Diploma in Education, had adapted flexibly to changing needs, this process needs to be maintained on a continuous basis and with a clear sense of direction.

Particular attention should be paid to fostering good partnership relations between the training institutions and the schools, in the interests of improving the school-based training experience of student teachers. The mentor/co-operating teacher assisting the student teacher's formation, in association with college supervisory staff, symbolises a productive form of engagement by the profession in its future members. It is in the interests of all concerned to try to ensure that good practices exist in the arrangements for student placement in the schools. It is undesirable, however, that student teachers should be regarded as trained teachers in the sense of being formally timetabled as if they were established staff.

The recruitment of mature applicants with varied work experience to teacher education was regarded as an enriching process and should be encouraged. However, it was held that a year was too short a period for the training of graduate applicants for primary school teaching. It was also agreed that the provision which existed in some denominational colleges of education for non-believers should be safeguarded and publicised.

11.3   Induction into Teaching

The Convention gave a general welcome to the Green Paper's proposal for a structured induction year into teaching, following initial training. The experiences of this foundation year, during which the beginning teacher was inducted into the full demands of teaching, were regarded as having many longterm consequences. The present ad hoc and adventitious circumstances which faced many such beginners were not propitious for success. The Convention regarded it as a healthy and beneficial development for the profession to be involved in the induction process. The principal teacher, in particular, could be of particular assistance, but it was regarded as unsustainable, within the circumstances of Irish schools, that he/she should be the sole assessor of the beginning teacher's suitability for entry to the profession. It should be the inspector or, if established, a professional extern assessor representing a Teaching Council, who should evaluate the probating teacher in relation to recognition or registration. If the desired induction process is to be a success, it is the view of the Secretariat and of many Convention participants, that much detailed planning needs to take place in advance and many practical implications must be thought through. These would include issues such as arrangements for the placement of probating teachers in schools, reduced teaching hours for those probating and those assisting them, demarcation of areas of responsibility between involved agencies, and general costing of the induction process. The role to be played by personnel from the colleges of education and university departments of education also needs to be explored.

If a Teachers' Council were in place it could play a useful role in the planning and implementation process of the induction years. Local education authorities could also have a helpful role to play. In the absence of such agencies, the Secretariat suggests that a committee of involved interests should be convened by the Department at an early stage to report on how best to introduce the reforms in teacher induction. A carefully managed induction programme would be of great importance in the formation of a confident, professional teacher.

11.4 Inservice Teacher Education

It was agreed that the case for inservice teacher education no longer needs to be made and that attention should be focussed on appropriate structures and best modes of delivery. Many interesting models are currently in operation and there should be an inventory and evaluation of these to guide future policy. It was felt that there should be a variety of forms of inservice teacher education, including an emphasis on school-based inservice provision. Inservice teacher education should take into account the personal and professional needs of the teacher, as well as those of the school system. A co-ordinating agency should be developed to plan inservice provision. This agency should include representation from the Department of Education, the teachers and the providers of inservice education, such as teacher education institutions and teacher centres. If a Teaching Council existed it would have important inputs to make to the planning of inservice education. Under a strategic plan for inservice education it was emphasised that there should be a harnessing of the providers of inservice education so that on a regional basis teachers and schools could have reasonable access to the provisions. The plan should set out priorities for action and it was endorsed that training for management and leadership in schools should be high on the list. Evaluation procedures should also be put in place. There should be flexibility of approach, and agencies should be invited to propose schemes or plans other than those on the priority list. With proper funding and personnel, the potential of new technologies and educational broadcasting for distance inservice education could be developed. More extended and structured provision of inservice teacher education could also allow for beneficial re-organisation within preservice courses, which, at present, tended to be very full because of the absence of a structured inservice scheme.

Appropriate incentives and means for rewarding teachers who obtain qualifications from participation in certificated inservice education courses should be put in place. In some forms of inservice teacher education better arrangements should be made available for teacher replacement/substitution. It was considered at the Analysis of Issues session that some of the proposals of the 1984 Inservice Committee Report would be beneficial in devising a future for inservice teacher education. Satisfaction and confidence were expressed at the National Education Convention that we might be entering a new era for inservice teacher education, which could yield significant breakthroughs in the general education of pupils and in the greater professional satisfaction of teachers.

11.5   The Teaching Career

A variety of issues arose at the Convention in relation to the teaching career in general.   It was regarded as desirable that post-primary teachers should, as far as possible, have taken their teaching subjects to degree level, particularly for the teaching of such subjects at senior cycle. In terms of promoting quality in education, it would be unwise to allow a situation develop whereby a significant proportion of subject teaching was being taught by non-specialists.   On the other hand, it was regarded as unrealistic to expect all primary teachers to be expert in all subject areas in the primary school.   In particular, it was considered that for arts subjects, physical education and science, a pool of peripatetic, supply teachers with specialism in these areas could be of great benefit to small schools, and might be beneficially deployed by a local educational authority.   In large schools scope exists for cultivating and drawing on specialist expertise through class exchanges by staff.

The very limited supply of support staff in Irish schools — of the secretarial, teacher-aide or caretaker character — means that a considerable proportion of teachers' time is distracted from the essential teaching and educational work to more routine and organisational issues.   A more generous policy regarding such support staff could be worthwhile in helping to ensure that the investment in teacher resources was yielding dividends by teachers having more time on teaching tasks.   Obviously, careful criteria would need to be devised in such a support scheme.

Teachers operate in very varying environmental contexts.   In some schools the context is very supportive of the work of the teacher, while, in other situations, the constraints and difficulties which exist make the task of the teacher extremely difficult and take a heavy toll on morale and professional satisfaction, over time. When considering the targeting of resourcing to disadvantaged schools, concern should also be in evidence for mechanisms to give greater in-career support for teachers who face daunting difficulties on a continuing day-to-day basis.   Teacher stress, job-related illnesses and a strong desire for early retirement are not symptoms congruent with promoting greater quality of education.

Early intervention mechanisms, career breaks, inservice education and secondment arrangements can also help to prevent persistent under-performance.   It is important to diagnose the underlying causes for such under-performance and preventative measures are likely to be more professionally satisfactory, and more economical. When serious under-performance is in evidence it should not be allowed to go unattended. Various organisations at the Convention accepted the need for a concerted, co-ordinated policy to be devised to deal adequately with such situations, in the interests of the individual teacher, the pupils and the profession in general. School managements and educational authorities need to combine efforts to deal with such longterm under-performance, regardless of the type of school in which it occurs. A broader scheme for conciliation and arbitration might allow such a co-ordinated policy to emerge. The general guidelines set out in the Green Paper need to be developed and made clear and precise. Calls were made for a welfare service for teachers and the general view was that a sophisticated process was required. The goodwill of relevant partners for reforming action seemed to be in evidence at the Convention.

The retaining of skilled teachers within the classroom, who could benefit from some form of promotion or special recognition, is an issue of importance in many school systems, as well as in Ireland. At present, those seeking career promotion tended to move on to administrative positions within schools. Some promotional outlets to use their professional skills should be devised for dedicated, highly skilled teachers who preferred to devote their efforts to high quality teaching. Posts such as heads of departments, or head of staff development, or mentors for inducting beginner teachers might be beneficial in this context. Furthermore, the Green Paper proposals of teacher secondments for periods to the inspectorate or for inservice education could give the professional recognition to such teachers which their expertise deserves. The secondment of teachers at present for curricular planning work provides a useful pattern which could be developed. Practising teachers and principals have also been contributing to the work of Eduction Departments and Teacher Centres for preservice and inservice education programmes, and this partnership has much potential for expansion. Such activities emphasise the continuing role of teachers as learners and researchers, and foster a benign cycle of self-renewal. The current supply and demand situation within the Irish system allows for the greater deployment of the teaching force in such contexts and this promotes greater width of experience and professionalism of approach.

The Green Paper proposal that teacher conditions of employment be incorporated in conciliation and arbitration procedures would seem to have won the support of the interested parties. As well as improving support resources for teachers in conciliation and arbitration, the changing roles of school in society and various new challenges require flexible, professional responses from teachers. The Secretariat considers that, at this period of great educational and demographic change, there is a need for a sophisticated, comprehensive, readily available, data bank on the teaching force. This would include age patterns, qualifications, teaching subjects, patterns of career breaks, early retirements, numbers qualifying annually, patterns of subject-teacher shortage, numbers of promotion posts and data on induction.

11.6   A Teaching Council

The proposal to establish a Teaching Council got widespread support at the Convention, although one teacher union had reservations about it. The general view was that such a Council was timely in Irish circumstances and would give the teaching profession a degree of control over and responsibility for its own profession and allow for its closer engagement in the process of change.   The Minister for Education also indicated her support for a Teaching Council in her final address to the Convention.   The main stumbling block seems to be some legal problems in its establishment. The Secretariat considers that the legal issues which may be involved should be examined openly, carefully and comprehensively by the education partners, with a view to resolution. The proposal to set up a Teaching Council has been pending for a number of years and it would seem very desirable that a determined effort be made to clarify the issues involved and bring the interested parties together to see if agreement can be arrived at on the establishment of a Teaching Council. Its powers might include establishing a register for all teachers, laying down the conditions for registration, administering disciplinary procedures, assisting in induction processes, offering advice on a wide range of policy matters relating to teacher-supply and demand, preservice training, inservice training and other forms of professional development. It might also propose or commission educational research studies on teaching issues. Such a Teaching Council could do much to promote a distinguished future for the teaching profession in Ireland into the new century.

12. Higher Education

12.1 Overview

The operation of the higher education system came under close scrutiny at the Convention with presentations by, and questioning of, representatives from the Higher Education Authority, the National Council for Educational Awards, the Committee of Heads of Irish Universities, the Council of Higher Education Directors, the Presidents of Colleges of Education, the Irish Federation of University Teachers and the Union of Students in Ireland. In addition, there were two Analysis of Issues Sessions devoted to higher education; one examined administrative structures and quality assurance, while the other focussed on research policy in higher education.

12.2 Participation

The dramatic rise in participation rates in post-compulsory education has brought about a four-fold increase in full-time enrolments in higher education, rising from 21,000 in 1965 to 84,000 in 1992. While the Green Paper did not explicitly set targets, it anticipated that by the mid 1990s over 45% of the age cohort would be transferring to third level and that total full-time enrolments would reach 100,000 by the year 2000. These ambitious projections have already been adjusted upwards by the Department of Education in its presentation to the Convention, when it projected an enrolment of 115,000 by the year 2000 with a further growth to 122,000 by 2005. In the light of the claim made by representatives from the universities and colleges that the recent surge in enrolments has stretched existing resources to breaking point, it is clear that significant additional resources will be required over the next twelve years to facilitate the projected expansion. The extent of additional provision to be made represents an important policy decision. The present strategy of making statistical projections on the likely future demand for places is not a sufficient basis for higher education planning. The setting of enrolment targets for higher education should be made on the basis of an explicit statement of policy objectives and should be accompanied by the appropriate implementation decisions.

Because of very high completion rates at second level and weak labour market demand, especially for poorly qualified school leavers, it is clear that there will continue to be strong social demand for increased provision. However, while successive studies have shown that levels of unemployment are inversely related to educational qualifications, it is not at all certain that our future level of economic development can, at least in the medium term, provide appropriate employment for the large proportion of labour market entrants who will be third level graduates.

Furthermore, while persistently high levels of graduate emigration serve to lower the social rate of return on higher education, it can be argued that a society which fails to provide employment for its young people should at least equip them with a high level of education to enable them to succeed abroad.   Equity considerations also arise in any determination of the appropriate level of provision.   Since participation at third level is highly selective by social class, the distribution of public expenditure on higher education is highly regressive.   However, both Irish and international evidence reveal that, while expansion of education provision for the post compulsory age group does not guarantee greater equality, it is an important element in any successful strategy in this area (Raftery and Hout, 1993).   If growth in enrolment is to be accompanied by greater equality, the provision of extra places needs to be supplemented by additional measures targeted at disadvantaged groups, to enable them to avail of higher education.

Thus, it is clear that there are a range of considerations which are linked to this decision on the appropriate degree of expansion of the higher education system. Because of these, and because of the very substantial resource implications for the taxpayer and the likely higher proportion of the education budget going to third level, it is imperative that higher education policy-makers develop an explicit analysis of the implications of the enrolment targets which are set.

12.3   System Differentiation

The growth of higher education systems into mass systems has been accompanied by structural differentiation.   The Green Paper endorsed the binary system stating that, it is important that the distinctive mission of the university and the non-university sectors should be maintained, and pointed to the danger of academic drift.   At present the sectors differ in their mission, their organised delivery structures, in the level of programmes and qualifications which they offer, in the role of research within institutions and in their prestige.   Many third level staff are conscious of differences in prestige which are perceived as being directly related to differences in levels of programmes and qualifications offered, and to levels of research activity.

Representatives of the university sector expressed themselves happy with the binary divide and indicated a willingness to facilitate linkages with non-university institutions, while acknowledging the inadequate student transfer arrangements which currently exist.   However, it is clear that there is strong pressure within the Regional Technical Colleges sector to resist any capping in the level of courses which they offer.   In response to the question raised in the Green Paper as to whether degree level courses in the RTCs would benefit from or require an association with a wide base of postgraduate work and related research in a university, RTC spokespersons pointed out that this perspective overlooks the benefits to a particular college of having some degree level work.   It is unlikely that the resolution of this tension will admit of any single panacea.   Optimum decisions will be taken in the light of local circumstances and in the context of national labour market needs. However, in the Analysis of Issues group which discussed this question, it was agreed that if too great an emphasis was placed on degree work, the certificate/diploma work of the RTCs might suffer, and the colleges would fail in their mission to provide the level of skills which they were set up to provide.

12.4   Role of the Higher Education Authority

The question of the appropriate balance of courses, by level and by discipline, and the related one of facilitating student transfer between sectors, are matters which can best be addressed if there is a single co-ordinating body for all higher education. The Green Paper had suggested that the remit of the Higher Education Authority might be extended to all third level colleges.   This suggestion met with unanimous approval at the Convention, and should be acted upon.

However, a consequential matter which was not explored at the Convention was the respective role of the Department of Education and an expanded Higher Education Authority.   In the Green Paper it is envisaged that the Department of Education, having divested itself of its excessive involvement in day to day administration of the educational system, would concentrate on strategic educational policy-formulation. It may be that, in relation to higher education, this role definition may bring it into conflict with the HEA, part of whose statutory function, as set out in the Higher Education Authority Act 1971, is as an advisory body to the Minister with an obligation to monitor, advise and play its part generally in furthering the development of higher education, and in the co-ordination of state investment therein.   Tensions have arisen between government and the HEA on a number of occasions during the past decade, revealing a desire on the part of Ministers of Education to regain some of the powers which had previously been devolved to the HEA.   These relationships need to be examined afresh in the context of new legislation and new structures.

It is the view of the Secretariat that, in addition to the proposed extension of its executive role to all universities and colleges, the Higher Education Authority should retain its broad advisory role in relation to higher education policy. It is, of course, ultimately a matter for Government to determine the overall direction of policy. However, operational decisions which determine how these policy objectives are to be achieved are best left to the Higher Education Authority, with due regard to the autonomy of the individual institutions.

12.5 Quality Assurance

The question of quality assurance was an important theme in the Convention's deliberations on higher education. The Green Paper proposes three mechanisms for quality assurance; the development of performance indicators and of internal quality review procedures, appropriate external monitoring, and a proposed academic audit unit within the HEA. There was total agreement on the need for quality assurance, although it was recognised that its meaning was problematic, and that it might mean different things to different people. There was not broad agreement that assessment of quality was primarily a task for the institutions themselves. Representatives from the universities and colleges tended to emphasise the range of quality assurance procedures currently in place, such as the system of extern examiners, external involvement in academic appointments and promotions, requirements of international professional bodies, and peer review of research for publications. There was not agreement on the appropriate location of the proposed academic audit unit. The Committee of Heads of Irish Universities (CHIU) is concerned about the implication for autonomy of locating such a unit within the HEA. It argues that such a unit for its institutions should be located within the university system and that the most appropriate role for the HEA would be that of monitoring the effective operation of the system devised by the universities, rather than exercising a direct role in devising and imposing an academic audit unit of its own. The Irish Federation of University Teachers questioned the adequacy of the performance indicators mentioned in the Green Paper. It was especially concerned about the danger of attempting to assess quality without taking account of the resource constraints under which teaching staff operate.

The issue of quality assurance brings into sharp relief the conflicting demands of autonomy and accountability. In general, higher education staff accept the need for accountability for the use of public funds, but argue that accountability and efficiency do not extend to relinquishing control over central academic issues, such as the right to determine their educational objectives and the best means of achieving them. Recent international trends in higher education governance are broadly supportive of this position, which gives priority to institutional self-evaluation. However, this autonomy can only be justified if appropriate and rigorous peer review procedures are put in place. These review procedures should involve assessments of individuals and departments. If third level institutions are to be self-evaluating, the public interest demands that the mechanisms put in place are manifestly adequate for this purpose. The Secretariat noted that the CHIU was engaged in discussions with the HEA on these matters and that it adopted a positive approach to them. A necessary complement to the process of evaluation is the need for a development programme which will assist third level staff in improving their teaching skills. Quality teaching is no less an imperative at third level than it is at first and second level.

12.6 Governance of Higher Education Institutions

The development of good quality assurance procedures is a central task of management in higher education institutions. Some other aspects of college management were also examined at the Convention. In relation to the role of University President, it was argued that analogies with the role of Chief Executive of business organisations were inappropriate. However, while it is easy to identify some of the distinctive organisational features of third level colleges, such as the emphasis on collegiality, it is more difficult to find agreement on the administrative and managerial implications of such complexity. It was acknowledged that third level institutions are difficult to manage and require constant reappraisal of management structures and functions.

The Green Paper pointed to the desirability of rationalising the composition and functioning of Governing Bodies, and proposed to bring forward the necessary legislation, following consultation with the HEA and the university colleges. It is clear from the responses to the Green Paper, and from the discussion at the Convention, that there is, as yet, no consensus on this matter. Many respondents take comfort from the assurance given that the legislation will be preceded by consultation with the interested parties, and that it will not attempt to impose uniformity.

The main contentious issue concerns the balance between the number of college staff and the number of external representatives. Those who advocate strong external representation, stress the need to safeguard the public interest, while those who advocate a preponderance of college staff argue on the basis of appropriate expertise and primacy of interest. However, as was pointed out at the Analysis of Issues session, the function of a Governing Body should determine its composition. Thus, this should become the initial focus for consultation. For example, there is a need to explore the ways in which the remit of a Governing Body might differ from that of an Academic Council. Does the hierarchy of authority imply a hierarchy of expertise? Or is it appropriate to think in terms of a differentiated hierarchy, where different levels in the hierarchy exercise a unique competence which is specific to this level? If agreement can be reached on these matters it will be easier to take decisions on the appropriate balance of membership.

The most explicit commitment to legislation for the third level sector which was made in the Green Paper, concerns the agreement to amend the Irish Universities Act, 1908, on the basis of proposals put forward by the Senate of the National University of Ireland. Spokespersons for the N.U.I. colleges welcomed this commitment and would urge its early implementation. They were also reassured by the undertaking that any new legislation would not seek to impose rigidity or unnecessary uniformity. The sentiments expressed in the *Programme For A Partnership Government* have been equally reassuring in their commitment to protect the independent and traditional democratic decision-making structures of the universities, and to enact legislation which will preserve their diversity, and enhance their developmental role. The Secretariat considers that this apparent consensus between Government and the universities on the question of third level legislation is likely to be more beneficial than the situation which existed a decade ago, when many in the universities were deeply suspicious of the Government's intentions in respect of legislation.

12.7   National Education and Training Certificate Board

The proposal to establish a single National Education and Training Certification Board was discussed at the Convention. Delegates did not reach any final agreement on this matter and concluded that there was a need for further discussion with interested parties before making any final decision. The Green Paper proposed to constitute a new Council for Education and Vocational Awards by combining the functions of the National Council for Educational Awards and the National Council for Vocational Awards. The new Council would have a wide remit covering all aspects of vocational training, provided by both the education and training agencies, including apprenticeship training, as well as taking over the role of the NCEA in relation to third-level courses outside the university sector.

While there is widespread approval for the notion of a unified national awards framework, the disagreement arises over the appropriate institutional framework which should be put in place. The NCEA argues strongly for the retention of its title, suggesting that it would be unwise to cast aside a "brand name" which had acquired international recognition over the past twenty-one years. It proposes the extension of the ladder of NCEA award by the addition of a National Vocational Certificate which would provide certification in the areas currently being certified by the NCVA. However, in respect of this proposal, it is not clear that it would have the support of all of the RTCs, its main client institutions. The NCVA argues for its continued separate existence, suggesting that the desired co-ordination would be better achieved through a federation under a co-ordinating council. It points to the danger that the higher education sector might exercise undue influence in those areas which fall within its remit. The different options suggested are not merely reflections of territorial disputes, they represent real alternative strategies, each with its attendant advantages and disadvantages. On balance it appears preferable, at least in the short term, to retain the separate councils and achieve the desired co-ordination through a National Board which would develop overall certificate policy.

12.8 Research Policy

In spite of the Green Paper's identification of research as one of the cornerstones of higher education, there is a great deal of disquiet about the condition of research in Irish higher education. While much of this concern arises from dissatisfaction with the low level of funding for research, this concern is part of a wider perception that the research effort in higher education, and its importance to national development, are grossly undervalued. It is clear that there would be a general welcome for the development of a more explicit national policy on the funding of research in third level education, as promised in the Green Paper.

However, in relation to the direction of future policy, there is very little support for some of the proposals contained in the Green Paper. There appears to be unanimity among academics that university colleges should get a unified budget to cover teaching and research. It was argued strongly that the proposal to establish separate funding for teaching and research would not be in the best interests of either activity. The preference for a unified budget did not imply a resistance to the evaluation of research output. It is significant to note that Convention participants seemed to accept the need for a systematic evaluation of the research output from higher education. Such evaluation, which was perceived to be primarily a matter for each institution, would involve peer review, both within departments and institutions and across institutions. Participants in this discussion were less certain as to how the outcome of these evaluations would influence subsequent resource allocation. There was a desire to avoid the use of negative sanctions and to seek to avoid the development of a rigid differentiation between staff who are research oriented and those who are identified primarily as third level teachers. It was asserted that, frequently, the best researchers are also the best teachers.

It is envisaged that the unified budget which forms the block grant given to colleges would provide the basic level of research funding. It is accepted that selectivity would arise in relation to additional funding for which academics would be encouraged to bid. A strong recommendation emerged from the Analysis of Issues Group which examined research policy, that two National Research Councils should be established, one for the Natural Sciences and one for the Humanities and the Social Sciences. It was argued that the arrangements currently in place for the Natural Sciences are entirely unsatisfactory, while there is no provision at all for the Humanities and the Social Sciences. In respect of research in the Humanities and the Social Sciences, it was felt that both government and the public must be convinced that such research is part of our culture and needs to be supported, just as other cultural pursuits are supported through the Arts Council. It is the view of the Secretariat that this recommendation for the establishment of two research councils is timely, and should be implemented.

Science policy analysts have made a variety of distinctions about different types of research in Science and Technology. One view which commends itself to the Secretariat is, that the distinction between applied and basic research is no longer the most useful, and should be replaced by the distinction between research which is primarily knowledge-oriented and that which is primarily production-oriented. Within knowledge-oriented research it is appropriate to distinguish further between the research undertaken at the initiative of the researcher (bottom-up research) and that undertaken as a consequence of a pre-established set of priorities that may be part of a national research policy. Using this distinction it is suggested that if a Natural Science Research Council is to pursue a balanced national science policy, it should divide its budget between bottom-up research and targeted or strategic research. In contrast, it is suggested that, academic involvement in production-oriented research should be funded directly by industry as a form of contract research. As a general principle such research should be on a full cost recovery basis. The higher education budget should not be expected to carry the overhead costs for such research.

The foregoing discussion on research relates primarily to the situation in the universities. Notwithstanding the new legislation, there is no statutory provision for research in the block grant for the RTC/DIT sector. Accordingly, it is appropriate to seek an increase in the block grant for these colleges to provide some core funding for research. It may also be appropriate, particularly in the case of the RTCs, to apply different criteria for the carrying out of contract research. Since these colleges have been given a specific mandate to assist in the economic development of their regions, they frequently provide research and consultancy to many small firms which cannot fund such assistance on a commercial basis. The colleges have put some seed money into this activity and, while there can be some cross subsidisation from one project to another, there may be a need for some targeted funds to support this activity.

Collaboration in research and development is merely one aspect of a broader programme on college-industry interaction, which was emphasised in the Green Paper. Among the other initiatives called for were greater co-operation in management and technical training, the further development of campus companies, increased staff mobility between colleges and industry and greater professional recognition by academic institutions of work carried out by academic staff for industry. While these issues were not the subject of extensive discussion at the Convention, it is clear from the responses to the Green Paper that colleges accept the mandate to foster increased interaction with business and, thus, to contribute to the development of knowledge-intensive industry.

importance of the role of Adult Education Officers was also emphasised. Within schools, there should be appropriate arrangements for teachers with responsibility for the co-ordination of adult education programmes.

13.8 Accreditation

Problems relating to the accreditation of adult education courses were discussed at some length. Although many excellent initiatives have taken place, no co-ordinated system of accreditation exists, neither does a comprehensive system of credit transfers or a recognition of prior learning. A rationalisation of the system should occur.

The need for the induction, training accreditation and support of adult education tutors also emerged as important. The skills and expertise involved in the area of adult and basic education are of a high order. Ireland has been fortunate in the calibre of many of the people who have devoted themselves to this work. It is the view of the Secretariat that facilities for training for this work should get high priority.

It was argued at the Convention that there is a need for the provision of an accreditation system which takes account of vocational and non-vocational education, of formal and non-formal education. It must also allow for entry at different levels. It was suggested that the National Council for Vocational Awards could assist in the development of an accreditation structure for adult education — for example, that it could initiate research on adults' needs, and then devise a structure which would meet those needs. Bodies such as the National Council for Educational Awards and the Higher Education Authority have already initiated some work in this area and could play an important role in the further development of a framework for accreditation, so that there could be more flexibility and movement from one level to another. The Secretariat considers that distance education could also have an important role to play here, although it was not discussed in detail at the Convention.

13.9 Budgets

With the exception of the Adult Literacy and Community Education (ALCE) budget, other sources of funding to adult education are sporadic and varying in size. Within the statutory services, it was argued, the self-financing rule has been a major disincentive to the development of adult education. There was agreement that this should be modified in order that greater flexibility be built into the structures. This would allow for greater possibilities in the prioritisation of disadvantaged groups.

In addition, access to further and higher education for mature students is currently limited by financial constraints. For example, there are no grants available for students taking part-time courses in further or higher education. It was emphasised at the Convention that there should be distinctive and separate funding by the state for the development of adult education within an overall structure.

13.10 Policy Options

One of the central problems in Adult Education, until now, has been the lack of a coherent policy. It is clear that a policy framework for adult education is essential. Adult, Community and Continuing Education will be further disadvantaged unless it is brought into the mainstream. One of the central recommendations at the Convention concerning Adult, Community and Continuing Education, was that there should be an entitlement to a certain quantum of education, after compulsory education. It was suggested that citizens would have an entitlement to a certain number of educational "credits" or vouchers which could be redeemed, over life, in any institution. This is an important and longterm proposal which deserves serious consideration and which would also provide a minimum budgetary framework. For the present youth population, and for cohorts over the last decade or so, this entitlement is already availed of, in effect, by the vast majority who remain in school well past the minimum school leaving age. However, there are sizeable numbers of adults who left school at, or before, the minimum school-leaving age, and who are seriously disadvantaged as a result of their low levels of educational achievement. Consequently, such a proposal would need to be targeted to these most disadvantaged adults. In addition, careful consideration of the most appropriate mechanisms for implementing such an entitlement would be required. It is clear that any a policy development should also be accompanied by a comprehensive survey of adult educational needs, especially in the area of basic literacy. The current survey under way should provide useful information. Also essential is the development of a coherent information and guidance service.

In relation to the question of structures for the delivery of adult education, it is evident that this also needs to be addressed as a matter of some urgency. There is obvious potential for an intermediate educational tier here, perhaps through the development of Adult Education Boards which could form part of a local educational structure.

More adequate accreditation procedures are also required. A framework for accreditation needs to be developed which takes account of the particular needs and experiences of adult learners, and which provides a comprehensive system of credit transfers. Bodies such as the NCVA, the NCEA and the HEA would play an important role here.

There appears to be a need for more comprehensive budgetary provision for adult education at a national level, in order to put it on to a more solid footing. It also seems to be essential to introduce more flexibility into the "self-financing" rule for schools and colleges.

There are also major equality considerations relating to adult education. Information from Ireland and elsewhere gives rise to the seemingly universal "law" that learning opportunities for adults tend to be dominated by the already educated:"without attention to lifelong education and continuing training in explicitly equity terms, the reproduction of earlier by later inequalities will be untouched" (OECD: in press, p.107). In the light of the experience of the main organisations involved in the delivery of adult education in Ireland, there is a strong argument for prioritising the needs of socio-economically disadvantaged groups and communities, and of low income women, in the provision and resourcing of adult education. In so doing, and in its organisation and delivery, it would appear crucial to develop its potential for critical reflection, empowerment and emancipation.

14.   Equality Issues

14.1   Overview

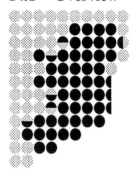

The Green Paper signalled the priority which was being accorded to equality issues, both by its location as chapter two of the Paper and by the extensive treatment which it received. In this Report, the nature of the proposed changes in the education system are set out first before considering the issue of equality of participation and achievement within that system.   However, the Secretariat is at one with the Green Paper in endorsing the priority of concern which should be accorded to tackling the problems relating to equality within the Irish education system.   This section of the Report treats of four elements of inequality: socio-economic; gender; education for special needs; and the education of Travellers.

14.2   Socio-Economic Inequalities and Educational Underachievement

(i)   The General Context

The PESP (1991), Green Paper (1992) and the *Programme For A Partnership Government* (1993) all placed high priority on effectively tackling the high levels of socio-economic inequalities in educational achievement, particularly correcting for educational failure, which is so highly associated with socio-economic disadvantage. The educational system cannot and should not be held responsible for the high level of socio-economic inequality in society nor for the level of unemployment present in the economy.   These are due to much more deep-seated, historical, structural causes. Nevertheless, the system can both reinforce, and even make worse, a problem that is already there, and the most recent evidence indicates that it can intervene effectively in children's lives to reduce or increase their levels of educational achievement, and consequently substantially affect their life chances.   Given, however, the depth and increased level of economic and social inequality in our society, due mainly to the increased levels of unemployment (Callan, Nolan et al 1989), it is essential that the burden of tackling the increasing inequality problem be not left to education alone, but shared more widely over the whole spectrum of governmental policy.

The individual and social costs of educational failure are now so great, the effects on individuals, the economy and society so serious, that it requires urgent attention from government (see Breen, Shortall, 1992 for estimates of the exchequer unemployment costs of educational failure; see also NESC, 1993).   So, against the cost of correcting educational failure has to be put the price the economy and society eventually pays

- The greater difficulty in entry requirements and access routes to the Irish higher education system, difficulty with regard to recognition of alternative entry qualifications to the Leaving Certificate Examination and inadequate transfer arrangements from courses in Regional Technical and Technological Colleges to University.

It would appear, therefore, that we need substantial improvements in grants, particularly for the lower income groups and larger families; more flexibility in access qualifications and routes; substantial expansion of the college-school linkage programmes; substantial improvements in the access and first year "care" programmes by universities and other colleges for students from lower socio-economic backgrounds; and, finally, the necessity for the higher education colleges to set serious targets for recruitment of students from working class and disadvantaged backgrounds, identify what the constraints are that prevent such students attending, and remove those within their power to do so.

(vi)   General Policy Guidelines

Given the seriousness of purpose and detailed specification of government proposals for educational reform to achieve greater socio-economic equality in educational achievement, as well as the evident will to tackle the very serious problems of educational failure, and the very wide level of consensus amongst the educational partners and the general public in supporting such a directive strategy of intervention, it should now be possible to put policies in force which should substantially impact on reducing both educational inequalities and educational failure levels.

The government, however, may be underestimating the serious difficulties involved in tackling effectively the educational failure and inequality problem. It is very deepseated and very difficult to tackle. The following policy issues appear central:

- Tackling the educational underachievement problem as early as possible in primary education, and, therefore, finding solutions to the significant resource allocations that are required for that purpose;

- Identifying children at risk of failure on a national basis as early as possible in their school careers, and intervening effectively to reduce substantially that level of failure;

- Increasing significantly the level of "success" in ordinary level subjects and reducing social class inequalities in achievement at junior cycle level;

- Increasing the level of achievement of working class children at Leaving Certificate level, as well as improving the quality of vocational/technical education for those not going on to higher education.

The Secretariat considers that the Department of Education and Government should set quite clear objectives, which can be easily monitored, to reduce the level of failure and the level of inequality in the educational system.   While the Secretariat considers that there is no acceptable level of educational underachievement, it would suggest that, at least, the following four objectives should be achievable over the next five to seven years:

- Substantially reduce, say, at a minimum by half, the proportion of pupils with serious literacy/numeracy problems in early primary education, over the next five to seven years;

- At least halve the proportion of pupils at second level who do not, for instance, get at least five "Ds" at Junior Certificate (ordinary) level;

- For those still under-achieving in the junior and senior cycle, significantly improve the quality of educational provision and certification at Foundation and other levels, so that their educational achievements and certifications are both appropriate and "marketable," providing access to the labour market and to further training;

- Closely monitor the effectiveness of any new changes in primary education and the current junior and senior cycle curricular/examination changes to see that these do, in fact, work to the advantage of those currently under-achieving in education;

- Accept, at a minimum, the HEA objectives to increase the number of students from lower working class or disadvantaged backgrounds by at least 500 a year over the next five years.

To do this the following policies seem essential:

(a)   An effective programme of pre-school education, targeted initially on disadvantaged areas which are more widely geographically defined than just in the large cities. This should be an effective and enriched learning programme with well resourced and trained leaders/teachers, which involves parents and the community, and is closely linked to schools;

(b)   Rapid target reduction of the pupil-teacher ratio in "disadvantaged schools," defined in terms of the proportion of children from disadvantaged backgrounds in the school, to less than 20:1, but only where a clear strategy of intervention is agreed with the school. Such enriched resources and programmes should first be targeted toward infant and junior classes;

(c)   The role of an Intermediate Tier, if established, could be of strategic importance in such intervention programmes, so as to ensure the interests of the common good, and protect the weakest members of the society. Each such agency should assess the level of educational under-achievement and inequality in its area, set targets, allocate additional resources and intervention programmes, where necessary, monitor and report on achievement of objectives, and should be held accountable to the state for achieving its targets;

(d)   Rapid expansion of the Home-School-Community-Liaison scheme to disadvantaged schools outside disadvantaged areas, but only if adequately resourced, only if schools "opt in" to the full objectives of the scheme, and only if adequate inservice is given to all teachers in such schools. Such Home-School-Community-Liaison programmes should be closely linked to adult/community education schemes running in the communities concerned, so that parents and the community are empowered, and more confident to deal effectively with the education of their children;

(e)   Resourcing of disadvantaged schools to be increased significantly, so that their resources, at least, start to approach those of the average school, where local voluntary resources have been effectively used for additional facilities;

(f)   A co-ordinated plan of intervention for families and children who are seriously disadvantaged, initially in disadvantaged areas, then disadvantaged schools. This would need to be agreed, first at a national level with the Departments of Education, Health, Welfare, Housing, Justice, so that at local level these agencies can work in a co-ordinated way to maximise the welfare and development potential of seriously disadvantaged families and communities. Otherwise, the school and the Home-School-Community-Liaison teachers will find themselves doing, not only a social worker's job, but perhaps a housing officer's as well.

The significant costs involved in doing the above need to be set against the price paid for not intervening in the past, and the cost that will almost inevitably be paid for "creating" an "underclass," disproportionately recruited from the lower working class, whose parents are unemployed, and suffer all the economic, social and psychological stresses resulting from this; whose children fail disproportionately in school, and which failure results in very high levels of persistent unemployment, and failed migration and emigration, (NESC, 1991; Breen, 1991; Hannan, Shortall, 1991; NESC, 1993; Breen, Shortall, 1992; Hannan, O'Riain, 1993) the consequences of which almost inevitably lead to higher levels of crime and social disruption in society.

14.3   Gender Equality in Education

(i)   The Socio-Economic Context
The 1937 Constitution provides, in Article 40.1 that "All citizens shall as human persons be held equal before the law." However, a qualification to Article 40.1 which allowed discrimination on certain grounds meant that the successful claim by women to an entitlement to equal rights in relation to work did not emerge until after entry to the European Community.   A series of Council Directives, under the relevant articles of the Treaty of Rome, together with judgements of the European Court of Justice enforcing the Treaty of Rome, have obliged the Government to ensure that laws, regulations and administrative provisions are compatible with the principle of equal treatment of men and women as regards access to employment, vocational training, working conditions and occupational Social Security schemes *(Second Commission on the Status of Women,* 1993). The Report of the Commission points out that "legislation is required dealing with discrimination on grounds of sex or marital status covering areas such as education and training, the provision of goods, facilities or services, the letting or management of premises, and in general discriminatory advertising" (p.34).

However, the legislative changes that have taken place in relation to the area of employment and employment-related issues have brought about relatively limited change in the socio-economic status of women. Women still constitute a majority of those in the part-time labour market and of those engaged in home duties. Within the paid labour force, women are crowded into a relatively small number of occupations, and tend to be concentrated in the lower echelons of the occupational hierarchy. Female earnings are, on average, still considerably less than those of men. Nevertheless, there have been some gains. There are considerably more married women in paid employment than there were in the 1970s, and women are slightly more likely to be in senior management than they were previously (Drudy and Lynch, 1993).

Therefore, while it is important to have the right to equal pay, working conditions, education and so on, it is evident that one cannot fully exercise these rights without greater equality of condition. It is likely that the formal elimination of barriers mainly benefits the more privileged (middle class women, for example), unless it is accompanied by some form of positive intervention. Consequently, the education system has a vital role to play in the formation of attitudes in society and, thus, in the development of more egalitarian and democratic structures and processes.

(ii)   Policy Statements on Gender Equality in Education

The Green Paper states the following aim for education: "It is the fundamental aim of the Irish educational system that each person be enabled to achieve her/his potential as a human being. Principles of justice, freedom and democracy demand that no individuals should be handicapped by their sex from full participation in the country's social, cultural and economic life" (p.67). *The Programme For A Partnership Government* reaffirms that "the promotion of gender equity will be one of the main aims of educational policy" (p.31). Both documents make a series of concrete proposals under the headings of "a campaign for gender equity" (Green Paper) and a "programme of affirmative action" (*The Programme For A Partnership Government).*

The Report of the *Second Commission on the Status of Women* also contains a very detailed set of proposals for the implementation of gender equality in education (Chapter 9). These proposals range from pre-school to adult education. The Commission recommends that the proposed Education Act should incorporate a gender equity provision.

Most of the submissions received prior to the National Education Convention directed their comments to the Green Paper. The proposals on gender equity were welcomed in all of the submissions which commented on them. Comments on gender equity were received from teacher unions, school management bodies, parents, third level and adult education bodies, and the main social partners (employers and unions). Some comments (particularly, but not exclusively, from the teacher unions) not only affirmed but significantly developed the Green Paper proposals. The key issues emphasised were the implementation of gender equality in the curriculum; textbooks; school organisation; subject provision and choice; Boards of Management and selection boards; school plans and reports; management and administration in schools, colleges and the Department of Education; the inspectorate; teacher education; third level education; adult education and schemes such as the Vocational Training Opportunities Scheme. The need for guidelines from the Department and for inservice education for teachers was emphasised repeatedly.

(iii)   Debate at the Convention

The issue of gender equality was raised in presentations and questions at the plenary sessions. It also formed part of an Analysis of Issues session on inequality in education. Greatest emphasis was given to gender equality in the presentations of the teacher unions, that on adult education, and that of the Council for the Status of Women. Under questioning, management bodies also made clear their commitment to gender equality. The matter of gender inequalities and imbalance in senior management and in the inspectorate was raised with representatives of the

Department of Education. Some of the factors underlying this imbalance were outlined: for example, there was a "time lag" for women, after abolition of the marriage bar in 1973, to percolate through the system; the general slowdown in recruitment and promotion in the Civil Service since the beginning of the 1980s affected promotions. However, it was also pointed out that the Department is an equal opportunity employer. It was argued that this precludes positive discrimination as such.

This point highlights a dilemma for future equality legislation in the education area and in other social spheres. There are limitations to equal opportunities legislation. These are particularly evident where groups (women or other disadvantaged groups) are at very different starting points. This perhaps underlies the fact, alluded to earlier, that the legislative changes in the employment area have not dramatically altered the socio-economic position of women in Ireland. There is a danger that equal opportunities legislation merely offers, as it were, an equal chance to become unequal.

This problem is referred to in the Report of the *Second Commission on the Status of Women* where it recommends that the Constitution should be amended to prohibit all forms of discrimination, either direct or indirect, based on sex: "There should, however, be a provision to protect positive measures designed to address imbalances resulting from past discrimination so that these measures could not themselves be held to be discriminatory and hence unconstitutional" (p.27). It would be necessary, therefore, that future equality legislation (whether of a Constitutional or other kind) should bear these considerations in mind.

In the Analysis of Issues group on inequality there was general agreement on the future thrust in the area of gender equality in education. There was a great emphasis on the need for guidelines on good practice, and for teacher education. The importance of the curriculum, subject take-up, school organisation, good practice in single-sex and co-educational schools and colleges were agreed. Examples of good practice include such things as positive intervention programmes to encourage girls and boys to take up "non-traditional" subjects, and appropriate time-tabling to facilitate this; staff development which includes advice on classroom management in co-educational schools; recognition of the contribution of women in the various areas of the curriculum; elimination of gender stereotyping in textbooks and so on. The need for the Department to play a monitoring role on progress at second level, and the Higher Education Authority at third level, was also emphasised.

(iv)   Implementation

It is generally agreed that the promotion of gender equality should be a fundamental educational aim. The key issue is how this should be implemented. It would appear to be essential to incorporate principles and provisions relating to gender inequality into the forthcoming Education Act. The "principle of equal treatment" which has underlain much of the current employment equality legislation would appear to be adequate to meet the needs in certain areas, such as the curriculum, school organisation, subject provision, allocation and choice, and school plans and reports. However, it is hard to see that it would be adequate to redress the imbalances in management and administration in educational institutions or on selection boards. Even in areas such as the curriculum and subject choice, positive intervention programmes have proved to be quite effective in encouraging girls and boys to move into non-traditional areas. There would seem to be a great need for such programmes to continue, as well as intervention programmes aimed at parents, teachers and employers. It would also appear to be essential to examine the content of knowledge itself in a variety of subject areas, since this has been a major influence in the formation of self-image and stereotypes and may well be closely related to stereotyped subject choices. In relation to better gender balance on Boards of Management, higher education governing bodies, selection boards and at senior administrative levels, possibilities which should be considered include positive intervention programmes, positive discrimination and the establishment of quotas.

14.4   Education For Special Needs

(i)   Definition and Numbers of Children with Special Educational Needs

The term "pupils with special educational needs" as used here refers to a wide variety of children with disabilities, i.e. children with mental or physical disabilities (including hearing and visual); children with emotional or behavioural disturbances; children with specific learning disabilities; children with specific speech and language disorders.

Figures provided by a survey for the Special Education Review Committee (1993) indicate that the number of pupils with special needs (as defined above) being catered for in ordinary classes in primary schools is currently 7,999 — with a total of 9,657 disabilities. Some children have multiple disabilities. Of these disabilities, 17% are physical, hearing or visual disabilities; some 19% are defined as moderate, mild, or borderline mild, mental disabilities (of whom the majority are "borderline mild"); and 64% are defined as emotional, behavioural or other disabilities (Special Education Review Committee, 1993, p.261).

The total number of children with disabilities being catered for in special schools and special classes is estimated by the Special Education Review Committee at just over 10,200. Of these, the figures supplied would indicate that about 13% are in special schools and special classes for the physically, hearing or visually disabled; 80% are in schools and classes for those with mild, moderate or severe mental disabilities; and 7% are in schools specialising in emotional, behavioural or other disorders (Special Education Review Committee, 1993, pp.88-134). There are approximately 2,000 children of school age with severe mental disabilities. At present just 207 of these are receiving a service from the education system, in 16 pilot projects. These children are included in the figure above. It is suggested that, while some are in schools for the moderately handicapped, up to 1,500 children with severe mental disabilities are not serviced by the education system (Special Education Review Committee, p.130).

(ii)   The Policy Framework
The Green Paper stated that policy will seek to provide for children with special needs in mainstream schools as far as possible and according as it is appropriate for the particular child, on the basis of assessment. It also suggested that there will continue to be children with disabilities for whom enrolment in ordinary schools would not be appropriate. The issues it identified as important were: identification of students in special schools who might be more appropriately provided for in ordinary schools and vice-versa; arrangements for ensuring students can be moved from special to mainstream or vice-versa; effective identification and assessment; adequate support services for special and ordinary schools providing for these students.

The *Programme For A Partnership Government* appears to take a somewhat different approach. It states that there should be an educational programme based on the principle of choice — integration into mainstream schools and classes for those children whose families want it, and improved staffing and facilities in special schools for others. It also proposes the re-classification of special national schools, as junior and senior schools, to recognise the fact that students attend such schools up to the age of 18 and, over time, the equipping of such schools to the same standards as all primary and secondary schools. Also proposed is the establishment of a vocational training centre for people with a mental handicap on the campus of one of the universities, as a pilot project, to enhance the rights and perception of people with a mental handicap, and to encourage and facilitate research into their training and developmental needs.

The commitment to accelerate integration which is made in the Green Paper, and implied in the *Programme For A Partnership Government* is related to commitments made by government under the articles of international agreements and in European

Community Resolutions. In May 1990, the then Minister for Education proposed a resolution to the Council of Education Ministers of the European Community that the integration of children with disabilities into ordinary schools be accelerated.

This policy reflects, among other things, increasing demands from parents for the same educational opportunities for their children with disabilities as for their other children. Such a policy also takes greater cognisance of the rights of the disabled child under the articles of international agreements and under the Irish Constitution. There is also an argument from the point of view of moral education:

> If we wish to promote mutual concern and respect among young people, regardless of gender, race, religion, social background or ability, then we must at the same time provide them with constant opportunities for the exercise of these attitudes, and that must mean a substantial degree of integration. For most young people, everyday life affords little or no contact with the problems of physical or mental disability. Conversely, those with disabilities (or indeed any other "special" group) cannot learn properly to participate with others without actually participating. In neither case can appropriate attitudes be developed as abstractions, for exercise later on or elsewhere. (Gaden, 1993)

Ireland's commitment to international agreements has significant implications for educational policy. In 1992, Ireland ratified the United Nations Convention on the Rights of the Child (UN CRC). Article 23 of this Convention states that: "a mentally or physically disabled child should enjoy a full and decent life" and that:

> the disabled child (should have) effective access to and receive education, training, health care services, rehabilitation services, preparation for employment and recreation opportunities in a manner conducive to the child's receiving the fullest possible social integration and individual development, including his/her cultural and spiritual development.

Article 28 affirms the recognition of member States to the right of the child to education and affirms that:"primary education (be) compulsory and free to all" and that second-level education and training be accessible and available; and that third-level education be accessible to all on the basis of capacity (UN CRC, 1989).

With regard to the Irish Constitution, a couple of points seem to emerge. When the Constitution speaks of "the child" it makes no distinction between children of different abilities. It would appear that the Constitution (Article 42.1) enshrines the rights and obligations of all children, (disabled and non-disabled) to an education. Secondly, the rights of parents are given primacy in relation to the education of their children. However, the implications of this for the disabled child have not been set out in legislation. The Report of the *Special Education Review Committee* (1993) points out that the "lack of a legal framework for education means that the right of access to education, more particularly in the ordinary education system, is not statutorally guaranteed" (p.56).

(iii)   Debate at the Convention

In their presentation, the representative group for people with disabilities — the Forum for People with Disabilities — declared that their preferred policy was an education programme based on the principle of choice: integration into ordinary schools for those children who along with their families want it, and improved staffing, facilities and minimum standards of certification in special schools if chosen by, or for, other young people. This position is identical to present government policy as stated in the *Programme For A Partnership Government.*

The Forum for People with Disabilities went on to argue that equal access to an education for all children must become a right enshrined in legislation. While the Forum for People with Disabilities favours integration, it argues that integrated and segregated education are not mutually exclusive: special education should be seen as part of a continuum; greater mobility between special and ordinary schools must be fostered.

While arguing for the importance of positive attitudes, teacher training and appropriate assessment, the Forum for People with Disabilities also emphasised the importance of the provision of sufficient resources to allow people with disabilities to participate equally in the ordinary environment. It was also suggested that co-operation, linkages, sharing of resources and co-ordination between special and mainstream schooling could be facilitated by the establishment of local educational structures. There was widespread agreement on this at the Convention.

Another issue on which there was widespread agreement was that the basic principle which should govern policy is that every child is educable. Each child has a right to education. There was agreement that there needed to be a continuum of provision ranging from integration into mainstream schools to special schools.

In making a decision on any child it was agreed that the emphasis should be on parental choice. However, it was stressed that parents should have the opportunity to make an informed choice which would follow psychological assessment and involve consultation with teachers. It was agreed that it should be virtually impossible to overturn parental choice. However, the possibility of an appeals procedure was also advanced to deal with cases where the integration of a pupil might present grave difficulties for a particular school.

The provision of necessary support services was seen as imperative. The importance of adequate resources was emphasised strongly in the presentations of the primary school management bodies and teachers' union and by all other bodies. It was accepted that with integration there was a danger that pupils would not have access to the same range of resources which are provided in special schools. The necessity for a structure to transfer the relevant supports for pupils from primary to post-primary school was also emphasised. However, if there were planning at a local level it might be a more realistic way to provide access to the range of specialist services which are required.

(iv) Policy Options

Some of the problems posed in discussions at the Convention present dilemmas for people with disabilities and their families. It is clear from the views of their representative body that people with disabilities wish to participate as fully as possible in the life of the community and to have a life that is as near "normal" as possible. This involves at least having the option of integrated education. But if such an option is to present a real choice it has to mean more than simply getting the child into an ordinary school. It is clear from all contributions that unsupported, unresourced integration is not a satisfactory option. Real integration involves identification of the child's needs, an appropriate curriculum, resources such as support staff, and inservice education for all involved teachers.

It is also worth mentioning that there are different models and degrees of integration and these should be explored. Examples of these might include (a) full integration; or (b) placement in a special class for part of the day and an ordinary class for the remainder; or (c) placement in an ordinary school for part of the week and in a special school for the remainder. It could also include a degree of specialisation in ordinary schools at a local level where support services for children with a particular kind of disability might be concentrated in one school, while another school might provide facilities for children with a different type or set of disabilities. Indeed, this model has already been operating successfully, on a limited scale, in the Dublin area.

There appears to be a strong case for increased integration, but also for the continuation of special provision. What is required is greater flexibility and greater resources. It can also be argued that where integration does take place that what is needed is the integration not only of the students but also of the resources and personnel from special education into regular education (O Murchú, 1993). This would imply adequate resource allocation, in order to ensure that special schooling is not impoverished or rendered less effective.

To provide choice and flexibility for children with disabilities and their families, there would need to be co-ordination at a local level. The Report of the *Special Education Review Committee* (1993) highlights the problems arising from the lack of an intermediate administrative structure. From the point of view of special needs, it is argued, this is inappropriate and inefficient. The Report points to the need for flexibility and contends that a local administrative structure would also be in a position to establish close links with other service providers in its area, such as the health services and the voluntary bodies. They consequently recommend the establishment of local educational structures and also resources to enable the establishment of on-going linkages between ordinary and special schools in an area.

Another issue is that many parents are fearful that their children will lose some of their entitlements in integrated situations. Unfortunately, it would seem that this has proved to be the case. Educate Together, the management group for multi-denominational schools, have some experience of integration in their schools. In their submission on the Green Paper they indicate that it has been their experience that children have lost entitlements to things such as school transport and special pupil-teacher ratios which they would have had in the special school. Again, this is an issue that merits close examination. Where a child with a disability transfers from a special school to a less segregated situation, such as special class or ordinary school, that fact should not result in the child losing a claim on resources.

Current government policy on the education of people with disabilities, as set out in the *Programme For A Partnership Government,* is one based on the principle of choice. Should parental rights to choice and consultation in the matter of the education and placement of their disabled children be incorporated in the forthcoming Education Act? It should be noted that, together with a series of very specific recommendations for children with a variety of special needs, the *Special Education Review Committee* recommend that:

> The right of pupils with disabilities and special needs to an appropriate education should be upheld and provided for under the terms of the proposed Education Act. (p.56)

Positive attitudes are essential to a successful policy of integration and to the removal of stereotypes and fear. This was reflected in the presentation of the representative body for people with disabilities and also in the Department of Education's responses to questions. The development of such attitudes, as well as greater knowledge relating to a range of disabilities, involves teacher education, both preservice and inservice. This too requires resources. Principles of justice and equality suggest that, to meet obligations to people with a disability, which would permit them to participate as citizens, education for special needs requires substantially more resources than it at present receives — both in integrated settings and in special schools and classes. This entails the prioritisation of special needs education and targeting of resources to it.

14.5   Education for Travellers

(i)   Numbers and Present Participation Rates
There are an estimated 5,000 Traveller children of primary school age in the country, although precise figures are not available. It is estimated by the Special Education Review Committee that approximately 4,600 children of Travellers attend either pre-schools or primary schools. Of these, approximately 650 attend pre-schools. This Report (1993) suggests that, of the almost 4,000 attending primary schools, about half are full-time in ordinary classes while the remaining 2,000 are in 160 special classes or in one of the four special schools for the children of Travellers, which have an aggregate enrolment of about 200 pupils (Special Education Review Committee, 1993, pp.155-156).

It is difficult to be clear about the number of Traveller children in second-level schools. There are no concrete data. Nevertheless, it appears from informed commentary that only a very small minority of children of Traveller families attend second-level schools. Some attend 11 Junior Training Centres These provide a curriculum which "attempts to maintain a balance between academic and craftwork education, together with an emphasis on social and sporting activities" (Green Paper, p.56). Senior Training Centres provided jointly by FÁS and the Vocational Education Committees cater for the needs of the Travellers in the 15-25 year-old age-group.

(ii)   The Policy Framework
The Green Paper proposed that there should be full participation in school life by all Traveller children. This implies, it suggested, integration into ordinary classes while respecting the unique culture of the Travellers. It outlined a number of requirements at primary level and at second level, and also concerning Junior and Senior Training Centres for Travellers. The Green Paper (p.57) proposed that steps be taken to increase participation at all levels and that"total provision will follow an integrated approach."

Responses to the Green Paper welcomed the concern to increase the participation rates of Traveller children at all levels. They also emphasised the need for support services. However, anxiety was expressed in a number of submissions, especially those directly concerned with Travellers or their education, that "integration" should not be equated with assimilation or "absorption" (Green Paper, p.8). Great emphasis was placed in these submissions on the value of the distinctive culture of the Travellers as a nomadic ethnic minority, and on the need for educational proposals to reflect and respect this, and to adopt an intercultural approach.

Although the *Programme For A Partnership Government* does not specifically address the issue of education for Traveller children, it pledges to create greater equality throughout society "for women, for the disabled, and for Travellers, and the elimination as far as possible of social disadvantage and poverty" (p.2). Two other documents are of direct relevance to the policy framework for the education of Travellers. These are the *Report of the Education and Training Sub-Committee of the Task Force on the Travelling Community* (1993) and the *Report of the Special Education Review Committee* (1993). Both of these reports contain detailed sets of recommendations concerning the education of Travellers.

(iii)   Debate at the Convention
Although there was not a Plenary session devoted to the education of Travellers, issues were addressed during some of the questioning sessions concerning educational inequality. During these it was suggested that, at post-primary level, the very small number of Travellers receiving education has been primarily the responsibility of the vocational sector. The view was expressed by the management body of the vocational sector that there is a need for all sectors to share more fully in the responsibility for educating Traveller children, and indeed other disadvantaged groups. These matters were raised with the representatives of teachers in the voluntary sector. Their responses indicated an awareness of the issues and an openness to addressing the problems. They indicated the need for education in relation to respect for cultural diversity at school level (pupils, teachers and Board of Management) and at the level of the community as well. This was suggested as necessary to avoid in-school segregation. They emphasised also the need for improved out-reach services, home-school liaison, remedial teachers and other support services to address the needs of these children.

These issues were also raised at the Analysis of Issues session which specifically addressed education for Travellers. It was suggested that the approach to the education of Travellers should be located within the broader context of respect for human rights. This would incorporate an emphasis on the right of Travellers to access to all levels of the education system, to consultation, to choice of school as they feel appropriate, and to significantly improved participation rates at all levels. However, it would also involve an emphasis on quality issues, such as the need for culturally appropriate materials and texts, and, across the curriculum, an intercultural approach to the education of all children — one which would include celebration of the culture of Travellers and other nomadic peoples. In addition, it would involve organisational adaptations, such as the use of detailed record cards which Travelling families could take from school to school and other measures which would address the specific needs of Travellers.

(iv) Policy Options

Travellers are a relatively small, but significant, minority group in Ireland. It is clear that their participation rates at all levels of the educational system are unacceptably low for a democratic society. There is an urgent need for positive interventions and affirmative action at all levels, from pre-school through to adult and third level education. Many of the problems and issues relating to Traveller education are similar to those relating to the education Gypsies and Travellers, and other ethnic minorities, elsewhere in the European Union (Liégeois, 1987). A 1989 Resolution by the Council of Education Ministers was highlighted at the Convention, and also by the Report of the Education and Training Sub-Committee of the Task Force on the Travelling Community. This specifically addressed the education of Gypsies and Travellers and gave recognition to cultural needs. This was followed in 1990 by the European Parliament approval of a budgetary line for intercultural education. A portion of this budget is specifically targeted for Gypsy and Traveller children (Task Force on the Travelling Community, 1993).

If the aim of increasing the participation of Traveller children in education is to be achieved, it would appear to be essential to address the qualitative aspects of their educational experiences. Submissions on the Green Paper, the work of the National Education Convention, and reports of expert committees such as the *Special Education Review Committee* and the Task Force on the Travelling Community suggest that this requires adequate resources and support services, outreach programmes, appropriate texts and materials, and a programme of intercultural education for all pupils. Indeed, such a programme of intercultural education should also reflect the culture of other ethnic minorities, as well as that of Travellers. The school population is changing and already includes minority groups such as Muslim, Vietnamese and Bosnian children. Appreciation of the value of other cultures has little to do with the numerical size of the group in the population.

15. Irish Education within its International Context

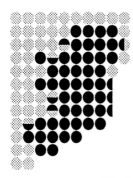

While the National Education Convention did not concentrate on the international dimensions of Irish education, it should be reported that the consciousness of this broader context was in evidence, and discussion on various issues such as the curriculum, teacher education, vocational and technical education and higher education made reference to the international context. Perhaps because of the multiplicity of cultural ties, political relationships and the strong tradition of Irish people going to work, in many capacities, to countries across the world, there is an outward-looking character to contemporary Irish education.   Ireland has participated very actively in the educational work of international bodies such as the UN, OECD and the Council of Europe. Since becoming a committed member of the European Community over twenty years ago, Ireland has been fully involved in social, cultural, training and educational aspects of EC policy. The distinguished involvement of Ireland in aid and education to under-developed countries, particularly through non-governmental agencies, has fostered a sophisticated understanding of the issues involved in promoting human resource development and social justice.   While, nearer home, the political upheavals and community divisions in Northern Ireland have prompted new educational initiatives involving agencies in the Republic, Northern Ireland and Britain, in fostering greater mutual understanding, in helping to define cultural identity and in promoting co-operation between people of different traditions. The Secretariat supports these initiatives and encourages as close a liaison as is possible, in the forthcoming years, between the two educational systems on this island.

Our membership of the European Community, now the European Union, involves us closely with its educational and training concerns and initiatives.   Responses to the Green Paper endorsed the thrust of the chapter dealing with Irish education within the European Union.   There was also a welcome at the Convention for the new possibilities opened up by Article 126 of the Single European Act, which, for the first time, provides a legal framework that allows the community to propose co-operative actions in the area of education and, in particular, in school-level education. Hitherto, Ireland has participated well in various schemes to promote European co-operation in education, although its geographical position has made it difficult for Irish students to participate in various student-exchange schemes.   As so much of the political, economic, social and cultural policy of Ireland is intimately affected by decisions of the European Parliament and the European Commission, it is a right of

Irish citizens to understand the nature and workings of the European Union with a view to being informed citizens of Europe, as well as of their own state. This has implications for the curricula of Irish schools and the reforms over recent years have incorporated a more specific European dimension within the school subjects.

Article 126 of the Single European Act stated that the European Union would contribute to the development of quality education by encouraging co-operation between member states. Specifically, it would support the teaching of the languages of states, encourage mobility of students and teachers, promote co-operation between educational institutions, develop exchanges of information on educational issues, develop youth exchanges and promote distance education. The Commission's *Green Paper On The European Dimension in Education* (1993) sees its initiatives as contributing an "added value" which would "contribute to a European citizenship based on the shared values of interdependence, democracy, equality of opportunity and mutual respect; it would also help to extend the opportunities for improving the quality of education; and finally, it would help pupils towards social integration and a better transition to working life"(p.5). In the context of a new era opening up in Irish-European Union relationships, it would be valuable if the forthcoming Irish White Paper gave some clear indications as to how it envisaged educational institutions here responding more effectively to this developing situation.

The variety of exchange co-operative schemes, such as Erasmus, Lingua, Petra, Comett, have fostered many useful linkages between Irish and other European educational institutions. As was indicated in section 10, there is potential for closer association of the Irish language with initiatives under the European Bureau for Lesser Used Languages (EBLUL). Greater mutual understanding and co-operative endeavour are also promoted by the links between professional educational associations in Ireland and their counterparts in other European countries. Thus, Ireland takes a significant role in such organisations as the European Secondary Heads Association (ESHA), the Association for Teacher Education in Europe (ATEE), European Association of Higher Education (EURASHE), the Conference of the Rectors of European Universities (CRE), and the Liaison Committee of National Rectors' Conferences of the member states of the EU. The Secretariat considers that such forms of liaison should be encouraged and supported as a matter of policy.

As well as European co-operation in education, there is also the aspect of improving our educational and training systems with support from the European Union Structural Funds. Article 130a of the Single European Act deals with the policy of reducing disparities between the various regions of the Union, and the Structural Funds are a key resource to help achieve that objective. The programmes for the Structural Funds from 1993 to 1997, as well as the new Cohesion Fund, allow flexibility for wider applications in the field of education. Having established a creditable tradition in the application of Structural Funds, Ireland has benefited from significant extra funding to help its development. The plans to utilise the resources are set out in the *National Development Plan, 1994-1999* (1993). These developments were noted at the Convention and there was a welcome for the opportunity which now existed, with the extra resources, to make significant improvements on some key areas of the education system.

While recognising Ireland's close ties with countries of the European Union, it should be noted that many responses to the Green Paper, and some submissions to the Convention's Secretariat, expressed concern about the danger of a Euro-centric view prevailing, to the detriment of more international concerns and responsibilities. The introduction to the Green Paper's chapter on the European Community had referred to wider international challenges — "the protection of the global environment, education for human rights and peace, and the needs of the Third World and its development." However, such concerns got no further attention in the Green Paper. Ireland's contribution to these challenges has been a distinguished one at the levels of political action, non-governmental organisations, and the contributions of funds and talents by many Irish people. There is also a circularity of interest in the promotion of social justice in under-developed countries and the cultivation of greater understanding and awareness of it within Irish society. Official policy ought to reflect more on the stance of contemporary Irish society on the broader issues of international education and development.

The Secretariat of the Convention wishes to support the proposal in the Green Paper (p.78) of centralising the distribution of information on activities and schemes of the European Union, the Council of Europe, OECD and UNESCO. Other countries have established such distribution and disseminating units and such a unit in Ireland could do much to develop further the genuine interest which currently exists in international education.

16. Legal Aspects

The forthcoming White Paper on Education is intended to pave the way for an education act or series of acts. The opening section of the Green Paper posed the question, "Why plan for new educational legislation?". In answering this question the authors pointed out how much of the current legal basis stems from the nineteenth century and stated that Ireland was probably unique among European countries in the degree to which it administers an education system without a comprehensive and up-to-date legislative structure. The Paper also pointed to concern in legal circles about rule by circular, without reference to the Oireachtas, and to doubts about some practices being in conformity with Articles 42 and 44 of the Constitution (Green Paper, pp.31-32).

It was the view of the Secretariat that the National Education Convention was not an appropriate forum to debate legal issues in current educational practice, nor to discuss varying legal opinions which exist on significant issues. Accordingly, no disputation was entered into on legal matters. The view taken was that the Convention could clarify and explore certain issues, which might be of benefit later to those charged with the authority to prepare new legislation.

As might be expected, in the context of some of the fundamental issues which were under discussion, participants made reference to legal and constitutional matters in their submissions and discussions. For instance, the Catholic Primary School Managers' Association and owners of voluntary secondary schools stressed that, in their view, legal and constitutional rights to the ownership of their schools severely limited the power of the Minister to introduce changes in their powers and responsibilities, except on a voluntary basis. The subsidiary role of the state regarding education, set out in the Constitution of 1937, was alluded to in some of the responses to the Green Paper and at the Convention. On the other hand, The National Parents' Council (Primary), emphasised the priority given by the Constitution to parents' rights regarding the education of their children and they wished this to be reflected in equal representation of parents with other partners on school management boards, and in other ways.

In its submission to the Convention the Department of Education drew attention to four elements which form the background to the legal environment regarding education — the Constitution, a limited amount of direct educational legislation, some international instruments and European Union legislation. It pointed out that it was the Courts which interpreted the Constitution and that comparatively little interpretation of the educational provisions had taken place. The Department was seeking further legal advice, but, so far, it had established that the ownership of schools was clearly a matter of legal fact, that state support for denominational education was constitutional and that, in all likelihood, the state had considerable regulatory and prescriptive powers on education.

During the Convention, debates on many specific issues arose which highlighted the complex character of legislative reform.   An instance of this was, reconciling the constitutional right of pupils who sought secular education to participate in national schools without interference with their views, with the rights of the majority to denominational national schooling defined as involving the permeation of the general life of the school with a religious ethos and spirit. In general, it was considered that new legislation should clearly set out the rights, responsibilities and powers of all key partners within the system.   Obviously, with such a limited and dated legislative framework in existence, much work needs to be done to devise a legislative basis for a system which has radically changed from the period when the existing constitutional and legal structures were devised.   Some participants at the Convention were in favour of a detailed Education Act which would be very specific on many rights and principles. Others considered that the Act should set out only the basic principles, with subsequent statutory instruments setting out more of the detailed issues.   In reply to questions, the Secretary of the Department of Education indicated that a choice existed between empowering and framework legislation as opposed to more detailed, prescriptive legislation.   However, he indicated that the approach would not be decided until a clearer designation of the functions of various educational partners had been decided.   The current situation provides an opportunity for questioning many existing practices and the Secretariat appreciates the Department of Education's on-going efforts in this regard.

The Secretariat would have a concern that too detailed legislation, in the long run, could be a straitjacket on a developing situation.   While being clear and precise on basic principles and rights, it would be inadvisable, in legislative expression, to relate issues too much to contemporary circumstances.   Flexibility, rather than restriction should be an aim so that the legislation may be responsive to evolving needs and developments.   The legislation should be forward-looking, remove existing anomalies and put in place principles linked to traditions of the past, reflective of current realities and enabling of future developments.   Legal provisions should themselves be subsidiary to, and supportive of, educationally defensible principles. The spirit in which the new legislation is devised and enacted is also important. Efforts should be made to foster, as far as possible, a sense of partnership on the legislation between the key agencies in education.   Concern for the common good should be the priority for all involved parties. The longterm impact of that legislation will be very significant, but if legislative reform can be managed responsibly and successfully it would be a major achievement of this generation and a most valuable contribution to the well-being of Irish education in the future.

17. The Resourcing and Implementation of Educational Change

17.1 Resourcing Issues

 The comprehensive range of proposals for educational change and improvement envisaged by the Green Paper, *Education For A Changing World* and the *Programme For A Partnership Government* involve significant increases in financial resources. When the latter document states government policy as follows, "We regard education as the key to our future prosperity and to equality and equal opportunities for all citizens," there is a price tag if the aspiration is to be converted into reality. The issue of funding cannot be marginalised in the policy decisions of the forthcoming White Paper. Increased resources are by no means the only ingredient for a major educational reform process, but they are an essential element if reform efforts are not to become frustrated and counter-productive. Just as society has greater expectations of, and places more demands on education, the educationalists are entitled to seek extra resources from society to enable them to fulfil a more expanded and complex role, while accepting the discipline of efficiency and accountability.

In discussing the proposals for change at the Convention, understandably, many proposals for improvements and extensions of educational provision were made. A great many of such proposals were legitimate, and in ideal circumstances, it would be desirable that they be implemented. The Secretariat would share most of the aspirations for such developments. However, it would not be helpful if it indulged itself in presenting a massive "shopping list," reflecting proposals made for a great accumulation of improved provision or services. The Secretariat believes that increased financial resources are necessary to the achievement of many important reforms. However, the reality is that, while it is worthwhile to have them on the agenda for future action, it is unrealistic and, perhaps, self deceptive, to presume that these can be provided all at once within the resources which can be made available at present. A policy of prioritising, and targeting to areas of most urgency or fundamental need, is necessary if real progress is to be made. The decisions on priorities are matters for policy determination. To operate within existing financial resources, even allowing for some redeployment, will not facilitate much development, but neither is it of great benefit to take the soft approach of presenting calls for greater resources for all kinds of desirable improvements, with no thought as to how these can be provided. Furthermore, to discriminate positively in favour of those least able to help themselves may require sacrifices from others who are more favourably circumstanced educationally. The Secretariat's report does not engage in costing exercises for proposals, nor does it intrude on policy determination. However, it is influenced by the awareness that a combination of vision and realism is required for serious progress on educational change.

The presentation of the Department of Education to the Convention was heavily weighted towards illustrative data on expenditure on education.   Many valuable tables were presented showing patterns of expenditure over time periods, expenditure by sector and expenditure on Irish education within a comparative perspective. From a number of viewpoints, the level of investment in education by the Irish public has been commendable.   However, expenditure per student as a percentage of G.D.P. is low by international standards.   In making the presentation, the Secretary of the Department stated, "One can certainly reasonably argue, as many participants have done, for spending increases in the education sector."   He went on to present a schedule of illustrative costings.   He stated that most of these "reflect the proposals at the Convention," but, it can be stated, that they are also implied by proposals of the Green Paper and of government policy.   Some participants considered that the costings were estimated conservatively, but, on aggregate they amounted to an extra £478 million.   This was a useful and sobering piece of arithmetic.   The Secretary of the Department drew the following conclusion, "Significant improvements in the education system are expensive, education is competing for resources with other policy areas and expenditure on education cannot be isolated from government policy generally on expenditure and taxation."   He pointed out that improved economic growth would be crucial for resourcing and that there would be a need for prioritisation among desirable inputs.

The Convention could not get involved in the process of prioritisation, but participants had much experience and knowledge of the educational system and of Irish society, and had a sense of realism as to what was attainable.   Not everything could be achieved in the short-term, but, it was important, that a coherent and balanced plan of procedure should be in place whereby genuine and pressing needs could be addressed, and be seen to be addressed, in an enlightened, consistent and systematic fashion over the years ahead.   While not a prioritisation *per se,* the Secretariat noted that there was a striking concordance of view that serious and sustained action needed to be taken to remedy various features of inequality of education which existed.   There was a sophisticated understanding in evidence of the problems of inequality in education and a genuine commitment to seek their resolution.   There was also a general realisation that primary and pre-school education needed greater investment and that the returns on this could be very significant.   In the context of the ambitious plans for increasing enrolment in higher education, prompted by rising social expectations, a concern was in evidence that an

Changing Patterns of Employment:
As well as the general issue of unemployment, there are many changes in the patterns of employment. One of these is the substantial decline in manual and service jobs which required only a minimal education and training. In many countries, a very high proportion of school leavers with no, or very poor, qualifications either remain unemployed or obtain very insecure and low paying employment. Over the decades ahead the minimum education level for employment will continue to increase and the growing long term unemployment levels amongst unskilled and semi-skilled manual workers' families pose a social and educational challenge which cannot be ignored.

At a broader level, public opinion is also increasingly of the view that the content and processes of the education system should be of such a character as to be in harmony with the creation and maintenance of employment opportunities. Closer liaison between the school and work experience is being fostered through a variety of initiatives. Close links are also being encouraged between higher education institutions and industry.

Inequality:
An impressive research data bank has been built up on the incidence and nature of inequality which exists in Irish society as regards patterns of participation and achievement in education. There is concern that in the interests of social justice, special intervention measures should be employed to redress the disadvantage experienced by many living in poor socio-economic circumstances. In particular, the extent of educational failure which is highly concentrated amongst the most deprived families and children, needs to be tackled in its wider social context and within the schools. There is also a much more informed and articulate concern in contemporary Irish society, than formerly existed, that greater gender equality should be promoted in many aspects of the education system. Class and gender inequalities, also evident at higher levels within the education system, pose a continuing challenge to resolve. There is also greater social awareness of the need for well-informed planning in the provision of education for minority groups, such as travellers. The travellers' voice requires to be heeded and appropriate planning put in place to tackle inequalities they face.

While significant strides have been made in recent decades in the education of people with various forms of disability, it is an issue of major concern in current educational debate that improvements be made in line with the best contemporary practice abroad and in keeping with the findings of current research in that area. In particular, the idea of integrating pupils with handicaps into mainstream schooling is much discussed, as are the conditions necessary for the satisfactory implementation of such a policy.

Role of the School:
In most countries the role of the school, particularly at post-primary level, has been expanding significantly. Changes in other social institutions and demands of contemporary living have increased the pressure on schools to take on new programmes or areas of study and skill, and to emphasise the socialisation and pastoral dimensions of schooling. Many countries have also been reforming their school curricula, seeking improvements in style of pedagogy and bringing assessment procedures into better alignment with curricular objectives. The achievement of many new educational objectives has implications for teacher-pupil ratios and for specialist resource staff, such as counsellors and remedial teachers. They also have implications for the support resources in schools such as psychological and referral agencies.

Leadership and inservice Education:
The changed role of schools calls for a high level of skill in school leadership and management. The range of responsibilities on principals and senior staff have become very extensive and the satisfactory performance of these functions is crucial for the effectiveness and efficiency of schools. International research on school effectiveness has stressed the importance of the quality of school leadership operating in association with collegiality of endeavour by school staffs. The extent of the changes involved for all school staffs has led to great emphasis on the need for a comprehensive provision of inservice education for teachers. There is more emphasis on the school as a community and on the quality of the working, learning and social environment within the school for all the personnel involved.

Partnership Within Schools and In Society:
Participative management, whereby school owners, parents, teachers and sometimes members of the local community, combine to form boards of management for schools, has become established in almost all national schools and in the majority of post-primary schools. The nature of the powers and functions of boards of management has come under public scrutiny and, in line with closer links between school and community, the use of school facilities as a community resource, has become an issue of public debate. An improved level of participation in school life by all, including the pupils, forms part of a wider issue which is the need in modern democracies for the more effective participation of citizens within their societies. The school can help prepare young people for effective citizenship and its responsibilities. The well-being of Irish society in the future will require a high level of civic participation in its affairs, and the knowledge, attitudes and skills which facilitate this need to be nurtured and developed.

Ireland, Europe and Changing International Perspectives:
In the wider political arena, Irish society faces new relationships with other states. On the island of Ireland there has been almost twenty-five years of violent conflict relating to Northern Ireland. In both parts of Ireland, the role of the education system, in fostering greater understanding, in helping to define cultural identity, in promoting co-operation between people of different traditions, is being emphasised. Through the formal and non-formal education systems, many initiatives are underway to try to build trust and tolerance, in place of suspicion and prejudice, between those of different religio-cultural traditions and political aspirations.

It is now twenty years since Ireland joined the European Community and, within that short time span, the links between Ireland and the Community have become very close, and the impact of the Community on Irish society has been very significant. The evidence of various measurements of public opinion has indicated the strong public support for Ireland's involvement with the European Community. Within the political, economic and social relationships which now exist between Ireland and the Community, the "European Dimension" has become a more prominent feature of our education system. Furthermore, financial assistance from the European Social and Structural Fund is of significance in relation to funding some of the developments of our expanding education and training system.

While playing a full part within the European Community arena, Irish political concerns are by no means Euro-centric. A striking feature of public attitudes and actions in Ireland has been the concern to assist people suffering hardship and distress in under-developed countries. Political engagement, the work of many aid agencies and the generosity with funds and talents of the Irish people have made significant contributions in such areas. While development education had its initial focus on under-developed regions, its ambit of concern has widened greatly to embrace issues of justice and under-development at home as well as abroad. In this, it coincides with many other agencies in contemporary Ireland, which view education and the promotion of greater social justice as intimately intertwined.

Thus, as this sketch of aspects of social change highlights, Irish society has been changing in many significant ways and the education system needs to be planned so as to respond to new challenges.

3. OUTLINE OF EVOLVING POLICY PROPOSALS AND ISSUES

In response to the social changes set out above, and to other considerations, the government set out its proposals for educational change in the Green Paper and in the Programme for a Partnership Government, and the Minister for Education has further elaborated on policy in various speeches over recent months. As in many other countries in recent years, the government considered that the time is ripe for a significant re-structuring and re-direction of the education system. Its agenda for educational change is very comprehensive. Furthermore, policy proposals have been evolving since the publication of the Green Paper in June 1992. The main aim of this section of the paper is to try to set out what the main government policy proposals are, to provide a synthesising framework within which to see interrelationships of such proposals, to indicate reactions to key proposals and to highlight issues which need to be explored by the partners in the lead up to policy determination by government. The Paper does not purport to cover all issues raised in the debate, nor does it set out solutions to problems, as such would be a pre-empting of the deliberation of the Convention.

A value of the debate over the last fifteen months has been the open way in which views have been expressed and entertained, with consequent shifts in policy attitudes. A less helpful by-product has been that a degree of confusion exists as to what is the current position regarding proposals in certain areas. It is essential that, in advance of the National Education Convention, an effort should be made to summarise the main issues as they now appear and to indicate the reactions of educational organisations to some of these policy proposals. Central objectives such as equity, quality, partnership, accountability, efficiency, devolution, autonomy, collegiality, innovation, recur throughout the Green Paper. One of the general concerns of all participants in the National Education Convention is, whether the proposals put forward are likely to lead to the realisation of such objectives within the system.

3.1 Aims and Philosophy

The Green Paper sets out a statement of educational aims (pp.33-35), which has been broadly endorsed in the responses to the Paper. However, criticism has been expressed that the statement of aims was not always followed through to inform other areas of the Paper. There has also been considerable criticism that the aims were not located within an encompassing philosophy of education, which underpinned specific proposals. Where such a philosophy existed, most commentators referred to its over-emphasis on utilitarian and individualist values, over stress on enterprise, technology and economic concerns and an underemphasis on cultural, moral, artistic and civic elements. Subsequently, Minister Brennan, in a speech in the Seanad on the Green Paper, enunciated a deeper and more liberal conception of "enterprise," than the Green Paper reflected, and also set out a much more enriched view of the arts as part of a balanced education, than was emphasised in the Green Paper.   The question of a commitment to a balanced education was again addressed by Minister Bhreathnach in a policy speech delivered in Tralee in March 1993.   It would seem that perceived imbalances of outlook in the Green Paper have been addressed in favour of the reinstatement of a view of education emphasising the moral, spiritual, intellectual, aesthetic, social and physical education of people in a harmonious and balanced way.   It is also felt that the value of enterprise, innovation, self-reliance, among other personal qualities, can be fostered through the range of educational experiences made available to people, without detriment to an initiation into Ireland's rich cultural heritage.   It is the conversion of the aim into reality for all our people which provides the continuing challenge to educationalists.

3.2   Administration of The System

Since independence, many aspects of the administration of Irish education have been very centralised.   Over the years, a great accumulation of powers, functions and responsibilities have come to reside within the Department of Education.   The rapid and widescale development of the education system in recent decades has placed increasing stress on the functional efficiency of the Department to fulfill its many roles, and, in particular, its strategic planning function.   It was also considered that decision-making on many school matters could be more beneficially employed at local level and that a culture of dependency had developed in relation to the Department of Education which was neither good for the "centre" nor for the local community.

Proposals for change, affecting the Department of Education, aim at concentrating the work of the Department on strategic educational policy formulation, the maintenance of educational standards and efficiency of the system, overall budgetary responsibility and support of those in need of special help and attention.   It is the intention of the Department to divest itself "of its excessive involvement in day-to-day administration of the education system."   As well as this, significant internal changes are planned for the administration of the Department, and in the operation of the inspectorate and the psychological services.   It is also proposed to harness educational research more closely to policy and planning.   If these policy proposals are to become a reality they will involve the most significant reorganisation of the Department of Education since its establishment.   They would also involve a fundamental change in the relationship between most individual schools and the Department.   Because of the long-term significance of such a change and its implications for many features of the system, it is an issue deserving careful attention.

The Green Paper declares devolution of responsibility to be a central principle of policy when it states, "It is proposed to devolve radically decision-making and responsibility in the education system, creating a new dimension of autonomy for schools.   The principle is that everything that can be administered effectively at individual school level should be done there; only matters which cannot be administered effectively at that level should be done elsewhere" (p.17).   Greater emphasis is being placed on the school as a self-reliant institution, acting with a greater degree of staff collegiality, a more central role for principals and middle management, working under boards of management, with greater powers.   The school is also envisaged as having close links with its local community and a more transparent accountability to its clients.

When one notes the intended withdrawal of the Department from the close, intimate relationships with individual schools, which can exist at present, and the extended responsibilities being placed on individual schools, many of which are small, the question arises as to the sustainability of this position. The Green Paper envisaged the setting up of a number of "Executive Agencies" to which various functions of the Department of Education would be devolved. The Vocational Education Committees were to be retained, no longer responsible for the direct management of schools, but with responsibilities for vocational education and training and for adult, youth and sport, and other services. Much debate took place on the adequacy of the planned structural changes, with many commentators pointing to a need for an intermediate tier of administration between the Department and the individual school. There was also concern at the lack of any agency with overall responsibility for the total public good of the community and all its children in a local catchment area. The *Programme for a Partnership Government* of January 1993 states that "democratic intermediate structures for the management of first and second level education," will be established. The functions and composition of such structures are not set out. However, this statement of government policy brings a significant new dimension to bear on proposals for educational administration.

In the course of the national debate, two main points of view were expressed. One view was that the intermediate structures should have comprehensive functions in relation to schools, including the employment of teachers. The other view was that the functions should be limited to the provision of support services for the schools and that they should have a co-ordinating rather than an executive role in relation to the schools. As well as these functions, the geographical area of responsibility and the composition of the structures, are issues of debate. The financial resourcing of such structures has a fundamental bearing on how effective they can be. The powers of new intermediate structures, vis-a-vis existing authorities of schools, need to be explored in depth, as well as how such private school authorities' interests and values could be represented adequately in such local structures. The implications of the establishment of such structures for Vocational Education Committees are also of fundamental importance.

The restructuring of the Department of Education, the establishment of intermediate tiers for educational administration and the re-constitution of boards of management in schools with more authority, represent major innovations which require careful analysis, thought and planning, if they are to be achieved successfully. The relationships and relative areas of responsibility which would exist between these three key administrative structures need to be carefully elucidated. As is to be expected, when such significant change is afoot, there is not agreement between all parties as to the best way forward.

3.3   The Position of Patrons, Trustees, Owners

There are other key partners in the education process whose rights and roles are under-emphasised in the Green Paper and associated documentation, and these are the patrons, trustees and owners of schools. The historical evolution of Irish schooling has shaped it as a predominantly state-aided system, with a subsidiary role for the state. The Constitution of 1937 set out very significant articles on educational rights. The situation now is that the ownership of schools rests with patrons or trustees, associated predominantly with religious organisations. The state pays teachers' salaries, most of the current expenditure of the great majority of schools, and the preponderant capital costs of school buildings.

In view of the financial and social circumstances of contemporary society, it is proposed in the Green Paper that the patrons and trustees should cede many of their traditional powers to the boards of management of schools, which would become the centre of authority at local level.   It may also be that some powers would be ceded to the proposed regional administrative tiers, and, if so, it might be profitable to explore what kind of safeguards for their values and religious ethos existing school owners might require.   It is also proposed that the composition of boards of management be altered to reflect a more equal and democratic balance between the trustees, the parents, the teachers and the local community.   Unlike the current system where the trustees nominate the chairperson of the board, in most instances, it is proposed that the chairperson be elected on a rotating basis by the board members.   The board would also have the power to appoint, promote and dismiss teachers, in accordance with departmental regulations.   These proposed changes regarding boards of management are of a very significant character.   The responses of various organisations of patrons and trustees to the proposals express dissatisfaction and concern at the diminution of their role which the proposed new arrangements involve.   A major aspect of this concern is the potential danger the new arrangements might involve for the denominational character and ethos of the schools.   The previous Minister for Education has sought to give reassurance on this aspect by proposing that school charters be devised which would set out and guarantee the ethos of the schools as envisaged by the patrons and trustees.   The Green Paper also proposes new conditions for schools to benefit from state funds, including non-selective entry and the availability of school premises for local community purposes.   Many issues remain to be explored about such proposed arrangements between owners of schools and boards of management.

There may be a number of other acceptable models of relationships between private school owners and the local, regional or national state authorities which could both guarantee the autonomous religious ethos and values of voluntary schools while, at the same time, incorporating them into an effective local system of school provision so as to achieve maximum coordination and collective effort to meet the educational needs and demands of local and regional communities.

As regards the Vocational Education Committees, it is also envisaged that they cede managerial authority to boards of management in vocational schools and community colleges. Under the 1930 Vocational Education Act these schools are intended to be non-denominational, non-selective, and non-fee-paying.   It would seem that if intermediate administrative tiers are established for all schools, the role of the V.E.Cs would be subsumed into such agencies.   Many of the adult education and support services, as exercised by the V.E.Cs at present, would be operated by the proposed new authorities for the future.   The V.E.C. authorities are concerned that any replacement of them would be of a character whereby their traditions and values in education would be safeguarded.

3.4   Provision of Multi-denominational and Secular Education
Another significant issue arises in the context of the changing character of Irish society which is becoming more pluralistic in religious belief, and that is a concern for the availability of non-denominational education.   The emergence of the parental movement in favour of multi-denominational schools, is a striking instance of this.   The Green Paper declares its support for the establishment of such schools on the same terms as are available for denominational schools, but this may place such parents at a practical disadvantage regarding the form of schooling they require for their children, vis-a-vis corporate agencies such as the churches.

There are other parents who wish for a secular form of schooling for their children, and who find the current situation, whereby the vast majority of schools are denominational, in effect denies them this. The Constitution guarantees the right of any child to attend a school receiving public money without attending religious instruction at that school. This, of course, can be safeguarded by withdrawal of a child from religious instruction classes, but, if denominational education is defined as education interpenetrated with a holistic concept informed by religious considerations and practice, then the demarcation is very difficult and the problem arises as to how such pupils' rights can be safeguarded, while, at the same time, the rights of the great majority to a denominational education be protected. While protecting the rights of majorities, the rights of minorities must not just be tolerated, but treated with respect and an out-going policy be adopted to facilitate the accommodation of their needs. The Convention may help to shape solutions to these problems.

3.5   School Rationalisation

A planning problem of significance which affects trustees, boards of management, teachers, communities and, if established, local educational authorities, is the rationalisation of school provision. The declining pupil population and changing curricular policies bring into central focus the issue of the closure of small schools, the amalgamation of schools and, in appropriate circumstances, the building of new catchment schools. The pupil decline at primary level is already significant. As the situation stands, almost half of the national schools are three teacher or less, and with further decline in the offing, the issue of small schools becomes acute. The Minister has modified the proposals of the Green Paper which indicated a policy of seeking schools of four teachers or more in rural areas and eight teachers or more in urban areas. Nevertheless, the issue of school size remains a significant issue for primary education. At post-primary level, the introduction of the six year cycle and higher retention patterns have relieved, temporarily, the pressure on many small schools. However, the emergence of new curricular policies at senior cycle level highlights the need for schools of a sufficient pupil enrolment to allow for the type of course options which are regarded as the entitlement of pupils. The Green Paper indicates that there may be a decline of between two and three hundred post-primary schools by the year 2000. Such a development would have massive consequences for the post-primary system. It is a matter of major concern for the good of education and for preserving the social fabric of local communities, that the issues are managed well; this will involve sustained co-operation, negotiating skills, diplomacy and the availability of resources. Timing will also be significant. However, the rationalisation challenge is occurring at the same time as significant new educational administrative structures are being proposed. The secure framework within which negotiations can best take place, may not be in position in good time, but it may add urgency to the planning.

3.6   Internal Management of Schools

Within the individual schools, particularly the larger ones, the issue of efficient and effective school management becomes all the more important as the education system becomes more sophisticated and complex. School management boards are, in the main, a growth only of the last two decades in Irish education. However, the concept of shared responsibility of trustees, parents and teachers has become generally established. Indeed, parents, teachers and the Department of Education now wish to establish boards with greater equity of representation for the different partners. It is also envisaged in the Green Paper that the boards should exercise significant powers and become the key responsible agency for the work of the school. School owners and trustees are at present reluctant to cede majority representation on the boards and see significant problems in handing over many of their traditional powers to the boards.   These are issues of considerable complexity and will require considerable discussion,clarification and good will if they are to be resolved satisfactorily.   Participation in boards of management requires a great deal of voluntary commitment and will require considerable expertise from board members.   If the projected responsibilities are to be well carried out, board members will require greater training and resources than have been traditionally available.

The key personnel within the schools who will relate with the boards of management will be senior management, principals and vice-principals.   Comprehensive international research has emphasised the crucial importance of quality leadership in the achievement of effective schools.   The Green Paper employed the term "chief executive" as reflective of the new role envisaged for principal teacher.   However, in the light of subsequent debate, it was considered that the term instructional leader was a more true reflection of the role of the principal, and the Irish term Príomh-Oide was also alluded to as reflecting the correct connotation.   The traditional role of the school principal was being elaborated in the Green Paper and a more precise articulation of responsibilities was set out.   While not disputing most of the features being designated, the debate highlighted the need for greater training and back-up resources for principals to help them perform such extensive responsibilities effectively.   The need for more vice-principals with specific duties in the larger schools, and for a reformed structure of middle management in many schools, has been emphasised.   The need for clearer designation of posts of responsibility and for improved modes of appointment has been raised in many of the responses to the Green Paper.

At primary level, the majority of principal teachers are teaching principals who carry out other professional and administrative responsibilities on top of their normal teaching. Teaching in small schools, many of them do not benefit from secretarial and caretaker services. These may be in limited supply in larger schools, but they can be non-existent in smaller schools.

The Green Paper proposed that the appointment to principalship ought to be for a fixed term, subject to renewal.   Reaction to this proposal has been mixed.   There is opposition to this as a compulsory measure and it has been pointed out that special arrangements in terms of salary would need to apply as a compensation for existing principals who vacate the principalship. On the other hand, some respondents consider the idea of fixed term principalship as of great potential value, both for principals themselves and for the career aspirations of other teachers with leadership talent.   The Green Paper also proposed that principal teachers be voting members of the boards of management.   Many of the responses to the Green Paper considered that such a role could be inhibitory to the exercise of professional freedom and flexibility by the principal teachers.   While exercising responsibility for many features of school life, the principal is also urged to foster a sense of participatory decision-making and teamwork among all staff. The Green Paper also stresses the importance of collaboration and collegiality among school staffs in the interests of better schools and professional satisfaction of staffs.

3.7   Quality of Education Within the Schools
While many of the proposed changes in administrative and managerial structures are important in planning a new framework for Irish education in the future, they all subserve the

most fundamental factor, namely improving the quality of education and the quality of the working and learning environment within the educational institutions, and in non-formal education. Among key proposals for schools is the fostering of greater collegiality and teamwork among school staffs. There is a concern to promote a greater sense of community within the school between teachers and pupils and also between schools and their parents and local communities. This is in line with changing conceptions of the school's role within a changing society referred to earlier. The concept of the health promoting school, in its most embracing sense, is being promoted.

One of the most concrete manifestations of the greater emphasis on collegiality is the Green Paper's proposal that all schools would prepare school plans on an annual basis. The Paper sets out a list of the type of aspects which such a plan should incorporate and stated that the Department of Education would issue guidelines to schools. The school plan would be complemented by the drawing up of an annual review, or report, on the work of the school at the end of each year. It is considered that the institution of school plans and school reviews would give to schools a more coherent sense of direction and a mechanism for assessing achievement.

Many schools, particularly at primary level, already devise school plans, and little opposition has been voiced to the principle of such plans. The key areas of concern relate to whose responsibility it is to draw up the school plan, as ambiguity exists on this score within the Green Paper. The Introduction states, "The first task of each Board of Management would be to draw up a formal School Plan....." (p.18) while in the text of the Paper it is stated that the School Plan will "be prepared annually by the principal, in consultation with the other members of staff and approved by the Board of Management" (p146). The responses emphasise that the formulation of the school plan is centrally a matter for the professionals involved in consultation with parents and management. There is also the question of time, resources and training, to foster and develop the process of staff collegiality.

The annual school report is conceived as part of the emphasis on greater accountability and transparency being proposed in the Green Paper. The main issues of concern with regard to it are the manner in which it is to be presented and approved and the nature of its content. Again, there is a divergence of view between the Introduction to the Green Paper (p.27) and the text (pp.146, 147) in this regard. The Green Paper suggests that the Department of Education will also issue guidelines for the review. An earlier proposal that the reports should involve the publication of the results of pupils' examination performances caused dissatisfaction among many agencies, which regarded it as educationally counter-productive, and the Minister has since declared herself against the publication of examination results. Linking the school plan with the school report has caused some anxiety, but the provision of guidelines on the content and format of both may alleviate some concerns. Too much rigidity and over-ambitious aspirations at this stage could impede the satisfactory introduction of what most respondents regard as potentially valuable innovations.

Other issues affecting the quality of school life include teacher-pupil ratios, time spent in school and support resources and equipment for schools. The Green Paper sets out an aim that the minimum number of school days is not eroded, and wishes to establish six days for curriculum development and planning activities. Teacher-pupil ratios are high in primary schools in Ireland by most international standards. In the immediate future the policy is to target improvements in teacher-pupil ratios on the basis of greatest educational need.   The Green Paper also stresses the value of harnessing educational broadcasting and new technologies for the use of schools, and the enrichment of the pedagogy therein.   There would seem to be much potential for improvement in this area. The needs for counselling and psychological services also have an intimate bearing on the welfare of pupils within the schools and a range of relevant issues need to be explored about the provision of such services. The Green Paper did not draw attention to the significance of local library services for the enrichment of school life, particularly in the area of self-reliant learning techniques, and future policy proposals could profitably place emphasis on this resource.

3.8   Curricular Issues

The Green Paper sets out many emphases and proposals affecting school curricula, pedagogy and pupil assessment, particularly in Chapter 4. The reaction of many organisations has expressed grave concerns, finding contradictions between the vision of the school as set out in p.129 and the earlier emphases which seem to imply a narrowing rather than a broadening concept of education.   In particular, many respondents were concerned with a too utilitarian, instrumentalist view of education, being led by economic considerations.   It was felt that a narrow view of "enterprise culture" was too pervasive, and, in particular, there was unease about the introduction of a subject termed Enterprise and Technology as a compulsory one for all students.   As mentioned above, there was considerable concern that a commitment to a balanced, holistic curriculum was being jettisoned and it was strongly emphasised by many that the role of the arts, in particular, needed much more articulation. It would now seem that a commitment to a broad, balanced curriculum right through schooling is endorsed in official policy. The general principles of the existing primary school curriculum are supported and are further developed in an appropriate way within the Junior Certificate courses at post-primary level.   The concept of a unitary, comprehensive type curriculum with a broad range of subjects is being sustained into senior cycle, with provision for a variety of options, including more vocational options.

The Green Paper proposals for the primary curriculum are generally in line with the recommendations of the Primary Curriculum Review Body Report (1990).   There has been general endorsement of the aims as set out in the Green Paper on pp.82, 83. The areas of most controversy have been the nature of the proposed delineated objectives and graded learning sequences, a tendency of an "adding on" syndrome to curricula and the institutionalisation of standardised tests for pupils aged seven and eleven years.

There has been general agreement with the principles set out and the general approach to the Junior Certificate courses at post-primary level.   Again, the main concerns lie in the area of its assessment. The Green Paper suggests that the assessment would consist of two elements; an externally conducted examination and a complementary but separate, school-based assessment.   The issue of school-based assessment for public certificate purposes has been an issue of on-going dispute for many years. The resolution of this issue is a matter of major importance, as the implementation of many of the approaches and methodologies proposed in the Junior Certificate courses would be in jeopardy without it.   The proposals for senior cycle are formulated on the basis of a three year senior cycle option.   There is a rejection of the "dual track" approach in favour of retaining an umbrella leaving certificate framework within which students would choose various clusters of subject options and levels.   The Leaving Certificate would remain a two-year course, and schools are encouraged to utilise a transition year programme. The situation regarding senior cycle provision has been evolving since the publication of the Green Paper. In summer 1993 the Minister for Education issued a circular to schools setting out the interim arrangements of options for 1994/95, and schools are to indicate their plans to the Department. A senior committee has been set up within the Department of Education, with consultation from the NCCA and the NCVA, to report on senior cycle policy by September 30, 1993, and the issue is under on-going examination by the NCCA. The outcome of planning for senior cycle will have many ramifications and the views of Convention participants should be informative and be influential in any such planning.

The place of the arts, physical and health education, and social and political studies are also areas of curricular concern in the Green Paper, and in the concerns of many commentators regarding the availability of a balanced education. Problems exist as to how satisfactory provision is to be made for such areas of experience. A very high degree of concern has been registered on the responses to perceived neglect of the role of the arts in education, in particular. Religious education is held to be part of the available programme for all pupils, with due regard to parents' constitutional rights concerning the participation of their children in religious instruction. While the Green Paper does not refer to it, some responses to the Green Paper suggest that religion should be a public examination subject. In general, many responses considered that the Green Paper did not pay sufficient attention to religion and its role within Irish education.

The Irish language, as the first official language of the state, receives specific attention in the Green Paper and has been given detailed consideration in the responses of a number of agencies. The Green Paper states that the national goal is that our people generally will be truly bilingual. However, it also stresses that, while Irish is of central importance to the education system, to be effective the schools' efforts need to be strongly buttressed by the general community. Each school is expected to set out a policy on the promotion and use of Irish as part of its school plan. New courses are to be introduced in primary schools with a strong emphasis on oral competence. This is also the approach taken at second-level, where it is proposed to allocate 60% of examination marks to oral abilities, though the wisdom of such a high mark for oral proficiency is contested by many interests. New schemes are proposed for Gaeltacht and all-Irish schools, and third-level colleges are expected to develop an "explicit policy" for the promotion, development and use of Irish among staff and students. The Green Paper also accepts the importance of co-ordination and liaison between the Department and other involved agencies.

A clearly perceived need appears to emerge from the responses to the Green Paper for a more concerted approach to co-ordinate the various efforts of state agencies and voluntary organisations in their work on the Irish language in the education system. In order to achieve this a number of new structures are proposed in some of the responses.

The position of Irish in the education system, from primary school through to Leaving Certificate level, is considered and questioned from many points of view. There is an underlying agreement about maintaining and strengthening this position. It would be further enhanced by the initiation of further incentives to provide a wider range of courses through Irish at third level. It has been commented that the National University bears a disproportionate responsibility in maintaining Irish as a matriculation requirement, as an aid to the promotion of the language in post-primary schools. The question must be asked what solutions might be considered to spread this responsibility more evenly? The special position of UCG with regard to the Irish language, the vibrant growth of Irish-medium schooling with a resultant need for research and planning in this area, the current status of Irish in Gaeltacht schools, literacy in the Gaeltacht, adult education in the Gaeltacht, curricular changes, teacher training, are all issues which are raised in response to the chapter on the Irish language in the Green Paper.

Questions need to be asked about the practical planning process necessary to initiate the progress envisaged by more emphasis on partnership between the education system, the broader state system and the public.

Positive attitudes, an awareness of cultural identity, a sense of pride of heritage as well as mastery of language skills, are seen as basic objectives in Irish courses in order to strengthen the pupils' self-confidence. The desire to achieve these is mentioned in responses, and questions are also posed as to how this might be translated into action.

3.9   Proposals Regarding the Teaching Profession

The proposals of the Green Paper pose a large number of challenges to the teaching force. They include curricular, pedagogic and assessment reform, new approaches to school administration, greater collegiality in working practice, responding to the widening role of the school, including pastoral care and health education, and establishing closer liaison with parents and the local community. The Green Paper recognises the centrality of the teacher's role and regards teacher education as "a continuum in which high quality initial training and properly structured induction are followed by well devised in-career training programmes, available periodically throughout a teacher's career." The Paper's proposal of a common form of initial teacher education for primary and secondary teachers was met with considerable opposition. Many responses urged that the concurrent model of training be maintained for primary teachers and for some secondary teachers. It would seem that official policy now may be in favour of retaining both the concurrent and consecutive models but to seek more flexibility in the way courses are organised, build in more modular elements and facilitate transferability into and out of the teaching career. There was a general welcome for the Green Paper's proposal of a re-structured induction year for beginning teachers, but the implications of the proposal need to be explored.

The Green Paper acknowledged the centrality of inservice education for teachers and stated, "The many proposed initiatives in this paper reinforce the need for an expanded and strengthened staff development programme." The vast majority of the responses to the Green Paper strongly reinforce this view and point to the need for more co-ordination and the utilisation of all available agencies to help provide a comprehensive programme of action on inservice teacher education. Good planning and sufficient resources are crucial issues which need to be examined. There was a general welcome for the proposal to second teachers to the inspectorate and for inservice work, but the practical implementation issues remain to be clarified.

The Green Paper makes suggestions on assessing the quality of teaching and on a career structure for teachers, about which divergent viewpoints exist. The issue of a Teaching Council has been an unresolved issue for quite some time and greater clarity on attitudes towards it, and problems about its establishment, is desirable. In the long run, the quality and morale of the teaching force are of fundamental importance to the implementation of change.

3.10 Higher Education Issues

In its review of higher education the Green Paper makes projections for a further significant increase in enrolments through the remainder of this decade. It endorses the binary system which has evolved stating that it is important that the distinctive mission of the university and non-university sectors should be maintained and fostered. However, it proposes that the remit of the Higher Education Authority might be extended to include responsibility for the co-ordination of both sectors. Such a change will have important implications for the respective roles of the Department of Education and the Higher Education Authority; the structuring of an appropriate interface between them will require detailed discussion and careful analysis.

An important issue which arises in the context of a differentiated system is the scope for co-operation between colleges in the different sectors. The need for co-operation is raised in respect of the provision of degree courses in the non-university sector, in research and in respect of mechanisms for student transfer between institutions. One of the proposals advanced in the Green Paper to facilitate such co-operation is to seek institutional links between the Regional Technical Colleges and the universities. Such a proposal inevitably raises concerns about academic drift, and about preserving parity of esteem and respect for the distinctive mission and ethos of different institutions. This development would also have significant implications for the remit of the National Council for Educational Awards, which is itself targeted for further transformation by the proposal that it be merged with the NCVA to form a new Council for Educational and Vocational Awards. The wisdom of this latter proposal is challenged in several submissions.

The Green Paper identifies research as one of the cornerstones of higher education. However, in spite of this endorsement there is a great deal of concern about the state of research in universities and colleges. Among areas of particular dispute are the proposal to separate funding for teaching from funding for research activities, a perceived trend to concentrate on applied research linked to industry's immediate needs to the neglect of basic research, and a failure to make explicit provision for research in the humanities and the social sciences. There is also concern about the low level of financial support for graduate students. It is clear that significant decisions need to be taken to develop an appropriate policy for research in higher education.

The issue of quality assurance in higher education has evoked considerable discussion. The Green Paper proposes the development of performance indicators and of internal quality review procedures, appropriate external monitoring, and the establishment of an academic audit unit in the Higher Education Authority. In contrast, the colleges point to the mechanisms currently in place such as external examiners and assessors, the requirements of professional bodies and peer review of research for publication. An issue of particular dispute is the degree of reliance on self-evaluation as opposed to external assessment and the appropriate role for the HEA in this process. The issue of quality assurance is linked to the review of management structures about which there are divergent views especially in respect of the proposed model of College President as Chief Executive. The Green Paper reiterates the Minister for Education's decision to amend the Irish University Act of 1908 in line with proposals made by the Senate of the National University. The Paper also proposes bringing forward legislation for the universities in general which "would be more compatible with the role, function and operation of universities in modern society." This potentially very significant development is left vague and would benefit from clarification and discussion.

Many of the divergent views on higher education issues are directly or indirectly linked to differences in the perceived goals of higher education. While the Green Paper aspires to maintain a balance between the technological and the humanities sectors many respondents argue that the balance has, to date, not been achieved and is not reflected in the Green Paper which, it is held, tilts decisively in favour of the technocratic and the utilitarian at the expense of cultural goals. The challenge which faces policy makers in higher education is to make possible the pursuit of multiple objectives and to ensure that goal enlargement does not lead to goal displacement.

3.11   Adult and Community Education

The Green Paper contains a number of proposals for Adult Education. It strongly encourages the use of adult education as a medium for "second-chance" education. It proposes the expansion of the existing Vocational Training Opportunities Scheme (VTOS) for the unemployed, and the opening up of vocational training programmes to second-chance students. It envisages expanded involvement of all secondary schools in extended programmes of adult education. Access to third-level education for mature students would be further extended. Adult literacy programmes would be expanded.

While submissions have welcomed the fact that Adult Education is discussed at some length in the Green Paper, some have suggested that the Green Paper does not set out any major proposals for development and have expressed regret at the absence of plans for Community Education as distinct from Adult Education.

Many of the submissions have expressed concern at the lack of financial support for adult education and the need for increased resources. Worries have been expressed about the self-financing aspects of second-chance education.

Responses have also emphasised the need for provision of information and for guidance for adults and, in particular, the need for support services to enable women to avail of adult education, such as child care and creche facilities. Submissions have also argued for the inclusion of more women in VTOS schemes, as well as their extension to much greater numbers. The role of the public library service for adult education has also been stressed in some responses.

Several responses alluded to the need to improve the structures of delivery of adult education. In particular, the need for the availability of adult education in a wide range of locations, has been argued. The need for specific training for teachers in adult education has also been presented.

There is widespread support in the submissions for the modularisation of courses in third level education and for the awarding of credits for part-time and evening courses. This is accompanied by a concern that in much adult education there are no agreed accreditation procedures. It is suggested that there is a need for a wide range of assessment techniques in adult education.

Thus, the key debates centre round the issues of the resourcing of adult education; measures to facilitate access, particularly by disadvantaged groups and by women; provision of adequate support structures and accreditation.

3.12   Equality Issues

Both in the location and treatment of equality issues in education the Green Paper signals the priority which is being accorded to such issues.   In this overview, the nature of the proposed educational changes are set out first before considering the issue of equity with regard to participation and achievement within the system.   Many research studies have endorsed the high levels of inequality which exist within our education system.   There are four areas of inequality highlighted in the Green Paper: socio-economic; gender; travellers and special needs.   There is considerable concern expressed about the levels of educational failure and under-achievement which are highly concentrated amongst children from the most socio-economically deprived backgrounds.   The substantial under-representation of working class youth in third level education, particularly within the universities, is accorded special attention.   A range of intervention measures is proposed to alleviate the problems, while it is also recognised that "tackling the problem requires integrated action and collaboration between education, health, social welfare, labour and training agencies, and, equally, co-operation between schools, parents and the wider community" (p.45).   Thus, an intersectoral approach is endorsed whereby multifaceted action by responsible agencies could alleviate the complex socio-economic issues which are operative. The problems in the activation of such an approach need to be explored.

A key issue in the approach to inequality is the specific targeting of additional resources to those most in need, and also focussing on inequalities which occur at senior cycle and entry to third level.   It will require a genuine commitment of society at large to a range of measures giving positive discrimination to those at risk as well as the other intersectoral interventions, if serious inroads are to be made on inequality in educational participation and achievement. The responses in general are favourable to the emphasis on alleviating inequalities in the Green Paper.   Recent ministerial statements have proposed that the provision of pre-primary education in disadvantaged areas could also play a role in tackling inequality. It is when the specific actions are taken, which may call for sacrifices, that the full degree of commitment may be measured.

The Green Paper lays great stress on the importance of promoting gender equality in education by stating, "Principles of justice, freedom and democracy demand that no individuals should be handicapped by their sex from self-realisation and full participation in the country's social, cultural and economic life" (p.67).   Changes are proposed for subject choices, syllabus and textbook content and the hidden curriculum, to promote greater equality of engagement by boys and girls.   They are also directed at the formation of attitudes and relationships reflective of equal status. Co-educational schools are favoured.   The career patterns of women in academic life and in management positions in education, as well as in the inspectorate, are seen to reflect significant imbalances which need to be addressed. There is a general welcome in the responses for measures to promote gender equity and equality, although some concern is expressed that teacher education, especially inservice education, and comprehensive guidelines on good practice can be made available in all schools, but, particularly in co-educational settings.   Thus, the implementation of gender equality has implications for a wide range of areas including the curriculum, subject provision and choice, school organisation, selection boards, management, the inspectorate, teacher education, third-level education, adult education and schemes such as the VTOS.   Some of the hindrances in the way of greater gender equality need to be explored with relevant agencies.

With regard to improving facilities for the education of travellers, the Green Paper states, "Further action is promised on the principle of full participation in school life by traveller children"(p.55). The policy of integration is supported "while respecting the unique culture of travellers." A number of specific proposals are set out for primary and second-level schooling and for teacher education, to help realise the general principle. A number of responses have focussed in a detailed way on the education of travellers, and a number of issues need to be explored with regard to the policy and perspectives of involved parties in the field. The responses have generally welcomed the concern to increase the participation rates of traveller children at all educational levels. The need for support services has also been emphasised. However, concern has been expressed that "integration" should not be equated with assimilation or "absorption." Great emphasis has been placed, in a number of the submissions, on the value of the distinctive culture of the travellers as a nomadic ethnic minority, and on the need for educational proposals to reflect and respect this.

A sub-section of the chapter on equity and access in the Green Paper, is devoted to children with special educational needs. In the course of the nation-wide debate, and in written responses, it was very evident that widespread concern exists on this subject. Furthermore, the Report of the Committee on Special Education is due shortly and will provide valuable perspectives on the special education issues. Key issues which should be explored include whether Departmental policy is:

> that accelerated integration is desirable but only on the basis of individual assessment, and accepting "that there will continue to be children with disabilities for whom enrolment in an ordinary school would not be "appropriate," as set out in the Green Paper, or whether it is:

> An educational programme based on the principle of choice - integration into mainstream schools and classes for those children whose families want it, and improved staffing and facilities in special schools for others, as indicated in the Programme For Government.

Other issues of importance are whether rights should be "attached" to the child and enshrined in legislation. It is also worth exploring whether parental rights to choice and consultation should be set down in law. The policy of integration, to be successful, requires very substantial resources and the question arises as to whether there is a social and political will to provide them. In general, positive attitudes are very desirable in relation to people with special educational needs, and exploration of how these can be promoted and facilitated could be beneficial.

3.13   Resources

While many of the government policy proposals involve changes in procedures, structures and attitudes, it is also the case that the implications for increased financial resources need to be understood clearly. The great majority of the responses to the Green Paper emphasise the need for significant increases in funding if many of the new developments are to be realised. This issue only gets a few sentences in the Green Paper (p.41) where it is stressed that "effective and efficient management at all levels, (is necessary) in order to ensure the most effective and equitable distribution of resources." The better distribution of "available resources" is a desirable goal, but, unless the available resources are sufficient to give real impetus to the many changes planned, then there is a danger of heightened expectations being deflated and goodwill and effort at reforms being frustrated. The issue of funding cannot be marginalised in the debate leading up to the White Paper. Furthermore, the policy decisions of the White Paper will require some costing and indications of budgetary strategy.

3.14 Implementation of Change

One of the significant lessons learned from international research is that it is a difficult and complex task to bring about significant educational change and the time-span involved may be frustrating for impatient reformers. Resourcing, timing and attitudes are very central elements of the process. The extent of the changes being proposed for Irish education, in many facets of the system, is very comprehensive and would lead to a large-scale recasting of the system. Even if Irish society had very much greater resources available to it for educational reform than appears likely, the process of achieving such widescale change requires sophisticated and sustained strategies for implementation. The Green Paper sets out to provide a framework for development and it is hoped that the White Paper, following all the debate and refinement of proposals, will set out a coherent pattern to that framework.

It is important at various stages in the development of an education system that a stocktaking take place which leads to the mapping out of a new way forward. This is the process in which Irish society is currently engaged. The actual final outcomes of the planning rarely end up exactly as the initial blueprint sets out. There are many variables which make themselves felt, and adjustments need to be made along the way. The timing and priorities of various elements in the change package are significant, as well as a flexibility of approach. A sense of commitment to, and ownership of, many of the proposals is important if key educational agencies are to deliver on the implementation of new policies. Thus, a partnership of effort becomes significant, even if agencies do not agree on all aspects of the plan. If that partnership is not forthcoming, the consequences for Irish education and for Irish society over the decades ahead will be fundamentally undermining. To have a plan which gives a sense of direction and which has coherence and a defensible, well-based rationale is a sine quo non for significant change. Within that overall plan, different elements may progress at different paces, and adjustments may be made along the way, but these occur within a demonstrably clear framework of reference.

In the last resort, it is the satisfactory implementation of worthwhile plans for change which is the crucial thing. This process of implementation will require long-term sustained attention and nurturing and the voices of those charged with the implementation of change, in whatever sector, need to be heard and heeded. The National Education Convention is a valuable forum in which consultation, reflection and areas of agreement can take place to assist in the process of educational reform.

Monday 11th October

9.30	**Registration**
10.00	**Opening of Convention by the Minister for Education, Ms. Niamh Bhreathnach, T.D.**
10.20	**Chairperson's Presentation**
10.40	**Secretary General's Opening Address**
11.15	*Coffee*
11.45	National Parents Council — Primary
12.15	Questions from Secretariat
1.00	*Lunch*
2.15	Catholic Primary Schools Managers' Association
2.45	Church of Ireland Board of Education
3.05	Questions from Secretariat
4.00	*Coffee*
4.30	Questions from Secretariat
5.00	Educate Together
5.15	Gaelscoileanna
5.30	Questions from Secretariat
6.00	Conclusion

Tuesday 12th October

9.00	Catholic Episcopal Commission for Education
9.30	AMCSS/JMB
10.00	Secondary Education Committee
10.20	Conference of Major Religious Superiors
10.45	*Coffee*
11.15	Questions from Secretariat
1.00	*Lunch*
2.15	Irish Vocational Education Association
2.45	Association of Chief Executive Officers of Vocational Educational Committees
3.05	Association of Community and Comprehensive Schools
3.30	*Coffee*
4.00	Questions from Secretariat
5.45	Conclusion

Wednesday 13th October

9.00	Irish National Teachers' Organisation
9.30	Questions from Secretariat
10.45	*Coffee*
11.15	Association of Secondary Teachers of Ireland
11.45	Questions from Secretariat
12.55	*Lunch*
2.10	Teachers' Union of Ireland
2.40	Questions from Secretariat
3.50	*Coffee*
4.20	Association of Principals and Vice-Principals of Voluntary Secondary Schools
4.40	Association of Principals of Vocational Schools and Community Colleges
5.00	Association of Principals and Vice-Principals of Community and Comprehensive Schools
5.20	Questions from Secretariat
6.20	Conclusion

Thursday 14th October
- 9.00   National Parents Council — Post-Primary
- 9.30   Questions from Secretariat
- 10.20   Irish Congress of Trade Unions
- 10.35   Irish Employers and Business Confederation
- *10.50   Coffee*
- 11.15   Irish Farmers' Association/Irish Creamery Milk Suppliers' Association
- 11.30   Irish National Organisation of the Unemployed
- 11.45   National Youth Council
- 12.00   Questions from Secretariat
- *12.45   Lunch*
- 2.00   Bord na Gaeilge
- 2.15   Comhdháil Náisiúnta na Gaeilge
- 2.30   The Arts Council
- 2.45   Questions from Secretariat
- 3.05   Council for the Status of Women
- 3.20   Campaign to Separate Church and State
- *3.35   Coffee*
- 4.00   Forum of People with Disabilities
- 4.15   The Special Education Review Committee
- 4.30   Questions from Secretariat
- 4.50   The National Association of Adult Education (AONTAS)
- 5.20   Questions from Secretariat
- 6.10   Conclusion

Friday 15th October
- 9.00   National Council for Curriculum and Assessment
- 9.15   National Council for Vocational Awards
- 9.30   FÁS
- 9.45   Questions from Secretariat
- 10.00   Higher Education Authority
- 10.15   National Council for Educational Awards
- 10.30   Questions from Secretariat
- *10.45   Coffee*
- 11.15   Committee of Heads of Irish Universities
- 11.45   Council of Higher Education Directors
- 12.00   Presidents of Colleges of Education
- 12.20   Questions from Secretariat
- *1.00   Lunch*
- 2.15   Questions from Secretariat
- 3.00   Irish Federation of University Teachers
- 3.30   Questions from Secretariat
- *4.00   Coffee*
- 4.30   Questions from Secretariat
- 5.00   Union of Students of Ireland
- 5.30   Questions from Secretariat
- 6.00   Conclusion

6.00 — 8.00 Reception hosted by An Taoiseach *in The State Apartments*

Monday 18th October
- 9.30 Presentation by Department of Education
- 10.00 Questions from Secretariat
- *11.00 Coffee*
- 11.30 Resumption of Questions from Secretariat
- 12.00 Recapitulation of work of Convention by Secretary General and an Outline of procedure for rest of the Convention
- *12.30 Lunch*
- 1.45 Parallel "Analysis of Issues" Groups
- *3.30 Coffee*
- 4.00 Resumption of Groups
- 5.00 Conclusion

Tuesday 19th October
- 9.30 "Analysis of Issues" Groups
- *11.00 Coffee*
- 11.30 Resumption of Groups
- *1.00 Lunch*
- 2.15 "Analysis of Issues" Groups
- *4.00 Coffee*
- 4.30 Resumption of Groups
- 5.30 Conclusion

Wednesday 20th October
- 9.00 "Analysis of Issues" Groups
- *10.30 Coffee*
- 11.00 Resumption
- *12.30 Lunch*
- 1.45 "Analysis of Issues" Groups
- *4.15 Coffee*
- 4.30 Secretariat Prepares Reports

Thursday 21st October
- 10.30 Presentation of Reports on the "Analysis of Issues" Groups
- *11.30 Coffee*
- 12.00 Presentation of Reports on the "Analysis of Issues" Groups
- *1.00 Lunch*
- 2.15 Presentation of Reports on the "Analysis of Issues" Groups
- *4.00 Coffee*
- 4.30 Secretary General's concluding remarks
- 5.00 Chairperson's concluding remarks
- 5.15 Closing of the National Education Convention by the Minister for Education Niamh Bhreathnach, T.D.

SCHEDULE OF ANALYSIS OF ISSUES SESSIONS

		MONDAY 18th — p.m	
GROUP I	**A**	**B**	**C**
	Primary School Curricular Issues/School Size	Roles of Principals and Middle Management in Post-Primary Schools	Research Policy in Higher Education

		TUESDAY 19th — a.m	
GROUP II	**A**	**B**	**C**
	Adult and Community Education	Patrons/Trustees/Owners Relationships with Boards of Management	An Ghaeilge sa Chóras Oideachais

		TUESDAY 19th — p.m	
GROUP III	**A**	**B**	**C**
	Local Educational Structures	Problems of Inequality (1) —Socio-Economic Inequalities —Gender Inequalities	Administrative Structures and Quality Assurances in Higher Education

		WEDNESDAY 20th — a.m	
GROUP IV	**A**	**B**	**C**
	Post-Primary Curricular Issues	Teacher Education and In-Career Development	Problems of Inequality (2) — Education for Special Needs —Education for Travellers

		WEDNESDAY 20th — p.m	
GROUP V	**A**	**B**	**C**
	Quality/Effectiveness of Schools	Support Services for Schools	Post-Primary School Rationalisation

A NOTE ON THE ANALYSIS OF ISSUES REPORTS

The Analysis of Issues sessions were not intended to be negotiating sessions. They were to be more open, in the" think-tank" sense, with the outcomes assisting in the on-going work on planning and policy-formulation. The reports are not summaries of what was said, but aimed to be distillations of the deliberations, set against the work of the first week's presentations and discussions. The reports were to describe such things as the character of the discussions which took place, the issues which were discussed, the areas of agreement and disagreement which emerged and aspects which required further analysis. There were fifteen sessions in a very concentrated time-frame. The Secretariat chaired and acted as rapporteurs, with some valued assistance from the following people: Caoimhe Ní Mhairtín , Dympna Glendenning, Breda Coyle, Helen Lane, Brother Patrick Morrissey, Sr. Pat Murray, and Michael Ryan. The time constraints put great pressure on the Secretariat to have the reports planned and written up in time for presentation to the last plenary session of the Convention. The reports were not formally agreed by the session participants, but an option was given for participants to submit reservations to the Chairperson if they considered that a significant misrepresentation had occurred in the reportage. Some comments of this character were received,and have been borne in mind in the preparation of the Report on the Convention. The text of the Analysis of Issues sessions is as presented to the Convention.

ANALYSIS OF ISSUES : GROUP 1 — A
PRIMARY SCHOOL CURRICULAR ISSUES/SCHOOL SIZE

1. Curriculum Balance and Expansion

Commitment to the basic principles of the primary school curriculum remains strong, particularly its child-centred approach. But it is also recognised that as conditions in which children live change it is necessary to evaluate the adequacy of curricular provisions.

It was accepted that some areas of the curriculum receive little attention in some schools at present (e.g. P.E., science) and that the suggestion that new areas be introduced (e.g. a third language) necessitate some readjustments. A major limitation in curricular provision is time. There is a tendency to add on requirements to the curriculum without considering the implications for time. Another limitation in curriculum provision is teacher skills. A teacher may not have the competence to teach science or a third language. Another limitation, which arises, particularly in the final years of primary school, is the pressure that entrance examinations to secondary school generates.

In the context of an integrated curriculum it is perhaps misleading to speak of provision in terms of time allocation to individual subject areas. An alternative view of provision is one which focuses on children's competencies, the fostering of which does not bear a simple one-to-one relationship with curricular provision.

Given that there is a finite amount of time available, the addition of new subjects (or increased emphasis on existing subjects) will have to be done by displacing other subjects. Thus, for example, increased time for science would have to be within the existing time allocation for Social and Environmental Studies, while the teaching of a third language would have to be done within the present time allocation for language teaching. (It should be noted, however, that most people were uneasy about a third language in the primary school.)

There was a danger that subject enthusiasts working in subject committees would drive forward, not bearing the overall or integrated curriculum sufficiently in mind. The value of the media (particularly broadcasting) to enrich curriculum was noted.

Finally, given that practically all children transfer to a second-level school and remain at school until 15, there should be less pressure on the primary school to try to cover "everything."

Literacy and Numeracy

The failure of some children to achieve adequate levels of literacy and numeracy during their schooling was recognised as a very serious problem. A concerted effort to deal with problems of literacy and numeracy would involve a multi-faceted approach.

The remedial teaching service was seen as a key factor. However, it was also acknowledged that this service has not been adequately evaluated. It may be, for example, that the services of remedial teachers would be more effective if deployed at an earlier age. There seemed to be a need for a greater emphasis on prevention, especially in disadvantaged areas. Greater involvement of parents could contribute to prevention. So also could assessment, early identification, and planning in the context of the school plan. Practice in the early teaching of reading should also be re-evaluated. Pressure from parents may result in the introduction of formal teaching of reading at too early a stage. There may also be a tendency to assign to inexperienced teachers the important task of introducing children to reading.

The importance of team planning by the school team on a regular basis was stressed, so as to diagnose learning difficulties and to plan remediation and monitor progress through the pupil's school career. Teachers also needed more assistance from the psychological service for diagnostic aspects. A targeting of extra assistance to pupils with difficulties was emphasised. The importance of teachers being better prepared to relate to parents, particularly those in disadvantaged areas, was emphasised.

School size and rationalisation

Despite a major rationalisation programme in the 1960s and 1970s, there are still a large number of small primary schools, with three teachers or less, in the educational system. Further, demographic trends would indicate that the number of small schools will increase in the coming years. This gives rise to problems relating to the adequacy of curricular provision in such schools, and the cost of maintaining the schools

It was recognised that there will always be some small schools in the country, given the distribution of the population and the need to serve minority religious groups. Indeed, the demands of some groups (e.g. those who want all-Irish or multi-denominational schools) may contribute to the number of small schools.

While small schools and rationalisation policies relate primarily to rural areas, the question of closure or amalgamation can also arise in urban areas, when large population shifts occur. Several problems associated with small schools were identified: the breadth of curricular provision that it is possible to provide, the limited physical resources that are likely to be available, difficulty in providing services (e.g. remedial teaching), and the professional isolation of teachers. Small schools were also seen as having advantages: better discipline, closer relationships with parents and the community, and avoidance of the problems associated with travel to larger units, which is a serious problem for younger children.

A blanket bureaucratic decision that all schools of a particular size would be closed would not be satisfactory. What are needed are catchment area studies which will provide detailed information on the present situation in terms of distances between schools, age and condition of schools, and demographic projections. When such information is available, decisions should then be made, on an individual basis, in consultation with parents, teachers, and managers. In this context, it may be helpful to set minimum standards for schools against which arguments for amalgamation could be evaluated.

ANALYSIS OF ISSUES : GROUP I — B.
ROLES OF PRINCIPALS AND MIDDLE MANAGEMENT IN POST-PRIMARY SCHOOLS

The Role of the Principal

The group discussed the role of the principal looking to the future in a climate of change. The discussion was structured around three themes as follows:

(i)   The main areas of responsibility of the principal;
(ii)   Improving the selection, training and functioning of the principal;
(iii)   Obstacles to be addressed in order to improve the above processes and enable principals to function effectively and efficiently.

Main Functions

The main functions of the principal were subsumed under three areas — Academic, Pastoral and Administrative, and included —

(i)   Personnel Management;
(ii)   Acting as Secretary to the Board of Management;
(iii)   Finance and Budgeting;
(iv)   Plant maintenance and safety;
(v)   Developing links with the local community and industry;
(vi)   Providing instructional leadership, including the organisation of the curriculum, staff deployment and staff development.
(vii)   Fund Raising
(viii) Monitoring Staff.

Instructional leadership was regarded as the most important role. It was also seen as the most neglected, because of the lack of support systems and time pressures, with the urgent taking precedence over the important. It was agreed that the role was wide-ranging and complex, with the principal in many schools being directly responsible for all the functions noted above. This role was contrasted with that of the chief executive in a company, who had a more co-ordinating role with managers to whom the separate functions can be delegated.

The principal exercises responsibility for the control, organisation and administration of the school. Assessing the quality of teaching provided was included among those duties. This was seen as operating at three levels. In cases of serious misconduct, both the responsibility of the principal and the procedures for dealing with incidents of this nature were clearly defined. It was also stated that the principal had first responsibility for dealing with an under-performing teacher and providing advice directed towards improving performance. However, if the problem remained unsolved, the professional expertise of the inspectorate would be required to deal with such cases. At a third level, it was also agreed that the principal had an important contribution to make in promoting the professional advancement of all teachers. This role of principal as appraiser of the staff and facilitator of their professional development, all conducted in a non-threatening climate, required a major time commitment both on the part of the principal and individual staff members. At the moment this amount of time was not available and appraisal and development of staff occurs in an informal and ad hoc manner. It was suggested that this could form part of the school development process, as proposed in the school plan.

The solution was seen to lie in a restoration of the support services which existed up to the cutbacks introduced in the 1980s, the provision of school secretaries and caretakers, and a more creative allocation of responsibilities among promoted staff.

Selection, Training and Support Mechanisms for Principals

Having agreed that the effectiveness of the leader was an important variable associated with school effectiveness, it was stated that the role and functions of the leader should be derived from an analysis of the concept of leadership. This was described as the ability to formulate a vision for the school, to build a corporate structure embodying that vision, to engage in strategic planning at all levels, and to put in place effective communication systems with all the partners, both within and without the school.

An important distinction was made between the principal as teacher and the principal as administrator or C.E.O., and, because of the priority given to the role of educational leadership, it was agreed that the principal, first and foremost, occupied the role of first teacher — *primus inter pares*. It was stated that management skills don't come easily to teachers, and that only limited opportunities are available to acquire and practice these skills. More opportunities, both in the areas of training and application need to be developed. It was felt that the role needs to be specific before selection can proceed. Particular concern was expressed in relation to obtaining worthwhile information on the track record of applicants. This arises mainly because of the limited scope available to candidates to assume responsibilities and gain relevant expertise as their careers advance. This makes the selection process somewhat of a gamble and raises questions about the need for a probationary period for principals. However, where such a period obtains within the system, it is difficult to operate because of the absence of suitable exit mechanisms.

Relevant experience in different areas of the school, such as the pastoral, the administrative and the curricular, would go some way towards identifying potential candidates. Experience in different types of schools, and working with a number of principals, was also regarded as important when electing candidates. Developing systems to encourage greater mobility within the system, especially across school types, would be beneficial in this regard. Concern was expressed about the pool of talent available for selection. The perceived lack of clarity about the role, the work level involved, inadequate support systems, poor remuneration and the absence of suitable exit arrangements, may be important factors in deterring suitable applicants from applying for posts. On the other hand it was suggested that the exciting and challenging aspects of the job should be emphasised, as well as the degree of job satisfaction and advancement which if offers. Existing principals have an important role to play in this area.

Having decided that the selection process was difficult, it was generally agreed that members of boards should be appointed by virtue of their expertise and experience in selecting staff at this level. Local interests and external perspectives should be included and a gender balance should be ensured. There was disagreement with regard to parental and teacher representation on selection boards. One view stated that they should not be included in a representative fashion, but rather on the basis of their experience and expertise. Another view stated that parents had a sense of the ethos of the school and an intuitive sense of the kind of personal qualities needed for the role, and should be included on all selection boards. The issues was not resolved.

The inadequate nature of the preparation of principals for their role gave rise to much discussion. This was placed in the context of the absence of a career structure for teachers generally within the system, and a feeling that ambition to develop upwards was judged to be unbecoming and left some feeling guilty about seeking promotion. Ideally, it was felt that training and the assumption of responsibilities should be developed on a phased basis throughout a teacher's career. This would not only ensure that applicants for principalships would have a realistic expectation of what the jobs demanded of them, but would also allow a larger period of observation for those who would have to make the selection and would provide some objective evidence of the candidate's previous track record. Specific training for the role would then be required before taking up the post and at regular intervals thereafter. This training should be organised so that senior management in all sectors could come together and thereby share experiences, and, hopefully, break down artificial barriers.

(ii) Middle Management

The present system of middle management in schools evolved historically in an unstructured manner. Procedures for delegating duties to post-holders, advertising posts of responsibility and appointing staff vary across sectors. Many of the duties assigned to posts, especially in the case of B posts, were described as being task oriented and not involving real responsibility or accountability for school management. This did little to lighten the burden of the principal. Moreover, certain key areas of responsibility associated with the management of the school are not presently included in the range of duties which can be assigned to post-holders. These included curriculum organisation and development and the management of the adult education programme. The Board of Management and Principal frequently have little discretion either in linking duties to posts or in selecting post holders.

While there was general agreement that the present structure needs to be redesigned, little consensus was achieved, mainly due to lack of time, on how this might be done. Two different models, the traditional hierarchical model and an organic model were discussed but not in sufficient detail so as to arrive at more concrete proposals aimed at restructuring and improving the system. However, it was suggested that an over rigid specification which could not take into account individual school requirements would be unhelpful.

For the proper functioning of management at this level it was felt that adequate out of class time should be made available for post holders to perform their duties. Moreover, it was suggested that a degree of accountability should be built into the system and that regular reviews of performance be undertaken.

Selection of Candidates and Assignment of Responsibilities

This was regarded as one of the most contentious areas in the process. Considerable discussion took place as to whether posts should be advertised with specific duties attached or whether duties should be agreed after candidates had been selected. While it was generally agreed that criteria should be developed for the selection of candidates, opinion was divided on the relative merits of competence and experience or seniority. Even where the criteria are presently based on merit and suitability rather than seniority, considerable resentment has been expressed by staff when seniority is not upheld. Striking a balance between these criteria in the allocation of posts has been used to allay suspicion and contain resentment.

However, it was suggested that the status quo could not be maintained and that an alternative system should be designed. General qualities which were suggested as being appropriate for consideration as criteria included leadership skills, competence, flexibility, and a good degree of energy and enthusiasm. Much more work remains to be done in this area.

The lack of a properly structured system of inservice training for staff at this level was highlighted. Such training should be properly funded and locally based.

In conclusion it was agreed that the lack of an adequate management infrastructure in schools seriously impeded the effectiveness of the principal and, indeed, resulted in senior management positions being unattractive to worthwhile applicants. In this instance bottom up reform of the system was seen as desirable and urgent.

ANALYSIS OF ISSUES : GROUP I — C.
RESEARCH POLICY IN HIGHER EDUCATION

Three main topics were proposed for discussion in this group:

- Unified or separate budgets for teaching and research
- Provision for different types of research
- Post-graduate education

However, before examining these issues the group felt it was appropriate to start by highlighting the low level of funding for research in Ireland, and the widespread perception that the research effort in higher education, and its importance to national development, are grossly undervalued. It was noted that, among OECD countries, Ireland had the worst record for funding research. Furthermore, the research effort had suffered in recent years with the sharp increase in student enrolment. It was suggested that in spite of these adverse circumstances we got good value for the money spent, as evidenced by the record of Irish scientists in getting more than their proportionate share of E.C. research funds.

It was strongly felt that the higher education sector needed to make a better case for research funding and needed to strive to gain proper recognition for its research efforts. The first step in this process was to identify accurately the research effort which is supported by the present funding arrangements. It was argued that the estimate based on surveys by Eolas that 30% of the university budget could be assigned to research, had little validity. It was hoped that the recently proposed HEA study will provide the necessary data to establish current levels of research output and funding; a necessary prerequisite to enable the universities to making a strong case for additional funding.

Even following the recent legislation there is no statutory provision for research in the block grant for the DIT/RTC sector. Thus the block grant is exclusively in support of teaching. It was agreed that this should now change to reflect the changing circumstances which are illustrated by the fact that the RTCs now offer a total of 20 degree programmes. The block grant to the DIT and the RTCs should be increased to provide some core funding for research.

In the Green Paper it was suggested that consideration is being given towards separating funding for teaching and research activities. However, there was complete consensus among our group that colleges should get a unified budget to cover teaching and research. Both activities, it was argued, benefited from this synergy. While subscribing to the idea of a unified budget for funding there was agreement, however, that for the purpose of accountability, it was necessary to quantify the research output. Measures of output should include peer reviewed publications, success in attracting other funds from outside the university as well as the enhancement of graduate skills. It was accepted that the evaluation of research output was primarily a matter for each institution. For example, the strategic plan of any department should include a plan for research as well as teaching. However, it was also accepted that the process of evaluation should involve peer review, both within departments and institutions, as well as across institutions. The group did not discuss in any detail how this would be carried out and how the outcomes of these evaluations would influence subsequent resource allocation. The group did not favour giving heavier teaching loads to those staff who had a poor research record. It was felt that, for the most part, good researchers also tended to be good teachers. It was suggested, however, that incentives should be given to reward research productivity.

The unified budget which forms the block grant given to colleges should be regarded as providing the basic level of research funding. Individual academics would then be encouraged to bid for additional funding from outside agencies. At a national level, it is imperative that two National Research Councils be established; one for the Natural Sciences and one for the Humanities and Social Sciences. It was suggested that, for the Natural Sciences, the arrangements which were put in place in the 1960s were more satisfactory than was the situation with either the NBST or Eolas. A newly constituted Research Council for the Natural Sciences should endeavour to strike a balance between two types of research:

(i)   strategic research in areas which reflect nationally defined priorities and
(ii)   bottom up or Blue Skies research where the research topics are open, reflecting the initiative of the researcher

It was felt that the distinction between basic or fundamental research, and applied research is not the most useful distinction. This position is consistent with the distinction made by Professor Ramírez, who differentiated between production-oriented and knowledge-oriented research. It was suggested that if a National Science Council is established it should be open to all scientists, not just those working in higher education.

While the present situation in respect of research support in the Natural Sciences is very unsatisfactory, there is no provision at all for the Humanities and the Social Sciences. Both government and the public must be convinced that such research is part of our culture and needs to be supported, just as other cultural pursuits are supported, through the Arts Council.

It was suggested that careful consideration needed to be given to the method of appointment to these Research Councils. A broad span of representation was needed and government should consult with various interests before making appointments. The majority of those appointed should be distinguished scholars in their field. The social partners should also be represented. There was consensus in this group that the funding of the Research Councils should come from another government department, other than education — possibly the Department of the Taoiseach — although no specific recommendation emerged on this matter. It was agreed that the Research Councils should advise the government on science policy.

In addition to this research effort supported from the block grant and by funds from specialist research agencies and the E.C., higher education institutions also perform a good deal of contract research. In general it was agreed that such research should be on a full cost recovery basis. The higher education budget should not be required to carry the overhead costs of such research. It was noted that in the U.S. a figure of 40% is now accepted as appropriate to cover overheads. However, we discussed the dilemmas, particularly of the RTCs, which have a mandate to assist in the economic development of their regions and frequently provide research and consultancy to many small firms which cannot fund such assistance on a commercial basis. The colleges have put some seed money into this activity, and, while there can be some cross subsidisation from one project to another, there may be a need for some targeted funds to support this activity. The view was expressed that if you add new functions to an institution the appropriate resources must be provided.

It was agreed that post-graduate education was a priority. There is evidence to show that 80% of post-graduates who were supported by the Department of Education and by Eolas, subsequently gain employment in Ireland, whereas only 25% of Irish students who receive their post-graduate education abroad return to work in Ireland. Post-graduate students also contribute significantly to university teaching both as tutors and demonstrators, and provide an important intellectual stimulus to teaching staff. Furthermore, it was argued that we would lose many of our best academic staff if they were not given the opportunity to work with post-graduate students.

The decline in support for post-graduate students was greatly regretted. The group felt strongly that this should be reversed. In relation to the mechanism for funding, our group favoured the funding being directed towards students giving them the freedom to move, rather than giving the funds to departments. Any system of post-graduate support should extend to students in the Humanities and Social Sciences where, it was alleged, there are high drop-out rates because of the absence of funding.

It was noted that much of the increase in post-graduate student numbers was in the area of post-graduate diplomas and in taught masters programmes. In this respect the availability of ATS funding was significant, and it was noted there was scope for significant further growth in this area. Concern was expressed at the fact that the ATS scheme had not extended to the non-university sector. There was disagreement over whether firms who had been given funds by the state to carry out research should be obliged, or merely encouraged, to involve third level colleges in this research activity.

We discussed the question of some specialisation in post-graduate provision. There was no support for any radical specialisation which would involve the development of selected graduate departments. It was agreed that while there was some scope for specialisation and complementarity, as illustrated with the Programme for Advanced Technology (PAT), the country was not big enough to support large graduate schools. There was a strong feeling within the group that the support system should back individual staff members who were capable of attracting good post-graduate students.

ANALYSIS OF ISSUES : GROUP II — A
ADULT AND COMMUNITY EDUCATION

Character of the discussion

This group was noteworthy for its willingness to cooperate and its commitment to look at issues in a spirit of moving on. This is a testimony to participants. The principal areas dealt with in this group were:

- Adult literacy and community education — access and provision
- Second chance education and accreditation issues
- Structures, administration and resourcing

Adult Literacy

Issues concerning adult education, but with particular reference to adult literacy, identified by the group were:

1.   The lack of knowledge regarding the true extent of the numbers requiring literacy training.
2.   Also identified were the multiple and diverse number of organisations, both mainstream and voluntary, engaged in delivery provision
3.   The area of adult education is totally under-resourced.
4.   Problems raised, experienced particularly by firms and businesses was that of the management of people with literacy problems and the necessity to facilitate those wishing to avail of literacy courses.
5.   Specific groups need particular attention, for example:
        (i)   People who might have issues of literacy in Irish;
        (ii)   Parents of children who attend all Irish schools;
        (iii)   Parents of children taking examinations through the medium of Irish;
        (iv)   Travellers.
6.   There is a need to examine the roots of the problem and to start interventions, especially in targeted areas which are particularly disadvantaged.   Early schooling needs particular attention in this respect.
7.   Allied to the last point is the issue of materials being used for special groups.   These materials should both reflect and respect their culture.
8.   The scarcity of materials was also highlighted.
9.   The issue of tackling the aura of shame and low self-esteem surrounding the issue of adult literacy problems was also raised.
10.   The concentration of people with learning/literacy problems in disadvantaged areas was noted.
11.   The true cost of the provision of resources to address difficulties in learning and literacy has not been identified.
12.   The question was posed — how should this whole area be administered and through what agencies?

Ways Forward for Adult Literacy Provision
1.   It was considered imperative that a comprehensive survey be conducted in order to highlight the nature and the extent of the problem.
2.   Materials which are appropriate and which respect the culture of adults with literacy problems, and of minorities, should be developed.
3.   A media campaign could be used to counteract the feelings of shame, failure and low-esteem which surrounds this area.
4.   Adult Literacy programmes need substantial resources.
5.   There was a recognition of the need for coordination of this area.   No decision was taken as to how this would be achieved

Adult/Community Education
        Under the Topic of Adult/Community Education it was suggested that there are difficulties of definition in the area of "Adult/Community education" but, in general, it can be defined in terms of goals, objectives and of empowerment.   The potential of Adult/Community education in breaking the link between education and poverty was also highlighted.
        In considering the wider area of Adult/Community education, or as some might refer to it, continuing life-long education, the issues identified were:
1.   The need for a coherent, visible policy for this area.
2.   Sources of funding need to be identified and such funding needs to be targeted.
3.   There is a vast need to train the trainers in communities or to enhance their existing skills.
4.   There is a great for local support of initiatives within the community.
5.   Voluntary group initiatives in this area, have not been recognised in the Green Paper and have been overlooked by educational planners.

6.   The whole area of continuing life-long education needs coordination.
7.   Such coordination has implications for accountability.
8.   There is a need for real data and research in this area.
9.   Many of the pedagogies developed in adult education could very beneficially transfer to primary or even post-primary schools.

Accreditation Issues
1.   Although many excellent initiatives have been initiated, no common system of accreditation exists, neither does a comprehensive system of credit transfers or a recognition of prior learning. A rationalisation of the system should occur.
2.   There is a need for recurrent or continuing professional education.
3.   There is an urgent need for guidance and counselling for adults.
4.   There should be an entitlement, for all, to a certain quantum of education after compulsory education.
5.   The need for resourcing in this area was emphasised and the question was raised as to who should pay. Should it be—
                         —   Government?
                         —   individuals?
                         —   or employers?
        in whatever combination.

Ways Forward for Adult or Continuing Education
1.   A comprehensive survey of the area should be conducted.
2.   A clear policy framework should be developed.
3.   Adult/Community education or continuing life-long education will continue on the periphery and be further disadvantaged unless it is brought into the mainstream. It should, however, continue to be both need and person centred. A guiding principle should be that such coordination be both participative and democratic; that is to say that the affected population should be the deciding population and that it should become empowered by such participation.
4.   There was universal agreement on the idea of a person's entitlement to a certain quantum of education after compulsory education. One suggestion, in this regard, was that every citizen could be offered a certain number of educational credits which could be redeemed, over life, in any institution.
5.   Finally, it was suggested that organisations which run adult education courses and which make a profit on such courses should be allowed to retain such money in order to provide courses, at minimal cost, for those who might not, otherwise, be able to avail of them. At the moment such profit returns to the Department of Education.

ANALYSIS OF ISSUES : GROUP II — B.
PATRONS, TRUSTEES, OWNERS — RELATIONSHIPS WITH
BOARDS OF MANAGEMENT

Three interlinked issues were discussed:
(i)   The powers and rights of Patrons, Trustees and Owners and the possibilities of transfer of some of their powers to Boards of Management;
(ii)   The balance of representation of Patrons, Trustees, etc., teachers and parents on Boards of Management;
(iii)   The feasibility of the Green Paper proposals for Roles of Boards of Management.

Since the first two issues were closely interlinked they were discussed together.

In the course of a comprehensive and constructive debate it was made clear by all parties that they were not opposed to change. The key concern was that forward planning would respect rights which had their corresponding responsibilities, would be based on clear and realistic rationales for the exercise of authority of the various responsible agencies, and that it would be flexible and amenable to comply with aspects of tradition as well as an evolving social contexts.

The debate focussed on post-primary level initially. It was agreed that the Green Paper had paid insufficient attention to the rights, roles and responsibilities of Patrons/Trustees/Owners, and that when it stated that there should be "minimum intervention" from Patrons/Trustees it indicated a misunderstanding of their position.

It was pointed out that Boards of Management in **post-primary schools** were a relevantly recent development and that they still did not exist in all vocational or secondary schools. The models existing in vocational, voluntary secondary and community and comprehensive schools were discussed. In all cases, the Trustees considered that their establishment had been valuable, but all conceded that improvements were desirable.

There is a clear diversity of forms of relationships between Patrons, Trustees and Boards of Management in the different types of school; between the Catholic bishops and primary school Management; the VECs and their schools, the Catholic Religious orders and their schools, the Protestant Patrons and their school management. Given that variation, if the legitimate rights and interests of the Patrons/Trustees, etc. are to be satisfactorily protected in any new arrangement, while at the same time providing significant autonomy and partnership on Boards of Management, it appears unlikely that a single model for Boards of Management would be acceptable.

Trustees were prepared to promote Boards of Management and considered that more thought should be put into the functions they could perform beneficially, although difficulties existed for the minority religious groups. The general view from trustees, parents and teacher representatives was that the existing trustees did not interfere in any significant way with the working of the Boards. The view was that Boards generally created a greater sense of collegiality and engagement on the part of the partners and had great potential if developed further. The general view was that it was better for the school's operation if the Principal was not a voting member of the Board.

Teachers sought equal representation with parents and trustees and post-primary parents favoured the same, but would not insist on it in all cases. The Trustees stated that their responsibilities were different and heavier than the other partners. The reason for the Patrons/Trustees/Owners current insistence on majorities on Boards of Management is to protect the religious ethos and the social mission of the schools they own. Such an arrangement ensures that the Board of Management implements in school practice the ethos, values and mission objectives of School Patrons/Trustees/Owners. Such objectives might also be expressed in clear social policy objectives, e.g., to serve the local parish community or to accept Traveller children and pupils.

In such an arrangement the Board can be called to account and, in extreme cases, disbanded if it does not carry out itsmission or live up to the trust placed in it. It operates on delegated authority subject to a pre-defined ethos and, in most cases, clear rules of Management. Even in these cases residual authority remains with the Patron/Trustee/Owner; in the case of capital development projects, Bank loans, school rationalisation, etc., the Patron's approval being necessary for such action. In addition the Patron indemnifies members of the Board of Management acting on his/her behalf, provided they comply with Department Rules and Regulations and the policy laid down by the Patron.

Although appointing majorities on Boards of Management are their currently preferred means to ensure the ethos of their schools the Catholic Bishops and the CMRS are both open to discussions with the Department and other relevant bodies in order to find alternative effective mechanisms by which the continuing religious ethos and social mission of their schools can be secured. In addition they wish to ensure that Boards of Management would report periodically to the Patron/Trustee on their work and progress through the annual school plan and school review, for instance. In extreme cases the Patrons/Trustee wish to retain the authority to withdraw power from the Boards where they are in serious breach of their duties.

To work out what would be acceptable and effective alternative mechanisms to majorities on Boards of Management would require a lot of discussion with the relevant authorities. Both the Catholic Bishops and CMRS expressed their willingness to take part in such discussions and their clear commitment to such a process of discussion to find alternative effective mechanisms. If successful this would then allow greater democratisation of and partnership on schools' Boards of Management.

Protestant Schools

The situation of the Protestant minority is quite different with a very scattered and low density population, with less clear bonds to local parish communities at primary level, and almost no such connection at post-primary level. In addition a substantial proportion of children attending their schools are not Protestant. In such a situation they feel strongly that the Patron's right to nominate the majority on Boards of Management is essential to maintain the Protestant ethos of the school. Even if Deeds of Trust guaranteed the religious ethos of the school they feel strongly that a significant non-Protestant presence on the Boards of Management would not guarantee the continuing religious ethos of the school. In addition it was felt that the "reserve power" of Patrons/Trustees could not be effectively utilised to ensure the continuing Protestant ethos of their schools when Boards of Management were not effectively carrying out their duties.

At post-primary level also it was strongly felt that the current structure of Boards of Governors/Guardians had such substantial advantages to the welfare and ethos of their schools that they would not wish to lose the expertise involved.

VEC Schools

The VEC schools, on the other hand, are the only schools which operate under a clear legal or statutory framework in which Boards of Management operate effectively as subcommittees of the VEC (VEC Act, Section 21, 1930). Although there is substantial variation across VECs in the presence, composition, powers and operation of Boards of Management, in general it is, nevertheless, the policy of the IVEA to increase democratic representativeness of Boards of Management and to devolve more power to them.

All Patrons, Trustees, Owners, except minority religious, were in favour of Boards of Management with significant powers, but required a safety structure to intervene if Boards went "off the rails," altogether. Some controlling mechanism was necessary. The possibilities of a School Charter and of Deeds of Trust were touched on as possible ways of ensuring trustees' concerns. The School Plan could also be a source of re-assurance to Trustees. It was also thought worth exploring the rights of trustees to withdraw consent to arrangements with Boards which strayed from their trust, as a safeguard.

LEA

There was more limited discussion of the possible role that intermediate structures could play in legally guaranteeing the right of Patrons/Trustees to their schools with their jurisdiction. It was pointed out however that any statutory accommodation could be constitutionally vulnerable, although it may be possible to do so under other non-statutory mechanisms.

....

A good deal of attention focussed on the functions of the Boards.   Some backed the functions as set out in the Green Paper.   The view was supported, however, that the Boards should not be responsible for the evaluation of teaching.   This should be a responsibility of professionals, such as the inspectorate.   It was also emphasised that while Boards should have significant and clearly delineated powers, they must also accept responsibility and implement the sometimes, hard decisions which had to be taken, in an unambiguous manner. Autonomy of Boards could not be absolute, but Patrons/Trustees were in favour of a greater degree of independence.

The position of Patron **at primary level** was seen to have significant roles which could not be ignored.   It was held that the patron actually intruded little on day-to-day management, or the general work of Boards.   It was pointed out that many Management Boards at primary level lacked real authority and were not always effective.   Parents and teachers considered that they should have equal representation with Trustees' nominations.

New models of Boards of Management were put forward by the National Parents' Council — Primary, Educate Together and Gaelscoileanna, which reflected responses to changing social conditions in Ireland.   Gaelscoileanna unambiguously supported the idea of the Patron system.   While problems exist with the panel arrangement and rationalisation of schools the Patron arrangement guarantees the maintenance of all-Irish ethos of their schools. Educate Together also proposed a new model for Boards of Management with equal partnership for their schools.   The multi-denominational schools, now totalling eleven, each have a limited company as their patron.   They have an elected Chairperson based on the 4+2+2 model.   Their representative body, Educate Together, support the general policy that Patrons who opt for equal representation on Boards of Management should be allowed by the Department of Education to do so.

The question of devolution from the Department to Boards of Management of schools generally was more important than devolution from the Patron.   There was also a fear expressed that devolving of powers from the Department to Boards of Management, without sufficient budgets, might increase problems at local level.

The suggested size of eleven for many Boards of Management for primary schools was regarded as unwieldy.   The expectation of a vast pool of interested and informed people to become effective members of Boards was also questioned.   Accordingly, at all levels of the system, training and support was important to give greater centrality to Boards of Management in a new educational culture.   Extra support would be needed, particularly in areas of disadvantage, where parents could sometimes be alienated from schools or reluctant to get involved. In view of the competence and experience required for efficient and effective engagement in Boards of Management, it was questioned if a three year term of office was the most appropriate, in that it might be too short.   It was pointed out that to have credibility, Boards had to have real powers and the principle of democratic engagement should be promoted.

It was accepted that accountability for the application of public funds for capital expenditure on school, was important, and systems existed for the accountability, but these should be more public when schools were being disposed of.   It was also accepted as a responsibility of denominational Trustees and Boards of Management to ensure that a sensitive awareness and code of practice should be promoted in schools which would facilitate non-believing students to attend the school, with the school community respecting their attitudes to religion.   The importance of trust in evolving partnerships in school managements was stressed.

ANALYSIS OF ISSUES : GROUP II — C
AN GHAEILGE SA CHÓRAS OIDEACHAIS

1.　　Comhthéacs agus Rannpháirtíocht

Naoi nduine dhéag a ghlac páirt sa díospóireacht - ionadaithe bainistíochta agus múinteoireachta ag gach leibhéal den chóras oideachais, ionadaí forbartha curaclaim, ionadaithe na dtuismitheoirí agus ionadaithe na n-eagras Gaeilge a ghlacann cúram de ghnéithe scolaíochta agus oideachais. Laistigh de fho-théamaí a bhí dírithe ar chomhordú iarrachtaí na Gaeilge sa chóras oideachais, ar oideachas trí Ghaeilge agus ar fhadhbanna na scoileanna Gaeltachta a bhí an díospóireacht suite, agus d'eascair - mar thoradh ar an díospóireacht - tuairimí a chlúdófar anois faoi na teidil seo:

Cuid 1: An Bhunscolaíocht; An Iarbhunscolaíocht; An Tríú Leibhéal (Ardoideachas); Réamhscolaíocht; Aosoideachas; An Ghaeilge agus an ghné Eorpach ; Ceist an leanúnachais; Múinteoirí; Oideachas trí Ghaeilge; Fadhbanna na Scoileanna Gaeltachta.

Cuid 2: Polasaí agus Reachtaíocht; Reachtáil agus Struchtúir; Tosaíochtaí; Cothromaíocht.

2.　　Mar atá agus mar a mholtar

2.1　　*An bhunscolaíocht*

Fáiltíodh roimh an siollabas nua Gaeilge, go háirithe an tosaíocht atá tugtha sa siollabas seo don taitneamh mar phríomhaidhm ag bunleibhéal na bunscoile. Tuigeadh go raibh an siollabas faoi stiúir an NCCA ach nach bhféadfaí é a chur i bhfeidhm gan tacaíocht chuí. Aontaíodh freisin gur ghá an siollabas a lonnú i gcomhthéacs an churaclaim i gcoitinne .i. an tábhacht a bhainfeadh freisin le Gaeilge chaidrimh na scoile agus an riachtanas a bheadh ann múinteoirí a oiliúint chuige seo. Luadh freisin an tábhacht a bhainfeadh le fiosrú a dhéanamh ar ról na léitheoireachta agus na scríbhneoireachta (i nGaeilge) ag leibhéal na bunscoile. Fáiltíodh roimh an tuairimíocht láidir atá ann faoi láthair maidir le tús áite a thabhairt don chumarsáid: labhairt na Gaeilge agus an tuiscint dá réir go gcuirfí siar tús na léitheoireachta ó Rang 1 go dtí Rang 2/3.

2.2　　*An Iarbhunscolaíocht*

Pléadh go mion an moladh a bhí sa Pháipear Uaine chun méadú ollmhór a dhéanamh ar imroinnt na marcanna do na scileanna labhartha ag leibhéal na hArdteistiméireachta. Tuigeadh go raibh míshuaimhneas léirithe in aighneachtaí a seoladh isteach maidir leis an 60% a bhí luaite do na scileanna cainte. Ba léir freisin cúiseanna áirithe imní ag an seisiún anailíse:

• na héagsúlachtaí a bhrathfaí sa chóras measúnachta idir Gaeilge agus Béarla;
• na deacrachtaí a chruthófaí do mhúineadh na Gaeilge sa Ghaeltacht;
• an tionchar a bheadh ag an moladh sin ar Ghaeilge ag an tríú leibhéal.

Ba léir, áfach, go rabhthas i bhfábhar ardú mór do scileanna fíorchumarsáide na Gaeilge (éisteacht, tuiscint, labhairt) ach - cé go raibh an sprid laistiar den mholadh inghlactha - gur ghá dul isteach go mion sa scéal ó thaobh oidí agus daltaí de agus an chéatadán a fhiosrú arís i gcomhthéacs na leibhéal agus na gcaighdeán éagsúil (bonn, meán, ard) a leagfaí síos do na scrúduithe. Moladh go bhféadfaí dhá scrúdú a dhearadh: (i) Teanga agus (ii) Litríocht agus Cultúr.

2.3   *An Tríú Leibhéal*

Léadh agus pléadh dréachtaí de na hachtanna ardoideachais a bhí bainteach le Gaeilge. Ba ríléir na héagsúlachtaí maidir le polasaí agus riachtanais iontrála na n-institiúidí éagsúla. Glacadh leis go raibh polasaithe i bhfeidhm ach rinneadh cíoradh ar na gníomhaíochtaí sna coláistí éagsúla. Ba léir go raibh dua ar leith á chaitheamh ag coláistí áirithe le beartaíocht agus le feidhmiú i leith na Gaeilge ach ba léir freisin gur mhór idir cleachtais choláistí éagsúla ó thaobh na Gaeilge de. Cé go raibh míshástacht á léiriú i dtaobh na riachtanais iontrála ó thaobh na Gaeilge de i roinnt coláistí agus easpa iomlán do riachtanas na Gaeilge i gcásanna áirithe, nochtadh an tuairim go mb'fhéidir gur mhó an díobháil a dhéanfaí dá n-éileofaí éigeantacht na Gaeilge mar riachtanas iontrála ag an staid seo.

2.4   *Réamhscolaíocht*

Bhí tacaíocht láidir ag an ngrúpa don chóras réamhscolaíochta. Ba léir go mbeadh buntáiste ag baint leis an réamhscolaíocht a cheangal (i) leis na bunscoileanna agus (ii) leis an aosoideachas ar mhaithe le tacú le Gaeilge an bhaile agus le Gaeilge na scoile. Tuigeadh, áfach, go mbeadh deacrachtaí praicticiúla ag baint lena leithéid.

2.5   *Aosoideachas*

Tá gá le beart don phobal. Ba chóir an Ghaeilge a chur chun cinn mar ghné thaitneamhach, chultúrtha. Is gá freisin dearcadh agus meon na dtuismitheoirí i leith na Gaeilge a threisiú. Ní foláir ranganna Gaeilge a chur ar fáil do thuismitheoirí ar mian leo freastal orthu ach ní mór caighdeánú a dhéanamh ar na ranganna/leibhéil éagsúla ionas gur féidir leanúint go tuisceanach agus gan dua ó rang-leibhéal amháin go rang-leibheal eile.

2.6   *An Ghaeilge agus an ghné Eorpach*

Luadh an tionchar a bhí ag ár n-ionadaíocht Eorpach ar an nGaeilge ó na seascaidí i leith. Mothaíodh, áfach, go gcruthaíonn ár mballraíocht diminsean Gaelach-Eorpach dár bhféiniúlacht agus go bhféadfadh leas dearfach - ó thaobh na Gaeilge de - eascairt as seo. Aithníodh an tábhacht a bhaineann leis an ghné Eorpach mar chuid den churaclam agus an comhthéacsú do theangacha (Gaeilge, Béarla, teangacha Eorpacha eile) a bheadh ionmholta sa chóras oideachais. Bheadh tionchar aige seo ar mhúineadh na Gaeilge - go háirithe an riachtanas a bhainfeadh leis an gcultúr maraon leis an teanga féin a fhorbairt.

2.7   *Ceist an leanúnachais*

Moladh go ndéanfaí an leanúnachas ó bhunscoil go hiarbhunscoil agus ón iarbhunscoil go hardoideachas a scrúdú ar mhaithe le leibhéil agus le caighdeáin na Gaeilge a rianadh agus a chomhtháthú.

2.8   *Múinteoirí*

Léirigh suirbhé a rinne Cumann Múinteoirí Éireann (1983) go raibh múinteoirí fábharach go maith do Ghaeilge ach go rabhadar duairc faoi thacaíocht an phobail. Sa seisiún anailíse aithníodh go raibh an-mhúinteoireacht sa Ghaeilge fós ar siúl in ainneoin an chórais. Tá gá láithreach ag leibhéal na bunscoile le: (i) siollabas nua Gaeilge; (ii) cúrsa réamhullmhúcháin do mhúinteoirí a dhíreodh ar mhúineadh na Gaeilge agus ar mhúineadh trí Ghaeilge; (iii) cúrsaí fiúntacha inseirbhíse a thabharfadh tacaíocht agus treisiú don oide agus a dhíreodh go háirithe ar réimsí modheolaíochta don siollabas nua, agus (iv) áiseanna teagaisc do mhúineadh na Gaeilge.

2.9   *Oideachas trí Ghaeilge*
Tá borradh agus fás as cuimse tagtha ar an oideachas trí Ghaeilge le scór bliain anuas. Tá deacrachtaí áirithe, áfach, ag gach leibhéal de chóras na nGaelscoileanna, cé go bhfuil buntáistí áirithe bainte amach ag na scoileanna seo. Ag leibhéal na bunscoile tá gá le pleanáil agus comhordú ó thaobh na Roinne de. Níl sé inghlactha gur cuma ann nó as do scoileanna lán-Ghaeilge. Mholfaí go láidir go mbeadh réamhbheartaíocht ag teacht ón Roinn seachas an iarbheartaíocht a tharlaíonn go minic. Tá gá fresisn freastal ar réamhoiliúint múinteoirí don mhúinteoireacht trí Ghaeilge, agus tá riachtanas práinneach ann anois do chúrsaí inseirbhíse do na múinteoirí.

Ba léir sa díospóireacht go raibh ag éirí go maith le hiarbhunscoileanna a bhí ag feidhmiú go hiomlán trí Ghaeilge ach go raibh deacrachtaí le sruth lán-Ghaeilge laistigh de ghnáthscoil. Aontaíodh go gcaithfeadh eagras na nGaelscoileanna agus córas an Ghairmoideachais - atá ag freastal ar na sruthanna lán-Ghaeilge seo - teacht le chéile agus na fadhbanna a phlé agus a réiteach eatarthu féin.

Léiríodh an gá a bhí ann ag an tríú leibhéal go mbeadh plean don Ghaeilge ag gach institiúid agus go ndéanfaí tréaniarracht an Ghaeilge a fhorbairt iontu. Thar aon ní eile ba léir an tábhacht a bhainfeadh le slat tomhais a dhéanfadh iniúchadh ar na spriocanna atá leagtha síos don Ghaeilge : (i) an bhfuil na spriocanna insroichte? (ii) an bhfuil na spriocanna á sroichint?

Tá deacrachtaí ag gach leibhéal i gcóras na nGaelscoileanna le curaclam agus le téacsanna oiriúnacha, le scrúduithe (míthuiscintí téarmaíochta mar shampla) agus le soláthar siollabais trí mheán na Gaeilge. Ní mór pleanáil láithreach do shárú na ndeacrachtaí seo.

2.10   *Fadhbanna na Scoileanna Gaeltachta*
Léiríodh buairt ar leith maidir leis na fadhbanna atá ag eascairt le tamall i scoileanna na Gaeltachta. Tá, ar ndóigh, athrú suntasach tagtha le scór bliain anuas ar phátrúin cumais agus úsáide na Gaeilge i gceantair Ghaeltachta agus Bhreacghaeltachta, agus tionchar nach beag acu seo ar an gcóras oideachais. Tá de mhíbhuntáiste ag muintir na Gaeltachta go bhfuil

•   a lán de na scoileanna féin i ndroch-chaoi;
•   páistí ar ilchumais agus ar ilchaighdeáin teanga (Gaeilge/Béarla) ag freastal ar na scoileanna;
•   deacrachtaí leanúnachais in áiteanna ó bhunscoil go hiarbhunscoil lánGhaeilge;
•   fadhbanna bainistíochta, riaracháin, airgeadais mar thoradh ar an ngréasán de scoileanna beaga Gaeltachta (easpa sa chaiptíocht, i soláthar na n-áiseanna agus sa mhúinteoireacht fheabhais srl.);
•   ganntanas téacsleabhar trí Ghaeilge. Aithníonn scoileanna na Gaeltachta uathu na buntáistí a bhraitear ag scoileanna eile. Tá scoileanna na Gaeltachta tite siar go mór faoi láthair idir na haitheantais ata tugtha (i) do Ghaelscoileanna;   (ii) do cheantair aitheanta faoi scéimeanna feabhais, srl., agus (iii) don mhaoiniú agus do na háiseanna a bhíonn ar fáil do scoileanna móra. Tá gá ar leith ag scoileanna na Gaeltachta le tacaíocht phráinneach.

2.10.1.   *Struchtúir Áitiúla agus an Ghaeltacht*
Léiríodh sa seisiún anailíse nach rabhthas ar aon fhocal maidir leis an tábhacht, leis an ról nó leis na buntáistí a thiocfadh as na struchtúir oideachais áitiúla a chur i bhfeidhm. Bhí dearcadh institiúideach ar thaobh amháin a bhí ag moladh na struchtúr áitiúil seo ar an gcoinníoll go mbeadh aitheantas agus ionad ar leith ag an nGaeilge i ngach ceann acu. Bhí, ar an láimh eile, buairt á léiriú - go háirithe ó thaobh na Gaeltachta de - maidir leis an bhfreastal a dhéanfaí (nó nach ndéanfaí) ar chóras oideachais na gceantar Gaeltachta. Ní léir faoi láthair go bhfreastalaíonn aon struchtúr áitiúil (ar bhonn contae) ar riachtanais na gceantar sin.

3.   An Ród Seo Romhainn

Bhí tuiscint iomlán sa ghrúpa don riachtanas a bhí ann céimniú fiúntach, dearfach a dhéanamh anois ar an nGaeilge i gcomhthéacs an oideachais. Mar seo a leanas a dhéantar an ród atá romhainn a léiriú:

1. Polasaí agus Reachtaíocht
2. Pleanáil agus Struchtúir
3. Tosaíochtaí agus Tacaíocht
4. Cothromaíocht
5. Impleachtaí.

ANALYSIS OF ISSUES : GROUP III — A
LOCAL EDUCATION STRUCTURES

Intermediate Structures

There was general agreement among the group on the role of an intermediate structure in supporting the quality of educational provision within the system. It was felt that schools in a stand-alone situation would be unable to fulfil many important educational functions without such a service. It was regretted that a clearer view of the nature, responsibilities and functions of such a structure had not been previously outlined in official documentation.   This would have helped to provide a better focus to the discussion, especially since serious doubts were expressed about the range of powers which it was intended to devolve to a local tier.   Local authorities, it was stated, don't have authority unless they have budgetary discretion.

In the absence of a view from the centre it was understood that the intermediate tier would subsume the existing functions of the VEC system and add to these as deemed appropriate.   In the first instance, it was stated that many of the functions, at present controlled and administered by the Department of Education, could be more appropriately and effectively administered by the new structure.   It was agreed that the intermediate tier should have both support and some regulatory functions, and have a remit ranging from pre-school to adult education level.

Services which could be provided included the organisation of inservice for teachers, and other staff, psychological, medical, para-medical and social services (in association with the local health board), a counselling service for pupils and teachers, library services, remedial services, a teacher supply service, organisation of adult education, specialist visiting teacher services, legal and inservice advisory services, school/industry links and coordination of European Community intervention programmes and funding mechanisms. While the list in the area of support services could be endless, it was suggested that agreement could be reached on the minimum entitlements to services either on a school or pupil basis..   this would assist in defining more clearly, the range of services which could reasonably be expected.

The strategic planning role of an intermediate tier for its region was considered to be an important function. This would include taking an overview of needs and existing provision in its area, engaging in forward planning, responding to national objectives, tackling inequalities, targeting resources into areas of greatest need, facilitating and organising the rationalisation process and moderating competition between schools. To fulfil these functions, it was agreed that the intermediate tier would require regulatory powers. The authority and powers of the tier would need to be clearly defined. Considerable discussion took place as to whether a local tier would require to own the schools in its area and be the employer of all the staff in order to fulfil the educational functions assigned to it. One view suggested that the staff in an area comprised the major resource at the disposal of an intermediate tier, while the majority opinion was that it was possible to function in a system where the legal ownership of the schools rested with various bodies. It was felt that a model could be developed which would accommodate both differences in school types and variations in ownership, and it was suggested that a number of models should be drafted and examined by the various interest groups. Flexibility in the type of relationships which schools might have with an intermediate tier was seen to be very important. Different schools might wish to have different relationships with the local tier. For example, multi-denominational schools, special schools, schools owned by minority religious denominations and Gaelscoileanna, may wish to have different linkages with an intermediate tier.

While at this stage the majority view was that teachers should be employed by their Board of Management, support staff such as psychologists and counsellors might be employed by the intermediate tier. This structure could also play an important role in the redeployment of teachers and the organisation of supply staff to schools.

The intermediate tier was seen as playing an important role in developing a variety of links at all levels within the system, downward to local schools and communities, laterally with other local tiers and upwards with the Department of Education. In this respect the strategic role of an intermediate structure in identifying local needs and priorities and communicating these upwards, was regarded as very important and influential. Links could also be developed with other agencies serving the systems, particularly with a Teachers' Council, if established.

The issue of resources was discussed at length. It was stressed that power and decision-making in this area must be devolved from the centre. An Intermediate tier servicing schools by merely redeploying existing resources would serve no useful purpose and would quickly fall into disrepute. Significant additional resources would be required in order to nurture a cultural climate which would enable the new structure to develop and gain the confidence of those it served. Authority would be dependent on the budget allocation. It was suggested that a reasonable degree of realism was required with regard to resources, and that an important task for the new tier would be to draw up a five year costed plan of requirements for the institutions in its area.

The geographical boundaries of the new structures received only brief discussion because of time constraints. It was stated that the area should be small enough so as to facilitate real local involvement and that account should be taken of existing boundaries which people understood and could identify with. Representation on such authorities should reflect appropriately the balance of interests involved, including public representatives in a minority role.

It was stated that this was the first occasion on which all the different groups involved in education had the opportunity to discuss this issue. All the participants contributed to the discussion and felt that the sharing of views was both informative and beneficial. As a next step the group agreed that the different organisations should engage in negotiations in small groups on relevant issues, and also examine a range of models, including provisions of the 1930 Vocational Education Act. It was also agreed that the Department of Education should publish a position paper outlining its concept of the new structures and presenting a range of models for discussion. Both initiatives would help to create a more favourable climate of acceptance for this proposal and make a significant contribution towards the establishment of a structure which would serve the needs of the system in future years.

ANALYSIS OF ISSUES : GROUP III — B
PROBLEMS OF INEQUALITY (I)
- Socioeconomic inequalities
- Gender inequalities

ISSUES DISCUSSED: —
Social Class:

- Curriculum and school organisational interventions to correct underachievement — pre-primary, primary, post-primary.
- Correcting inequalities at entry to third level education.

Gender:

- School organisation and classroom practice.
- Management and career structures in education

CHARACTER OF THE DISCUSSION: —
The discussion was positive and constructive.

Pre-primary
There was unanimous agreement in the group that pre-primary education has an important role to play in combating underachievement connected to poverty and social class. However, there were some differences of emphasis in how this should be delivered.

One suggestion was that there should be a three-year cycle at infant level, that the primary school cycle should be lengthened downward by one year — this would imply an age range 3-6 (this was later modified by some members to age 4-7). This scheme should begin in socio-economically disadvantaged areas. However, this should involve additional funding and resources should not be drawn from the existing budget for primary schools in disadvantaged areas.

There were significant reservations expressed in the group about the appropriateness of existing primary school pedagogies for the pre-primary age group and, consequently, an alternative approach was suggested. This was that pre-primary education in disadvantaged areas should be primarily community-based. It was suggested that pre-primary education must involve parents, in order to encourage and support them in helping their children to learn. This approach would also involve the need for co-ordination between local communities, health boards, local authorities and other agencies to address the multiple problems that such areas have.

Ways Forward for Pre-Primary Education
The state should involve itself in pre-school community education and target it to disadvantaged areas. Other private pre-school provision should continue but there is a need for a system of regulations and guidelines for this.

After further discussion of the two alternative approaches (3 year junior infants and community based pre-primary) discussed earlier, the group arrived at the view that a combination of both strategies could be used.

There was an emphasis on the importance of an appropriate curriculum for pre-primary and on the need for professional training for the work.

Primary
Again, two possible mechanisms for prioritising the needs of socio-economically deprived children were discussed.

The first was the disadvantaged areas and disadvantaged schools scheme. While this was deemed to be a useful mechanism, there are still some problems with it which must be sorted out. The most seriously affected are the crisis schools within crisis communities. It was suggested that a higher capitation grant be available to schools designated disadvantaged.

Areas of high unemployment should be prioritised in this scheme, with targeting based upon clear criteria.

A different approach would be to focus on the child. One of the difficulties with the first method is that the needs of a high proportion of socio-economically disadvantaged and underachieving children in non-designated disadvantaged schools will not be addressed. It should be possible to identify children at risk of underachievement and to implement interventions at an early stage. These children would then have entitlements to grants and other resources which they would carry with them through the education system, at all levels.

Further discussion suggested that there is a need for flexibility in the mechanisms for targeting resources.

Ways Forward for Primary Education

The two strategies discussed above are possible and both should be implemented.

There was universal agreement on the need for inservice education for teachers dealing with disadvantaged children. This should involve appropriate pedagogies and curriculum. It should also include methodologies to deal with disruptive children. The need for some form of referral system for these children was also discussed. In addition, there is a need for a substitute panel for crisis schools as substitution is difficult to get for these schools. A crisis unit within schools was also mentioned.

It was suggested that a range of support services (e.g. remedial and psychological) to priority targeted schools could be co-ordinated and delivered through local educational structures.

Post-Primary

There are problems with some of the existing schemes to target resources at second level. In the schools which have been designated for additional staff, the criteria for allocation did not include educational underachievement. Designated voluntary schools received the allocation of a teacher but no allocation of additional materials or resources. Many schools in rural and small towns did not receive allocations. In many disadvantaged areas pupils pass from designated disadvantaged primary schools to second-level schools which are not so designated. Does the disadvantage disappear at post-primary?

Examination fees have placed a heavy burden on many low income families. Fees for examinations should consequently be removed — for low-income families.

The problems posed for low-income children by the low level of funding of voluntary secondary schools with significant proportions of disadvantaged children should be addressed. It was agreed that families need more money to send their children to secondary schools because the schools require more support from parents than VEC or community/ comprehensive schools. Consequently it is more difficult for low income children to participate fully in such schools.

Differential funding mechanisms by school types mean that this feature is structured by the state.

Ways Forward for Post-Primary Education

Certain curricular interventions could be used to combat disadvantage. For example, there are great possibilities within the arts. Through the arts children can identify talents within themselves and thus build their self-esteem and achievement. There is a need to further develop activities here.

There is a need for a great deal of pre- and inservice education for teachers working with low-income working class children at post-primary as well as at primary school, in order to eliminate bias. All teachers in low income areas should have some training in remedial education. Better ways of using remedial teachers should be devised - for example, a remedial teacher should be a resource teacher who diagnoses problems and then works with the class teacher or staff.

Guidance and counselling provision is very important to combat underachievement. If present restrictions on guidance counsellors were lifted there would not be enough to meet the needs of schools, thus there is an important need to increase the numbers being trained. Fees for examinations should be removed for low income families.

Entry to Third Level

There are particular problems for low income pupils at entry to third level, in particular to the universities.

Participation at third level presents a real problem to low income families. While grants are available, the real costs are higher, especially for 3/4 year courses and this is perhaps reflected in lower participation at universities than in the RTCs/DIT where shorter courses are available, as well as ESF funding.

There appear to be attitudinal/cultural problems in poorer socioeconomic areas also. Pupils may feel that university is not for them and peer pressure may be a problem. College school links programmes may well play a significant role here in remediation, but it is still too small and too early for evaluation.

The Higher Education Authority is very concerned about low participation of low income groups in their sector. They have consequently set a target to increase their participation by 500 students per annum.

Problems of access to third level have arisen in relation to Syllabus C, the Alternative Ordinary Course in Maths — a small number of third-level courses are open to pupils with this qualification.

Ways Forward at Third Level Entry

We need to work on curricular issues and accreditation at the same time. College/school links programmes could be further extended. There is also a need to develop mechanisms for access to third level which take account of PLCs, although some linkages already exist.

GENDER
School Organisation and Classroom Practice

There was a great deal of agreement both on the importance of the issues here and on the measures which need to be implemented.

Ways Forward:

Inservice education for teachers is a basic pre-requisite for the implementation of good practice in relation to gender equality. This needs to be intensive in the first instance and should be directed to the leadership within the school and thereafter on a whole-school basis. There is a need for resourcing also.

There is also an urgent need to provide good inservice in the case of amalgamating schools from single sex to co-educational. However, problems exist within single sex schools also. Issues should cover classroom practices, timetabling, other organisational issues and curriculum. In addition, research results, especially from action projects, should be disseminated more widely. There is a great need to raise awareness about the factors in the system which impede gender equality.

There was a strong call for good leadership from the Department of Education itself. Guidelines on good practice already exist but these have not yet been published. The Department should set up a structure to monitor progress on gender equality. It was proposed that a unit be established in the Department, headed by a senior member of staff, with staffing and a budget. Its role would be to monitor and support the implementation of gender equality. There is a need to set targets also and to monitor, for example, the balance of men and women in new management structures. In establishing this, reference should be made to recommendations of the Report of the Commission for the Status of Women.

Management and Career Structures in Education
Again there was a great deal of agreement on the nature of the problems here, and on the issues that need to be addressed. There are still male/female imbalances in management positions in schools. To address this a number of policy proposals were suggested.

Ways Forward:
-        Intervention programmes on leadership for female teachers
-        Training for selection boards
-        Development of clear criteria for appointment for selection boards
-        Further research on women and promotion patterns
-        Examination of role requirements of senior posts and the possible impact on family responsibilities
-        Strategies to make teaching (especially at primary) attractive to men as well as women, and, in this regard, to examine salary structures
-        Evaluation of the role of networking and "mentoring" in the career development of teachers
-        Provision of child-care facilities.

In third level education there is still significant under-representation of women in certain courses (e.g., engineering), at post-graduate level and in senior academic and management positions. It was suggested that in order to address these problems there should be an Equality Officer in all colleges. In addition the Higher Education Authority should play a monitoring role. If its remit is extended to the RTC/DIT sector, it can do this for the entire sector. It was suggested that the Department of Eduction should also play a monitoring role in the development of policy in this area, and in the compilation of statistics.

ANALYSIS OF ISSUES : GROUP III — C
ADMINISTRATIVE STRUCTURES AND QUALITY ASSURANCES IN HIGHER EDUCATION

1.   Differentiation and Co-ordination in a Binary System
The decision to set up regional technical colleges was a conscious one to provide an alternative to university education. At the time, it was decided not to establish further universities, and not to extend the scope of universities to provide courses in technical and commercial areas, which it was felt were needed to service the economy.
Regional technical colleges and universities have the common goal of helping bring students to a high level of achievement. However, it is also clear that the two sets of institutions differ in a variety of ways. They differ in their mission, in their organised delivery structures, in the level of programmes which they offer, in the level of qualifications which they confer, in the role of research within institutions, and they differ in prestige. There has, however, been some drift in the work of the RTCs. There was general agreement that RTCs should not be capped in the level of courses which they could offer. However, it was recognised that if too great an emphasis was placed on degree work that the certification/diploma work of institutions might suffer and that the colleges would fail in their mission to provide the level of skills which they were set up to provide.
While acknowledging that differences exist between sectors, the need for co-ordination of the higher education system by the Higher Education Authority was stressed. It was considered that a single funding authority would be a help in this regard. At local level, linkages between universities and regional colleges are to be encouraged.

One negative consequence of the binary system is the difficulty which arises for students who wish to transfer between sectors. At present, while it is not impossible to transfer from an RTC to a university, it is often very difficult. This sometimes is because of a lack of compatibility between courses. In some such cases (e.g. engineering) special provision may be needed to facilitate transfer. At a more general level, problems in transfer arise from the fact that mechanisms are not in place for institutions to establish procedures regarding equivalence and mobility. A further problem that inhibits mobility is the pressure on places in universities. The fact that British universities seem more open than Irish universities to applications for transfer from RTCs, may reflect the greater availability of space in British universities. The structure of courses in Irish universities also creates problems for the student who may wish to transfer. When courses are linear and non-modular, it is difficult for a student to enter at any point, other than the starting point, for the course.

It was generally agreed that the issue of student transfer between sectors should receive attention and that mechanisms to facilitate it should be established.

2.   Quality Assurance : Self Evaluation and External Assessment

It was recognised that the meaning of quality is problematic and that it might mean different things to different people (students, university staff, the HEA, business). However, there was total agreement on the need for quality assurance. There also was general, but not unanimous, acceptance that quality assurance needed to be improved, or at least made more transparent. There were some differences on the means that are necessary to do this.

While defining and measuring quality presents problems, there are many aspects of education where it seems possible to ask questions in a useful way; for example, the concern and care for students, the quality of teaching and support provided by staff, the proportion of students who proceed to graduation, the output and quality of research, the efficient use of resources, and the procedures in place, in institutions, to review quality on a continuous basis.

Three procedures to improve quality assurance were considered: self assessment by institutions, peer review, and monitoring by an outside body (the HEA), whose function it would be to ensure that an adequate system of quality assurance was being implemented by institutions.

It was accepted that assessment of quality was primarily a task for the institution itself. Students should have a major role in this. Internal assessment would be augmented by external peer review. At present, external examiners serve this function, though their role may need to be strengthened and specified more clearly. The nature of other forms of peer review was briefly discussed, but agreement was not reached on the form which it should take or who would be involved (academics or other interested parties). The HEA, as the body responsible for seeing that adequate quality assurance procedures are in place in individual institutions, would not itself be involved in the assessment of institutions. Neither would negative decisions about funding be based on the results of assessments. The function of assessment is not to provide a basis for penalising institutions for poor quality, which may be due to a variety of factors, but rather to identify where there are specific problems within an institution.

The role of performance indicators in quality assurance was briefly discussed. Performance indicators were defined as empirical, quantitative or qualitative data that point to an institution's success in achieving its goals. Indicators monitor performance and signal the need for further examination of issues or conditions. The emphasis is on the signalling function. Performance indicators in themselves do not judge on performance or quality. Other information is needed to define satisfactory levels of performance, or to make quality assessments.

It was suggested that quality assessment might take place at the level of disciplines (probably every year through the external examination system), at the college or faculty level, during which issues relating to resources and achievements would be considered (perhaps every four or five years), and at the institutional level (perhaps every ten years).

3.   National Certification Board

The responses of the NCEA and NCVA to the proposal that they should merge were not very far apart in terms of the structural arrangement considered to be most suitable. Further, it was recognised that the drive for a unified form of certification was strong in the education sector.

A number of reservations, however, were expressed about a possible merger between the NCEA and NCVA. First, a fear was expressed that the present relationship between the NCEA and regional technical colleges, particularly in terms of quality control, might be disturbed if the NCEA were to be absorbed into a wider body. It was also felt that there was a need to protect the status of the qualifications which are provided by the NCEA.

There was general agreement about some characteristics which were considered to be desirable in a unified system. First, a system that was heavily bureaucratic would not be suitable. Second, it is important that the new structure should build on what already exists. And third, it is crucial that any new body should stay in the education sector. It was agreed that there should be further discussion between interested parties before a final decision is taken about a national certification board.

4.   Management Structures in Third Level Colleges

In discussion of the role of the heads of universities, it was pointed out that the community of scholars and students, over which they preside, is unique and that, as a consequence, analogies with business organisation are likely to be misplaced. However, it was accepted that efficiency in the administration of resources was a vital part of the role of heads.

The role and composition of governing bodies evoked considerable discussion. It was pointed out that the function of a governing body should determine its composition. In one view, appointment or election to a governing body should be on the basis of individuals' expertise, the time they can devote to business, and their ability to contribute to the efficiency of an institution. The implementation of such a view might allow college staff to hold the majority of places on a governing body. An alternative view suggested the need for representation of individuals whose function it would be to safeguard the public interest.

There was considerable agreement that legislation should allow for flexibility, permitting diversity of structure and practice, and acknowledging the traditions and ethos of individual institutions. It was felt that there was need for further consultation on the composition of governing bodies before legislation was enacted. This could be assisted by calling witnesses at the committee stage of legislation.

The roles of deans and heads of departments were briefly discussed. It was argued that third level institutions are difficult to manage and that their level of complexity requires constant reappraisal of management structures and functions.

5.   Other Matters

The problems of part-time students have received little attention and should be examined.

There is a need to improve access to third level education other than through the Leaving Certificate examination.

ANALYSIS OF ISSUES : GROUP IV— A
POST PRIMARY CURRICULAR ISSUES

Curriculum Levels and Pupil Differentiation

There was unanimous agreement that there was a need for a period of "calm reflection" on, and consolidation of, the Junior Certificate of Education before any other further major changes were introduced. It was felt that teachers who had now experienced teaching the Junior Certificate for three or four years and had observed examination trends for two successive years, needed to consolidate their experience for a further period of time.

Several issues regarding curriculum levels and pupil differentiation were discussed. Firstly, there was a danger that students would be locked at an early stage within particular levels due to rigid streaming practices and inflexibility in some schools. This effect was considered contrary to the original aims and objectives of the Junior Certificate. There was consensus that the rigid "categorisation" of students should be minimised because of its serious implications for access to ordinary and higher level courses at senior cycle and because of difficulties which have already arisen, particularly in relation to the degree of recognition accorded syllabus "C" Maths by third level institutions.

Concern was also expressed that teachers' perceptions of students and their potential might be influenced by the level at which a student was studying a subject. This possibility could have serious implications for the eventual achievements of students. It was agreed, however, that some students could be facilitated to move to higher levels at senior cycle if there was an adequate system for reviewing placements.

The view was expressed, that within the Junior Certificate course, levels of ability within individual students should be the driving force of school policy rather than convenience in management or administration.

There was universal agreement that the "resourcing" of the Junior Certificate was inadequate in a large number of areas. A need for additional inservice training was noted. The need might vary from subject to subject. For example, the need seemed to be particularly acute in English, where courses have undergone radical change. Individuals responsible for setting and marking examinations also needed some "inservice" to deal with a perceived discrepancy (in some quarters) between syllabi and examinations. It was felt that inservice targeted towards the professional development of teachers and changing pedagogy was also needed. The resourcing of school administrations was also necessary if schools were to implement change to reflect the aims and objectives of the Junior Certificate programme. At a more specific level, the resourcing of practical subject areas (e.g. provision of equipment and photocopying facilities, etc.) needed attention.

Time will have to be set aside for teachers to engage in curriculum planning.

Particular problems arise in small schools in implementation of curricula. The range of options which can be offered at senior cycle is inevitably limited. This has implications for student choice, and may affect career options.

The scarcity of textbooks in the Irish language was highlighted as a problem for Gaelscoileanna. It is unlikely that this will be resolved by commercial publishers as long as the number of schools which teach through the medium of Irish remains small.

Another problem which was identified related to the curriculum requirements of students with special needs. It was felt that this issue had received inadequate attention in the context of a policy to integrate special needs students in the ordinary school.

In discussing assessment, some apprehension was expressed that the demands of the Junior Certificate Examination were interfering with the implementation of junior cycle programmes. There was general agreement, however, that the Junior Certificate Examination should remain in its present form. In support of this view, it was noted that the examination is the first occasion on which external objective information is provided about students. Such information can be helpful to students and parents in choosing further educational and career options. The examination also provided students who were leaving the system at the end of the compulsory period with certification. However, the problem of students who were not served by the examination and left school without certification was acknowledged. The Junior Certificate was also seen to have value in providing information to the Department of Education on standards in the educational system and in focusing and motivating students.

In discussion of issues relating to non-core examination subjects and non-examination subjects, there was a general feeling that subjects which are formally assessed in the Junior Certificate Examination are accorded a higher status than subjects which are not. Limiting the external examination to core subjects would make for a hierarchy of subjects and a neglect of subjects of low esteem.

Core Curriculum and Balance

Approval for the breadth of the Junior Certificate programme was widespread. However, it was felt that this could be distorted by paying inadequate attention to curriculum areas which were not examined. It could also be less obviously distorted by students' choice of subjects. For example, if students studied two continental languages, almost half their curriculum would be in the language area.

Since time is limited, student experience could be broadened by the provision of short modular courses. This might present problems when students transferred to senior cycle. However, students should not necessarily be locked into choices made at junior cycle level. It should be possible in the case of some subjects, for some students to commence their study at senior cycle level. Some time during a transition year might be devoted to helping students prepare for new subjects at senior cycle.

Senior Cycle

There was considerable enthusiasm for transition years. However, it was felt that practice varied considerably from school to school and that transition years in some schools were more successful than in others, and were more faithful to the objectives of a transition year. Provision during the transition year would be likely to improve if schools had to submit a programme annually, if schools were more readily inspected, if information on good practice was more widely disseminated, if additional resources were provided, and if more time was allocated to the co-ordinator's work.

It was noted that students matured during the transition year and sometimes revised their subject choices. Particular benefits, by way of improved self-esteem, seem to accrue to lower-achieving students.

Considerable discussion took place on the Applied Leaving Certificate. While the need for an alternative to present provision was universally accepted, lack of information on the precise nature of the applied alternative created some problems for discussants.

While there was general approval for keeping the applied programme under the general umbrella of the Leaving Certificate, a number of problems were anticipated. Would the Applied Leaving Certificate be perceived as having low status in schools? What prospects awaited students on completion of the programme? Would students be able to proceed to further education or to particular jobs? What effect will it have on the ordinary level Leaving Certificate? How can it be provided in anything but very large schools? These are all issues which need to be kept in mind in the design and implementation of the Applied option.

ANALYSIS OF ISSUES : GROUP IV — B
TEACHER EDUCATION AND IN-CAREER DEVELOPMENT

The session on Teacher Education focussed on the following sub-themes: structures for preservice education of teachers, induction procedures and inservice teacher education. A fourth sub-theme, A Teachers' Council, was on the list for discussion but pressure of time precluded this.

In the context of a teaching career being seen as a continuum of **Initial Induction and Inservice Education** there would be opportunities for new developments, which could require some changes:

- A four-year degree structure for the B.Ed.
- That colleges of Education and training institutions would change Themselves on two fronts:
  — to enable new elements to be incorporated into preservice education;
  — to enable practising teachers to get involved in a closer partnership with the colleges in the area of student teacher placement for formation and that this partnership would be further cultivated by the mentor system.

At this point it was suggested that perhaps the colleges of education and the teaching profession could draw up a schedule to show what changes would be effected in a restructured four-year B.Ed., how and where those course changes would be targeted, taking into account the variety of social contexts in which the degree qualification would be used. Areas such as teaching in all-Irish schools, developing a pedagogy for adult education, a component in remedial education and other special options, could be built into initial teacher education programmes. This would be necessary in order to make a demonstrable case that the change being recommended was meeting real needs.

The mentor/cooperating teacher assisting the student teacher's formation on teaching practice, symbolised a productive form of professional interest in preservice teacher education. It would not, of course, be on an imprinting modelling basis.

The current model of preservice teacher education at post-primary level was discussed, and satisfaction was expressed with the various changes that have occurred in the past ten to fifteen years. The school-based nature of the course was seen as very important in helping student teachers cope with the cultural shift they might experience in the emphasis towards greater collegiality in their approach to their work, and in their training to become part of a school team. The weaknesses in this model of teacher education were identified as follows:

- Too short a time-scale to cope with all the changes in the post-primary school today;
- The perceived need to improve the language standards of student language teachers, and the consequent aspiration to enable such students to spend some time in the host country of the target language;
- The need to continue the work currently being done by the Department of Eduction, the HEA and the Universities to get a balance between supply and demand in the post-primary sector.

The criteria for selection of student placement in schools for teaching practice, particularly in the context of the over-demand for reduced places which now exist, should be examined by the partners involved in the process. Allied to this it was felt necessary to express concern about the situation where some schools use student teachers as part of the teaching force of the school in a timetabled way. The issue of retaining quality recruitment to the teaching profession, particularly in the case of men, was raised with the concomitant questions of gender imbalance and role models within the profession.

Induction Year

There was a welcome for the greater emphasis in the Green Paper for induction as a significant support to the beginning teacher. However, it was felt that the emphasis being placed on the Principal, as being the arbiter of the beginning teacher's ability to teach, was unsustainable in the circumstances of many Irish schools. While the Principal could be of considerable assistance, it should be the role of an Inspector as a professional extern to evaluate the probating teacher in relation to certification. It was suggested that it was a healthy and beneficial development for the profession to be involved in the inducting of others into the profession.

The discussion focussed on many practical aspects involved in making the induction proposals a successful reality in the schools, e.g. reduced teaching hours, the nature of links with Colleges of Education and the Teachers' Centres. If the policy proposals for induction are to become a reality, many practical implications must be examined and worked through.

The issue was raised about the apparent contradiction on calls for the Inspectorate to be more present on this and other capacities in schools, while policy-makers sought a disengagement of this type of work in favour of inputs to policy-formulation and overall school inspection. International trends also seemed to be in favour of a reduced role for the Inspectorate in the general work of the school.

If there is to be a serious induction process following graduation from college, it will require the provisional placement of all graduating students in schools. A serious effort needs to be made on the costing of the induction process.

Inservice Teacher Education

It was agreed that the case for inservice teacher education no longer needed to be made, and that attention should be focussed on appropriate structures and best modes of delivery. Many interesting models are currently in operation and there should be an inventory and evaluation of these to guide future policy. It was felt that there should be a variety of forms of inservice teacher education, including an emphasis on school-based inservice provision. Inservice teacher education should take into account the personal development of the teacher, reconciling the needs of the individual with the needs of the system. A small co-ordinating structure should be developed to plan inservice provision. This structure should include representation from the Department of Education, the teachers and the providers of inservice education. Under a strategic plan for inservice education it was emphasised that there should be a harnessing of the agencies for inservice education so that, on a regional basis, teachers and schools could have reasonable access to the provision. Allowances for qualifications obtained from participating in inservice education should be available and updated. In some forms of inservice teacher education better arrangements should be made available for teacher replacement/substitution. It was felt that some of the proposals of the 1984 Inservice Committee Report would be beneficial in devising a future for inservice teacher education. Satisfaction and confidence were expressed by the group that we might be entering a new era for inservice teacher education, which could yield significant breakthroughs in the general education of pupils, and in the greater professional satisfaction of teachers.

Finally, in the course of the session it was clarified that provision existed in some denominational Colleges of Education for non-believers, and no restrictions could be placed in their path.

ANALYSIS OF ISSUES : GROUP IV— C
PROBLEMS OF INEQUALITY (2)
— Education for Special needs
— Education for Travellers

The dimensions of inequality chosen for analysis by this group were:

(i)   Special Education — with a focus on the issue of integration and/or special schooling : parental choice and assessment.

(ii)   Education of Travellers — with a focus on participation, curricular issues and quality of educational experience.

Initially these issues were discussed separately, while the final part of the session discussed support services and resources in the context of both special education and the education of Travellers.

Special education covers a wide spectrum. It includes the education of those with a range of physical disabilities, those with learning disabilities, emotional/behavioural disturbance and giftedness.

In our discussion of provision for children with special needs it was agreed that the basic principle which should govern policy is that every child is educable. The right of the child to education must be our first concern. It was suggested that there was a danger that the debate might be forced into institutional language.

There was agreement that there needed to be a continuum of provision ranging from integration into mainstream schools to special schools. There was also a case for the provision of special classes in mainstream schools, and possibly the provision of special units which would be associated with mainstream schools.

In making a decision in respect of any child the emphasis should be on parental choice. However, it was stressed that parents should have the opportunity to make an informed choice which would follow psychological assessment and involve consultation with teachers. The process of assessment should be linked to the planning process, which would identify the resources available and involve dialogue with the school personnel and how they might accommodate the child. It was agreed that it should be virtually impossible to overturn parental choice. It was accepted that in some circumstances this could create very real difficulties for the school. One person experienced the view that if parents insist on integration against the advice of all the professional staff, the school should have the right to refuse admission. It was pointed out that in the face of such a conflict there was no appeal procedure to resolve this dilemma. The need for such an appeals procedure was suggested, although this suggestion was not given unanimous approval. One of our group suggested that such an appeal procedure could generate conflict.

To support the right of parental choice it was necessary to have a continuum of provision options. This was not always available. Furthermore, it was stressed that initial placement decisions should be kept under review. There should be a constant monitoring of performance with the possibility of movement from special schools and/or classes, to mainstream education, and for movement in the opposite direction. If placement decisions are not seen as permanent, it helps to remove the stigma which some parents may associate with special schools and classes. It was also stressed that children should not have to travel too far to gain access to their preferred type of education.

Our discussion supported the call for coordination at local level. It was suggested that there was a need to formulate a plan for provision in each area. Schools in an area should be required to work together to plan a range of provisions for their area. All schools should have a responsibility to serve children with special needs. There was concern that any one school should become a designated school, although it was assumed that some specialisation and complementarity may be appropriate. At the level of the school, each school plan should strive to make their school inclusive institutions, aiming to meet the needs of all its pupils, including those with special needs. It was also suggested that there should be closer linkages between special schools and other schools.

Where children with special needs are integrated in mainstream education, it is imperative that the necessary support services are provided. If schools are providing a specialist service it must be supported. In this context, it was stressed, that the flow of extra resources should not be determined merely on the basis of a head count, but on the basis of support for plans and programmes which had been developed. It was accepted that with integration there was a danger that pupils would not have access to the same range of resources which are provided in special schools. However, if educational provision is planned at a local level, it is more realistic to provide access to the range of specialist services which are required. The development of a schools psychological service would be an essential requirement. Our group were very conscious of the distinction between "placing" and "integration;" the latter involves planning and support services.

The problems faced by third-level students with physical disabilities were also discussed. While acknowledging the progress made in this area in recent years, it was suggested that all third-level institutions should set targets for admission in all faculties. These students needed ongoing support services after admission. It was agreed that, in addition to meeting the physical barriers which inhibit their full participation in the academic area, there needed to be support for the socio-emotional integration of these students.

Our group did not discuss, in any detail, the position of special classes, although we did discuss the issue of special units. There was a suggestion that these special units were needed to cater for children who were emotionally disturbed. The desirability of such units, which would be separate from a mainstream school on the same campus, was challenged. It was argued that special units will break bonding, and that segregation may lead to prejudice.

EDUCATION FOR TRAVELLERS
Ethnic Identity
Before commencing our discussion on the education of Travellers it was noted and regretted, that Travellers had not been invited as a group to the convention. Their representation in our group was facilitated by the two parent associations. The discussion opened with the suggestion that Travellers must be recognised as a distinct ethnic, nomadic group. Consequently, the approach to the education of Travellers should be located within the broader context of respect for human rights. Thus the question must be one of how education can respect and endorse minority positions. In the case of Travellers, it is an issue of how their nomadic identity can be facilitated, reflected and respected.

Curriculum
Participants suggested that the focus on Traveller education to date has involved too great an emphasis on quantity questions (such as participation rates), and too little emphasis on quality issues (such as the curriculum). In particular there is a need to produce culturally appropriate materials for use with Traveller children, ones which celebrate and reflect Traveller culture. It was also pointed out that in the different subject areas of the curriculum, such as history, geography, languages, issues relating to nomadic peoples, can be incorporated for all pupils.

Problems Faced by Travellers
For many Travellers their experience of education has been very negative. Many have perceived prejudice from teachers and other pupils and have been subjected to bullying. For Travellers schooling is experienced as alien from their culture. It has not been easy for them to see the linkages between what happened in school and in the home. Furthermore, when the children of Travellers move from special school or class to mainstream classes, they lose their entitlements to additional resources. They have also found in many cases, that teacher expectations of Traveller children are low, with consequent effects on achievement.

As a group who have a significant experience of marginalisation and oppression, Travellers have very special needs.

Access, Consultation and Choice

Access to education for Travellers has a number of dimensions. It includes provision within the formal system. It was suggested that this right of access should be supported by a circular letter from the Department of Education which would set out parents' rights. Because of the special circumstances of Traveller families, access must also embrace the concept of the school going out to the families (through the visiting teacher service). Parental choice should be the basis on which placement is made, and there should be adequate consultation with parents in decision making about their children. At second level, choice should be available to Traveller children in respect of placement in training centres as well as mainstream second level schools. It was pointed out that there are no figures available on participation at second level, since Traveller children are not distinguished from others for administrative purposes. The need for linkages between the different levels of education was also emphasised, and it was pointed out that the NCVA could play an important role here in certification, with linkages to third level and to adult and community education.

Other Issues in Educational Organisation

It was suggested that there is a need for the educational system to adjust to the needs of travelling children. For example, it was suggested that schools operate on the assumption that all people are in a fixed location, and thus cater inadequately for nomadic children. One possible mechanism for facilitating academic progression through the system is that individual pupils would have a detailed record card which they would take from school to school. The lack of representation of Traveller parents on Boards of Management was noted, and the suggestion was made that in cases where they were not elected, the mechanism of the Patron's nominee could be used to ensure representation. The National Parents' Council could also play a role in facilitating more positive attitudes towards Travellers on the part of settled parents. It was also pointed out that there was a need for linkages between the education service and other government, health and welfare agencies dealing with Travellers. Local educational structures might also play a role.

Third Level

Access to third level institutions is as much a right for Travellers as for anybody else. There is a need for affirmative action directed to travelling families and communities in order to present third level education as a viable option. The HEA has a monitoring role on this, as on other equality issues.

Teacher Training

There was an emphasis on the need for the inclusion of modules on Traveller culture and education in preservice and inservice teacher education. This should emphasise the need for appropriate pedagogy, materials and homework strategies.

EC Resolution

The 1989 Resolution from the EC Council of Education Ministers on Gypsies, Travellers and nomads in Europe, gives clear recognition to cultural needs. It was argued that due account should be taken of the implications of this resolution in future policy.

In our discussion of support structures and resources, which was common to both special education and to the education of Travellers, it was suggested that it would be useful to think in terms of rights, responsibilities and resources (the 3 Rs). The former two should feature in the proposed legislation, which should specify the rights of children and parents, and specify with whom the responsibility should lie to provide the services to facilitate the realisation of these rights.

ANALYSIS OF ISSUES : GROUP V — A
QUALITY AND EFFECTIVENESS OF SCHOOLS

1. School Plans and Annual Reports

There was general support for the concept of a school plan although a variety of opinions was expressed about its nature and purpose. This arose, in part, because of the inadequacy of the discussion of this topic in the Green Paper, especially with regard to the process involved in the development of plans. The intended purposes of plans, particularly with regard to their publication for the wider community, and the relationship between the plan and annual report gave rise to some degree of concern. However, the process involved in devising a school plan was seen as a potentially valuable mechanism for promoting a collaborative culture in schools by engaging patrons, management, staff and parents in defining a mission and objectives for the school, devising policies for implementing programmes, monitoring progress and using the data collected as part of the process of in-school evaluation.

It was noted that school plans have been developed at the primary level since 1984 and that some post-primary schools have more recently become involved in this activity. The overall purpose of the school plan was seen as a way of enabling staff specify the aims and objectives which it wished to set down for the school. It was described as a working document to be drawn up by the principal in collaboration with staff and other bodies, and subject to the approval of the Board of Management. The involvement of parents in this process gave rise to much discussion. It was generally agreed that they would have a significant role in the development of general school policy, and especially in areas such as health and social education, religious education, discipline and homework policies. In general, the professional staff in the school would have responsibility for that part of the plan concerned with the delivery of the curriculum and implementation of policy. Parents would have a consultative role in these areas. The function of the Board of Management would be to ensure that the task was completed.

Opinion was divided on the degree of importance which should be attached to the two main dimensions of planning: Product and Process. While all agreed that the process dimension was a very important aspect of the plan, it was stated that the production of a final document, recording both the process and the progress already made, gave a greater sense of structure to the activity. Fears were, however, expressed that the production of a document might bestow a degree of finality to the exercise and thus impede further development. It was concluded that a balance needed to be struck between these two elements and that attention should then be focussed on implementing plans which have been developed, and monitoring their progress. It was important that national objectives and priorities, as well as local and school objectives, be included in the plan, that realistic and short timescales be set for achieving targets and that a whole-school review be conducted around the framework of the plan on a regular basis.

The publication of guidelines by the Department of Education, as mentioned in the Green Paper, would contribute significantly to the success of this proposal, especially for those schools which have not yet become formally engaged in this process. The provision of resources, particularly secretarial assistance and time, was regarded as essential, especially for schools about to become involved in developing plans of this nature. Support for staff in the form of relevant training was also important.

There was considerable divergence of opinion on the feasibility of making school plans and annual reports widely available to agencies outside the school, other than the Inspectorate. Fears were expressed that circulation at this level could lead to increased competition between schools and that, more importantly, plans and reports used for marketing purposes might give an exaggerated view of the school and do little towards improving the quality of education being provided. However, a majority agreed that all the partners, trustees, board of management, staff, parents, pupils and the Department of Education should have access to the plan and the annual report.

2. Assessment

The discussion on assessment was mainly confined to primary school children and focussed on the identification of pupils with learning problems and the provision of additional services to remedy these.

As a general principle, it was agreed that early diagnosis was important and that corrective action should be taken at a very early stage in the child's educational career. It was stated that teachers can and do assess and diagnose children using a variety of techniques including observation, questioning, class tests and standardised tests. Where particular difficulties arise, the expertise of the remedial teacher in administering more sophisticated tests could be used. The main problem arose in the post-diagnostic phase and related to the provision of remedial services. There was considerable discussion on how this might be done and it was suggested that this service needed to be evaluated. Many areas, particularly those served by small schools, have no access to this service.

At a more general level it was stated that every teacher should, at various stages, assess the progress of pupils against national norms and interpret and explain the outcomes to parents. The use of standardised tests in this exercise has financial implications for schools.

Assessment at the stage of transfer to post-primary school remains problematic. Some primary schools do not forward assessment information on the pupils to the schools and in other cases post-primary schools do not use the information passed on. The use of a pupil profile system from the early stages of schooling, covering both cognitive and affective domains was suggested as a means of improving the flow of information on the pupil, both through the school and from school to school. In view of the fact that some post-primary schools enrol pupils from a large number of primary schools, pupil profiles need to be standardised.

Parents need to be much more involved in the assessment process. The information derived from assessment is important if parents are to have more involvement in helping their children and supporting the work of teachers. Pupil records should be available for inspection by parents and the transfer of pupil records to other schools should be done in consultation with parents.

There was no support for the school-wide testing of children at ages 7 and 11 proposed in the Green Paper. It was felt that this would serve no useful purpose for schools or for children. This position was held, even with the assurance that the data collected would be aggregated and not linked to individual schools, or published. However, testing of national samples of children at various stages in their schooling was not seen as problematic. It was suggested that these tests should be conducted more frequently and regularly, and that they should cover wider areas of the curriculum.

3. Inspectorate

Inspectors were regarded as having an important supportive role to play in assisting teachers in their work. In this respect the advisory role of the Inspectorate was seen as having particular relevance. However, the capacity of the Inspectorate to provide this service at post-primary level was severely curtailed, due to shortage of personnel and the range of duties inspectors were expected to undertake. The rare visit of an inspector was frequently regarded as an indication that a school or teacher had some serious problem and gave rise to suspicion, even in the community. In short, valuable as the advisory service may be, schools no longer expect the Inspectorate to provide it. It was suggested that the secondment of experienced subject and pedagogical specialists from schools, as suggested in the Green Paper, might be a more appropriate way of providing services to schools.

The role of the Inspectorate as auditor of schools was endorsed, but practices in the conduct of this role varied between primary and post-primary schools, as well as between different types of post-primary school. In some cases, procedures for carrying out this role have been agreed and are clearly understood by the teachers; in other instances, where a degree of confusion exists, agreed procedures would be welcomed.

ANALYSIS OF ISSUES SESSION : V—B
SUPPORT SERVICES FOR SCHOOLS

This issue was considered under four general headings:
*   Administrative/Technical Assistance
*   Psychological and Guidance Services
*   Medical, Remedial and Referral Agencies
*   Pedagogical Resources, including Library Resources and Educational Broadcasting.

Administrative and Technical Assistance
School Secretary:
The provision of secretarial services for schools was seen as a basic requirement of all schools. The need for schools to have access to proper secretarial services was heightened by the emphasis which the Green Paper places on accountability and transparency. The need for such services will vary from school to school and, therefore, for some schools access to a service shared with other schools in their area might suffice.

School Caretaker:
The provision of a school caretaker was also seen as a basic requirement of all schools. The provision of a school caretaker was seen as a cost effective way of ensuring that school buildings did not fall into disrepair as was happening at present. Once again access to the services of a caretaker on a shared basis might be sufficient for some schools depending on their size.

Essential Equipment:
It was felt that a phone and photocopier were essential equipment in all schools, regardless of the size of the school.

Technical Advice:
Schools needed to have access to technical advice on matters relating to employment of personnel, school buildings etc. It should not be necessary to have to refer all of these matters to the Department of Education.

Administrative Structures within Schools:
It was felt that additional administrative services were needed, particularly in larger schools, as it was unreasonable to expect that a principal and vice-principal could cater adequately for the administration of such large organisations.

Psychological and Guidance Services
Psychological Service:
The provision of an adequate psychological service was seen as a priority.   The present psychological service, such as it is, was seen to be grossly inadequate and frustrating for those who are working in it.   It was felt that the provision of a proper service, would be cost effective in the longer term, as it would address problems at an early stage and thus avoid more serious problems manifesting themselves later.

Two successful models for delivering such a service were operating at present and it was felt that lessons could be learned from these. Pilot Projects have been running for the last three years in Clondalkin and in South Tipperary. These two pilot projects have shown that it is possible to provide a service which meets the needs of schools,

Dublin VEC also provides a service for the 17 schools which are under its jurisdiction. This service focuses on the identification and remediation of learning difficulties and also addresses the behaviour problems of pupils. Mention was also made of a successful programme operated by a unit attached to St. Vincent's Psychiatric Hospital. When necessary, this unit withdraws pupils from schools, assesses their needs, provides specialist therapy for the pupils, and/or their families, and then reintegrates the pupils into schools.

What is needed is an educational psychological service, provided by professionals with experience of schools. This service needs to be preventative as well as corrective. It must enhance the lives of children and not just label them.

Structure:

To provide an adequate service, a ratio of 1 psychologist to 5000 pupils was needed (1 : 3000 in disadvantaged areas). Building on the experience gained in the pilot projects, this service should be introduced on a phased basis, not just all at once. Disadvantaged areas would need to be targeted initially in the setting up of such a service. In order to provide an effective service, it would be necessary to build up a network in a local area where psychologists worked as part of a team and not just in isolation.

Service:
The service offered should incorporate the following elements:

*   Individual case work with pupil;
*   Consultation and work with teachers on more general issues, in order to help schools develop strategies for dealing with problems which occur on a regular basis;
*   Input into inservice;
*   Project work which would have a more preventative focus.

Guidance Counsellors:

The present system was seen to be inadequate, with many smaller schools having no guidance counselling. Where the service does exist, it is very often a fire brigade service offering career guidance at sixth year level only. Access to the services of a professional guidance counsellor was seen as a fundamental right of every student, regardless of the size of school he/she attended. The provision of such a service was seen as making economic sense, as ultimately the state would benefit from improvements in the provision of guidance counselling. It was also emphasised that there was a need for the two dimensions of the work of the guidance counsellor i.e. career guidance and counselling of students. Once again needs would vary depending on the size of a school, and the services of a guidance counsellor could be shared between smaller schools.

Medical, Remedial and Referral Agencies
Liaison between Services:

In looking at the school psychological service and school guidance services, the group also looked at the wider area of family support services, which the school needs to call on from time to time, in responding to the needs of pupils. These services include, social workers, Gardai, J.L.O., speech therapists, community welfare officers, local doctors etc. At present there is a variety of services operated by various agencies, but what is needed is some local structure which would co-ordinate the services offered by these agencies in so far as they relate to schools. This would ensure that the many agencies worked in a collective manner for the benefit of the child or family. The work of Home/School/Community liaison co-ordinators, who have been appointed to some schools in disadvantaged areas, was seen as a positive move in this area. It was also suggested that the role of the Director of Community Care should be looked at, to see how it could contribute to the co-ordination of family support services. On a very practical level, it was suggested that an information booklet could be made available to schools and to parents, outlining the various services which were currently available.

Remedial Teaching:
At present, at primary level, two thirds of schools do not have access to the services of a remedial teacher. It was felt that all pupils who need remedial teaching should have access to it. In smaller schools these services could be shared between schools but it was felt that a remedial teacher could not cope effectively, if the number of schools they were expected to cover was too large.

Resource Teachers:
Children who have special needs, and who live in some rural areas, need the support of a resource teacher in the classroom, if they are to receive an adequate service in their own local areas.

Visiting Teachers:
The current provision of visiting teachers needs to be examined. A co-ordinated service, whereby a team of specialist teachers could provide teaching services to hearing impaired or visually impaired children, was suggested.

Pedagogical Resources
Teachers themselves were seen as central to the education system. Teachers and staffs need support and backup in their work. The provision of the necessary supports for teachers would ultimately ensure that they were enabled to provide a quality service. These support structures need to be co-ordinated at local level. It was suggested that the provision of a Welfare Officer for teachers would assist individual teachers who had difficulties or were under performing. It was recognised that the inspectorate also had a role to play in supporting and advising teachers.

Teaching Principals at primary level were seen as having particular difficulties. There was a need to establish a mechanism which would allow teaching principals to be relieved of teaching duties for some time each day or each week, in order to give them the opportunity of dealing with the other aspects of their work. The panel of supply teachers, which was set up as a pilot project in three different areas this year, offered possibilities on this front.

With the many curricular changes that are taking place at present, especially at second level, it was recognised that there was a need to develop a structured mechanism to facilitate this change. There was a need to provide a support service to co-ordinate and implement curriculum change and there was a need for resource centres to support this change.

Many new courses such as Post Leaving Certificate Courses, transition years, VTOS and youth reach programmes incorporate elements of work experience. It was agreed that there was a need for an administrative structure to co-ordinate such programmes at local level.

The emphasis on practical activities in many of the new courses, highlighted the need for the provision of technical assistants in schools. The possibility of linking in with RTCs, where such existed, was mentioned.

I will notify each presenter with an amber light that they have five remaining minutes to complete their presentation. As their time allocation runs out, I will then notify the presenter to complete the presentation with a red light.

Presenters may select to use only some of their allocated time for presentation. However, they are advised that they may not run over their allocated time.

On completion of all the presentations in each subsection, members of the Secretariat will then direct questions at, and request points of clarification from all of the organisations seated at the top table. The participating organisations are free to select who from their delegation is most appropriate to respond to each question.

I should like to remind you that I shall not take questions from the floor without a prior knowledge of the question. This stricture is essential as time is of the essence.

Once again may I stress please feel free to contact me if you are unhappy, but preferably happy about the procedures.

I now call on Professor John Coolahan to present his opening address.

SPEECH BY THE MINISTER FOR EDUCATION
Niamh Bhreathnach T.D.

At The Opening of
THE NATIONAL EDUCATION CONVENTION
on Monday 11th October, 1993

Partners in Education:

Welcome to our National Education Convention, an event which will, I believe, be of enormous significance in the history of eduction policy-making in Ireland. This event marks a new point of departure in the process of research, reflection and debate about the place of education in our world of innovation and constant change.

We are about to complete a process which has taken us on a long journey beginning with the publication, in June 1992, of the Green Paper *Education For A Changing World*. There have been written responses from nearly 1,000 interested parties and a series of major public meetings throughout the country organised by my Department and attended by your members.

Education has now been debated in the public arena for 18 months. You have held countless conferences, seminars and symposia concerning the issue of education as it affects your particular interest group. The publication of the *Programme For A Partnership Government 1993-1997* by this Government, with its detailed commitments to Education, further advance the debate.

We are on the threshold of a historic occasion — a process which will become a landmark in the history of Irish education. Indeed this Convention is seen internationally as a mould-breaking initiative. It has aroused intense interest in educational circles in Europe and elsewhere and I welcome the many distinguished educationalists and commentators from Ireland North and South and from abroad, who are with us here today.

I wish to pay tribute to the Chairperson of this Convention, Professor Dervilla Donnelly, the Secretary General Professor John Coolahan, and all the members of the Secretariat. They have brought to the task of preparing for this Convention, not only their formidable expertise, but dedication over and above the call of duty. I know that our prospects of success are enhanced by their preparation. On behalf of us all, I offer them our sincere thanks.

The Convention is designed to facilitate genuine debate and discovery. Participants are invited to both contribute and listen, to clarify and analyse and arrive at the fullest possible understanding of ways forward to meet the challenges which confront us during this two weeks of discussion and facilitation. This marks a major change in the way education policy is to be formulated for the next generation of pupils in Ireland. It arises from our commitment to partnership as expressed in the *Programme For A Partnership Government,* and I quote:

The key to our whole approach will be to develop a strong sense of partnership, not only in terms of political structures but throughout the economy, our society and our community — a partnership that will be dynamic and creative and geared totally towards confronting the major challenges that lie ahead of us.

The *Programme For A Partnership Government* pledges us to commit ourselves to democracy, to devolution and openness, to a genuine and meaningful role for all partners in education and to a focussing of resources towards disadvantaged areas and groups.

Education is a major project of the state in which the resources of the community are mobilised to ensure that the life chances of our young people are enhanced, that the effects of inequality are alleviated, and that each young person will experience the opportunity of real personal growth. The resources which we mobilise for education in the community are not only financial but also resources of time, effort and expertise. Professional educators, parents and many other individuals and groups in our society have committed their skills and talents to this great enterprise. The level of response and debate in recent months bears witness to this commitment.

As a community we have always seen education as a priority, and have had an immense faith in the power of education to improve the welfare and well-being of the individual and of society as a whole. It is an appropriate recognition of this commitment throughout society, therefore, that we have present here today representatives both of the organisations directly and centrally involved in the process of education on a continuous basis and of the social partners and other organisations, whose input will anchor our deliberations in the wider context in our society. The Convention is designed to facilitate each of the 42 groups here present in exploring their positions relative to each other. It is a multilateral forum which allows for discussion and exchange in a positive and constructive way to encourage wide ownership of a White Paper which will address issues of real change in education. Each group here has its own insights, its own vision of education in our community and its own unique part to play in the process of the Convention.

The challenge which confronts us is the challenge of change. We may accept the reality of change or we may resist it, but change is an inevitable feature of our society, of our communities and of the education system, as we face the closing years of this century. The key issue is our management of this change. Bringing about change in education is a difficult and complex task. The stakes are high — the future of an entire generation of our young people. Sometimes, change may threaten our established positions. It often takes courage to move from the known and familiar to the unknown, with its attendant risks. In education, we need to move with vision, but with care. Change may well be a matter of evolution rather than revolution. As we respond to altered circumstances and build for the future, we build on the strengths of an education system which has earned the confidence of the Irish people. To retain this confidence, our system must adapt to the challenges of the future. But in facing these challenges we must recognise, value and affirm our cultural and spiritual heritage. If we fail to do this our education system will lose the characteristics which attune it to the Irish psyche and the Irish spirit.

The process of change, then, is multi-faceted and complex. Yet we must not be daunted by this difficulty and complexity.   In the words of Michael Fullan, the well known Canadian educationalist: "We do not have the choice of avoiding change just because it is messy." Change is inevitable, and it is our duty to manage it in the interests of our young people. We must focus on how best to face this challenge.

Speaking at the Association for Teacher Education in Europe Annual Conference in 1990, Professor Coolahan stated, and I quote:

> In any professional activity, inertia and complacency need to be challenged, and self-examination fostered.   To this extent.... critiques are valuable. However, there is a grave danger that simplistic, short term solutions may be devised, which are not well enough grounded in research, experience and reflection.   Efforts must be made to face all the relevant issues and to shape a coherent model which relates to the many inter-connecting elements involved in a genuine solution.

What is true of teacher training, to which Professor Coolahan is referring in the above, is even more true of the wider education system.   We, therefore, need to establish a coherent plan which will set the context for decisions on policies, on priorities and on resource allocations. This is the task which faces each of us at this gathering today. We must have a real dialogue at this Convention — a dialogue which will allow all of us, and especially those centrally and directly involved in the process of education, to develop an ownership of and a commitment to this plan.   Our dialogue involves a recognition that we all have our varying responsibilities and obligations to those in the education system. We all have our different parts to play, some centrally in the system itself and others in the wider context in our society. We all have an interdependence in cooperating to provide the best possible educational experience for the next generation.

As Minister for Education, I appreciate the thoughtful responses to the education debate which all of you here today have formulated. When I reflected on how to determine Government policy in the White Paper, I concluded that this could best be advanced by a process which builds on and enriches the valuable insights in these responses. We are engaged, therefore, not just in a reiteration of positions but in a qualitatively different process, a process which involves listening to each other, clarification, communication, and a genuine search for understanding through discussion and debate. The concept of partnership is central to this process.

My invitation to you to participate in this Convention is a tangible recognition of the importance of openness and transparency in the policy making process and of the involvement in this process of all of us who contribute to education.   I thank you for the serious preparation you have undertaken in response to my invitation.

As Minister for Education, it is my duty to determine policy in the White Paper.   I believe, however, that this Convention has the potential to enormously enhance the quality of this policy-making process.   As trustees of the education system, we have a tremendous responsibility to our young people and to future generations.   Those of us who are in positions of influence, authority or control in education, do not have absolute ownership rights.   Our tenure is temporary.   Thus, we hold our offices in trust for the generation now going through the education system and for those coming after them. Let us then make this concept of trusteeship central to this Convention. We need to recognise our common interest in education, our interdependence and the responsibility we have to exchange information and work together to meet the challenges ahead. We must remember that the undertaking in which we are engaged is not merely shaping of policy for the next few years. We have here the opportunity to fundamentally influence the education of future generations in ways beyond the imagination of any individual here today. This demands of us all that we work together to help devise policies and structures which will have the flexibility to respond to the changing circumstances of the future. The obligations of our trusteeship require us to do our utmost to meet this challenge.

As trustees of the system, we are accountable for our stewardship of education. We are accountable to society, to our community but most of all to the young people whom the system is designed to serve. Central to our endeavours in the coming days must be the consciousness of this tremendous responsibility we have to the current generation and to future generations of pupils and students in the system.

We must not lose sight of the student. I have a vision of a system which allows each student to have a rich and satisfying school experience here and now while preparing for full participation in work, in family, in the community and in the society of which she/he is part. I know you will share with me the image of the student in the poem:

> Aoibhinn beatha an scolaire
> a bhios ag déanamh a leinn;
> Is follas daoibh, a dhaoine,
> Gurbh do is aoibhne in Éirinn.

We want to make the pursuit of learning, of personal growth and of development, a happy experience for all our students. This is our aim. This is our vision. As our Convention begins, I invite you all to reflect again on the historic nature of the process in which we are engaged. We are privileged and challenged by our trusteeship of education at this time. Change is inevitable. Change must be managed. I believe we must broaden the management of change to include all those who are affected by that change. That is why we are here today.

When we contemplate the importance of the task in which we are engaged, the significance of its outcomes and the consequences for our students, for our nation and for our future, we may well be daunted by our endeavour. Yet, rather than being intimidated, I believe we should take courage from our collective strengths, which this Convention is designed to harness, so that we can work together. No one person here has a monopoly of wisdom. No one person can face the challenge alone. Yet together, working in harmony, recognising our interdependence, respecting and hearing each other's insights, we can and must succeed.

The vision of a new type of policy process, a new type of dialogue and a new type of partnership, which this Convention represents, demands new and creative responses from all of us. I will remain at this Convention throughout the week to carefully listen to the contributions of each group. As Minister, I have extended an invitation to you to participate in this most demanding endeavour which will have the most profound consequences. You have responded to my invitation. I am confident that, working together, we can prove ourselves equal to the task.

OPENING ADDRESS
To
THE NATIONAL EDUCATION CONVENTION

By
THE SECRETARY GENERAL
Professor John Coolahan

GEORGE'S HALL, DUBLIN CASTLE
11th — 21st October, 1993

A Chathaoirligh, a Aire agus a dhaoine uaisle go léir. Fearaim fíorchaoin fáilte romhaibh go léir go dtí an chéad Chomhdháil Náisiúnta Oideachais anseo i gCaisleán Bhaile Átha Cliath. Is ócáid thábhachtach í agus táimid buíoch díbh go léir as bheith i láthair.

San obair phleanála atá beartaithe ag an Rialtas i gcúrsaí oideachais, tá béim á chur anois ar iarraidh ar dhaoine dul i gcomhairle le chéile in ionad polasaí a dheachtú ón mbárr anuas. Léiríonn an chomhdháil seo go bhfuil staid nua sroiste anois sa phróiseas comhairleoireachta do réir mar atá an Roinn Oideachais ag druidim i dtreo críoch a chur leis an bPáipéar Bán. Is é an fhreaghracht atá ar bhaill na Comhdhála ná iarracht a dhéanamh oiread comhaontaithe agus is féidir a chur ar aghaigh chun dul i gcionn ar shocruithe polasaí.

Chun toradh fiúntach a aimsiú in obair na Comhdhála beidh gá le comhoibhriú, dea-thoil agus muinín eadrainn go léir. Dá réir sin, déanfaidh an Rúnaíocht a ndícheall caidreamh fónta a bheith acu leis na comhpháirtithe éagsúla.

Tá súil agam go mbeidh rath ar ár gcuid oibre.

Education, A Trust Bonding The Generations
The National Education Convention takes place here in Dublin Castle, the centre where for many, many years plans were drawn up and promulgated for Irish education, but not under the control of the Irish people.   For instance, it was in rooms nearby, in this same month of October, in 1831, that plans were prepared which led to the establishment of the Irish national school system.   The plan was later released from his London office by the Chief Secretary for Ireland, Lord Stanley, in the famous Stanley Letter.   Of course, the Irish heritage and achievement in formal education extends for well over a millennium before that, but the Stanley initiative was a significant landmark in the state's intervention in the provision and co-ordination of education as we know it in modern Ireland. Much of the basic framework of modern Irish education — national, secondary, technical and university — was shaped in the nineteenth and early twentieth centuries.   Much of the planning and many of the initiatives took place in these rooms.

It is also the case that some of the organisations represented here have their origins in the nineteenth century. For instance, the INTO is celebrating its 125th anniversary this year, and the Irish Schoolmasters' Association is just one year younger.   We also have with us organisations of more recent origin, such as the National Parents' Council, dating from 1985, and reflective of changes in modern Irish society.   Old or young, all the organisations and their representatives are very welcome. While a great many of the major interests in Irish education are represented here, there are many other organisations which contribute valuably to the education system, which could not be accommodated. However, that is not to say that their concerns will be excluded from our deliberations.

As we gather here in George's Hall in Dublin Castle for Ireland's first National Education Convention, in October 1993, the **past** nudges at our shoulders to look back briefly and note from where we have come, the **present** presses upon us to deal with its realities and the **future** beckons to us to plan the improvement of our education system. One is conscious of the historical landmarks in the development of our education system. One is aware that, even in times of great political oppression and economic deprivation, Irish people cherished education and sacrificed a great deal to attain it. One is reminded of policy makers who, with a sense of vision, broke old moulds, took risks and chartered new ways forward. One remembers many thinkers and leaders who contributed so much to our educational heritage. One also honours the quiet dedication and commitment of so many men and women who worked, often in difficult and unpropitious circumstances, in the cause of education. Above all, it was the quality of such personnel and their unselfish commitment which achieved so much. On an occasion such as this, we salute their endeavours, and take pride in and build confidence from their achievements.

As we focus on the **present,** our first reaction is one of celebration. Your presence here at this remarkable assembly symbolises the great richness and diversity of our contemporary educational system. It represents the spirit of partnership which should be a rich feature of an enterprise so intimately affecting our people, as education. The fact that we gather here in Dublin Castle emphasises that our education system is now under the control of the Irish people. Surely this is one of the valuable consequences of independence: our education can reflect our distinctive values, culture and aspirations.

Any society which hopes to develop and improve the quality of life of its citizens needs to plan for the **future** of its education system in a sophisticated and sustained way. The future beckons, and the future challenges us. Decisions, which will have long-term consequences, need to be taken. **How** we decide, and **what** we decide, are of crucial and urgent importance. The responsibility is ours, in our generation, and should not be shirked. We are part of the bonding of the generations, which education as an on-going process and trust exemplifies. Undoubtedly, the challenge is significant, but it also represents an opportunity. I think that we should set our sights high so that what we do at this National Education Convention is worthy of those who went before us, worthy of the issues which face us, and worthy of our current and future citizenry, whose interests we are called upon to serve.

The Convention: A Challenge and an Opportunity
What we decide in planning our educational future is significant; but **how** we decide it also has central importance for us as a people, and for the manner in which decisions may be implemented. In this context, the process set out by the Irish government is one which lays great emphasis on consultation, rather than dictat. Already, the process of consultation and discussion has been extensive and impressive. Since the publication of the Green Paper, in June 1992, a remarkable degree of engagement in debate on educational issues has taken place at venues all over the country. It is also reflected in the vast amount of written responses which has been lodged with the Department of Education, commenting on the

Green Paper proposals and on the *Programme For A Partnership Government.* This level of interest reflects well the quality of democratic debate in Ireland. The time involved has not been long in view of the range of issues which is involved, and of the significance of the issues for Irish society. The National Education Convention represents a **new** stage, and, in a sense, a rounding off stage of the consultative process. It provides us with an opportunity to put a tighter focus on the debate, to clarify and analyse the key issues in a structured, multi-lateral framework, to establish areas of common ground and to identify and seek to narrow areas of disagreement. It allows the major partners in education to influence significantly the decisions which it is the responsibility of the Department of Education and of the Government to make in the near future. The Minister has established the Secretariat as an independent agency and the Secretariat is anxious to protect this independence in the wider interests of all concerned. The Secretariat is in many ways, the servant of the Convention, and seeks to facilitate dialogue, to analyse issues, to listen attentively, to be faithful to the facts and to explore possible ways forward. Arising out of the Convention, the Secretariat will prepare its final independent report, present it to the Minister, and publish it for all Convention participants, and for the general public. In the process of its work during, and subsequent to the Convention, it will seek to act constructively with all parties, but retain its independence, which is the trust placed upon it.

In my view, the Minister for Education is to be commended for taking this initiative, and, by so doing, has provided the opportunity for the education partners, operating in a cohesive and public way, to influence strategic decision-making at a crucial stage in its formulation, without prejudice to other forms of negotiation at a later stage, on policy decisions and implementation. The Convention is, thus, a distinctive opportunity, but it also presents a unique challenge to the partners. The Secretariat will seek to assist the partners to meet that challenge, but a great responsibility lies on the participants themselves as to whether they can seize the opportunity and work co-operatively to help shape reform. The Convention helps give education a centre-stage position in Irish public life at a vital time. The government and social partners are about to engage in the planning of another partnership agreement on future social and economic development. The National Economic and Social Council has just completed its report, *Education and Training Policies for Economic and Social Development.* The Government publishes its *National Development Plan* to-day, to cover the next six year period. *The Programme For A Partnership Government* stated, "We regard education as the key to our future prosperity and to equality and equal opportunities for all our citizens." It is a time in Irish education when low expectations should not be allowed too much sway, but, based on realism and serious analysis, idealism and a vision for the future ought to energise our efforts.

It is a great credit to the organisations which were invited by the Minister that they are represented by so many of their leading members. It also reflects their sense of responsibility to the Irish public on this national occasion. We thank them for their presence and we also thank them for the time and thought put into their preparation for the Convention. The quality of documents submitted in response to the Green Paper bears testimony to much reflection and clarity of view. We are glad to be able to accommodate some observers at the Convention and we are very obliged to the media for their strong presence so as to mediate the proceedings of the Convention to the public at large.

SPEECH BY THE MINISTER FOR EDUCATION
Niamh Bhreathnach, T.D.

At The Closing of
THE NATIONAL EDUCATION CONVENTION

IN DUBLIN CASTLE
on Thursday 21st October, 1993

Partners in Education,

Sna laethanta seo, bhíomar ag dul i gcomhairle le chéile, ag plé, ag éisteacht, agus ag malartú tuairimí.   Inniú, ag an seisiún deireannach seo den gComhdháil Náisiúnta Oideachais, tá an próiséas seo ardaithe againn chuig leibhéal nua ar fad.

Gabhaim buíochas libh uile, a chomhpháirtithe san oideachais, as chomh dáirire agus a ghlac sibh páirt sa díospóireacht seo.   Dhírigh sibh mór-chúram agus dúthracht iomlán agus muid ag plé leis na ceisteanna is bunúsaí a bhaineann le oideachais na hÉireann, anois agus sa todhchaí.

I pay special tribute to the Convention Secretariat who facilitated and challenged us as we shared, as we listened and as we learned from each other.   I particularly thank Professor Dervilla Donnelly for her astute and impressive chairing of the Convention.   I pay tribute to Professor John Coolahan for his focused and visionary approach to the overall structure and workings of the Convention, and to the members of the Secretariat for their resourceful and rigorous examination of positions on the issues which confront us. Without their dedicated commitment and their formidable expertise, this Convention would not have provoked the very thoughtful response from the participants, the observers and the media.

The *Programme For A Partnership Government* states, and I quote:

> The key to our whole approach will be to develop a strong sense of partnership, not only in terms of political structures but throughout the economy, our society and our community — a partnership that will be dynamic and creative and geared towards confronting the major challenges that lie ahead of us.

We have seen the reality of this dynamic and creative partnership at this Convention.   The Convention has proved to be an enormous success.   It has harnessed energy and commitment beyond our most optimistic expectations.   It has radically changed the way in which education policy in Ireland will be formulated in the future.   And all of us, each one of us, has contributed to this landmark event, this moment in history.   Let us pause for a moment to reflect on some of the characteristics of this Convention.

At this Convention, we experienced participation.
The Convention has been marked by the involvement of a broad range of groups, all of whose role in education has not always been acknowledged by the State.   These groups have now

demonstrated their right to have a very real role in the formulation of education policy.   I believe that the fundamental change experienced at this Convention is that their voices have been heard as enriching the debate, rather than as competing for attention.   This Convention marks a realisation that attention to the contribution of other groups does not weaken our own contribution.   On the contrary, we can move together to a deeper understanding, a better insight and enhanced capacity to generate responses to the challenges which face us. And indeed, listening to the voices of others can help us define our own position, what is of fundamental importance to us and what is not essential.   This is the reality of partnership and this is the reality of the Convention.

At this Convention, we experienced openness and transparency.
It is not every day that this Government Department or, indeed, any of the partners in education submit themselves to rigorous examination under the glare of both public and media attention.   Your open and generous engagement in this process has been matched by a unique contribution by the Department of Education.   The willingness of all the senior Department officials, not only to make a public presentation, but also to undergo a lengthy public debate with the Secretariat on the issues raised has earned universal praise from commentators.   I believe that over the last nine days, the Irish people became aware of the realities facing us and the choices that are to be made in the forthcoming government policy on education.   For that I thank all of you who have been involved in the open debate on the education project, and in making the government's commitment to transparency very real.

At this Convention, we experienced the democratisation of the policy making process.
As I attended the Convention daily, I gained a real opportunity to listen in a very public way to the stated positions of the partners in education.   I believe that over the past nine days we have seen real openness of mind and attitude expressed by the education partners who have participated here.   And this openness of mind and attitude is the heart of the matter.   Real change stems from change in our attitudes, our approaches and our way of doing things. Change begins in the heart.   I believe that the most fundamental and lasting effect of this Convention is this new way of looking at things, which has effected all of us and which will be reflected in the White Paper on Education.   Together, we have produced a most powerful and influential dynamic during these days of intense debate.   The forces unleashed by this dynamic will ensure that policy making in Irish education will never be the same again.

We have tangible and encouraging results of this process
During the public sessions we saw convergence of opinion on a range of issues.   The reports of the Analysis of Issues Groups today indicates further convergence and consensus.   Even where opinions vary, there is a note of acceptance of diversity of view and of a belief that solutions can be found, not at the lowest common denominator of compromise, but at the highest level of new and imaginative solutions which meet our multiple objectives.

Let me give some practical examples:

This Convention has addressed the needs of our community.
There has been a striking convergence of opinion on targeting of resources towards disadvantaged individuals and groups.   This has created a momentum, a new way forward for providing access to education, full benefit from the system and second chances for all.

Is mór ar fad agam an tacaíocht a tugadh agus an cúran a rinneadh de cheist na Gaeilge. Léiríodh roinnt moltaí úrnua faoi thábhacht agus áit na teanga dár saol agus dár timpeallacht, dar, ndúchas, agus mar chuid bhunúsach dar gcine mar phobal. Tuigimid gur féidir leis na scoileanna straitéis a úsáid chun an teanga a chothú agus a fhorbairt, ach ní féidir leis an gcorás oideachais amháin an cuspóir seo a bhaint amach. Chur an díospóireacht faoin nGaeilge an córas oideachais ina suíomh sa phobal í gcoitinne. Mothaítear práinn ar leith le ceist na Gaeilge go bhfuil an t-am ag sleamhnú thart agus go bhfuil uair na cinniúna ann. Tháinig moltaí praiticúila ós ár gcomhair a bhfuil tacaíocht laídir leo, moltaí gur feidir linn a chur i gcríoch gan mhoill.

The increasing plurality and diversity in our community is exemplified by the contributions from representatives of the Gaelscoileana and the multi denominational schools. We have made real progress on the issue of how we move from a relatively homogeneous system to one which accommodates diversity of provision.

The place of the school in the community received much attention. I have heard the arguments that any rationalisation proposals must proceed with care and sensitivity, with full consultation with the community and with special attention to the requirements of minorities who have a scattered population. I am convinced that an inflexible standardised approach in terms of four and eight teacher schools, which has been criticised at this Convention, is not the way to approach this issue. The widespread concern we have heard for the place for the arts in education provides us with an agenda for action in this area. We have had a valuable highlighting of the issues of educational broadcasting. And we have widespread agreement about the establishment of Local Educational Authorities. We have consensus that they have the potential to genuinely enhance our education system and that they must have a strong local role to succeed. There is a heightened awareness that local power means local responsibility, local choices and local accountability.

This Convention has addressed the needs of the student.
The student is and must be at the centre of all our debate and endeavour. Indeed, at this Convention we spoke not just **about** the students but **with** the third-level students who have participated fully and have enhanced the quality of the proceedings with thoughtful insights on a broad range of issues. This Convention has shown widespread concern that far too many people who leave the formal education system and experience major problems with numeracy and literacy. Specific approaches to this problem have been highlighted — many of which can lead to action in advance of an Education Act. The Convention has focused on quality in education, not in terms of crude measures such as league tables but in terms of subtle and demanding analysis of curricular outcomes, their measurement and the role of the inspectorate. Quality measurement is not simple for education is a complex process. But it cannot be ignored and I am impressed at the commitment of a large number of groups to make progress on this issue.

This Convention addressed the needs of our teachers
We have been reminded at this Convention that the quality of education of our students relies fundamentally on the quality of our teachers. I am impressed by the strength of support for a Teachers' Council and for the valuable range of issues concerning the role and functions of this council, which we have heard. I already indicated my commitment to the establishment of such a council; this Convention has dramatically advanced the potential for rapid progress on this issue.

The other major theme emerging from this Convention concerning the teaching profession is inservice education. We have made significant progress in the last nine days in spelling out an action plan to provide the structures, the programmes, the monitoring mechanisms and the local networks to deliver an enormously improved inservice provision. I intend to incorporate these outcomes of this Convention into our planning for major advances in inservice education, which will begin in this school year.

The future.

We have reached the end of a long journey which has marched through countless debates, seminars, conferences and symposia over the last two years, which has brought almost 1,000 submissions to my Department and which has culminated in the most intense activity over the last nine days. Many of you, I know, are tired, drained after the intense effort of mind and intellect, of concentration and attention over the span of this Convention. But your weariness is tempered with the consciousness of achievement, of a job well done. As I go forward to determine the shape of the White Paper and the Education Act, I will rely immensely on the outcomes of this Convention. This Convention provides a momentum, an impetus and a groundswell of support which will aid me in moving to the White Paper stage.

I would like to refer particularly to the Secretary General's Report on the issue of **Intermediate Structures** and, in particular, to two specific proposals contained in his report on the outcome of work in the Analysis of Issues group.

The second proposal was that an official position paper should be published, prior to the publication of the White Paper. I heard the proposals for the first time at the Convention just after mid-day. I consider these suggestions to be a very positive development. I have decided to act on them. This allows me to underline in a very practical way the undertaking I gave to all of you participants, that I would give the most serious consideration to the outcomes of the Convention. The synchronisation of continuing negotiations with the publication of an official paper is obviously a matter on which I would need to reflect. I would be concerned of course that the publication or expectation of an official paper might limit the boundaries of discussion. But I do accept the clear implication of the group's conclusion that clarification of Ministerial thinking on this issue would help to progress discussions. I will need to reflect on this point and I will ask the Secretary General for his advice. The Convention issued me with a challenge on this issue. I will take it up. This Convention is a watershed in the history of Irish education. The policies which emerge and the process by which they have been formed will have a profound effect on the education and life chances of generations to come. Indeed, this Convention is a landmark in the policy making process not only in Ireland but in the international context. Together we have seen history in the making. We have participated fully in this historic Convention. And we have seized the opportunity to shape events.

Partners in education, as I go forward to frame Ireland's first Education Act, I am challenged by the great burden of expectation, of trust and of faith we have in our education system. I am conscious of the great privilege it is to be Minister at this time of momentous change. I know that each of you, by your participation here, has shown that you too share this sense of privilege as we stand at this moment in history. And at the close of this Convention, you can all, partners in education, feel satisfaction and pride that you have played your full part in helping me shape the future of Irish Education.

Partners in Education, I congratulate you.

Wt. P33818. 10,000. 1/94. Cahill. (M10752). G.Spl.